Applied Artificial Intelligence in Data Science, Cloud Computing and IoT Frameworks

(Volume 4)

AI-Driven Competitive Intelligence and Next-Generation Security

Edited by

Suneeta Satpathy
Center For Cybersecurity, SoA Deemed to be University, Bhubaneswar, Odisha, India

Sachi Nandan Mohanty
School of Computer Science & Engineering, VIT-AP University, Andhra Pradesh, India

&

Subhendu Kumar Pani
Computer Science & Engineering Krupajal Engineering College BPUT, Odisha, India

Applied Artificial Intelligence in Data Science, Cloud Computing and IoT Frameworks

(Volume 4)

AI-Driven Competitive Intelligence and Next-Generation Security

Editors: Suneeta Satpathy, Sachi Nandan Mohanty and Subhendu Kumar Pani

ISSN (Online): 3029-2247

ISSN (Print): 3029-2255

ISBN (Online): 979-8-89881-213-3

ISBN (Print): 979-8-89881-214-0

ISBN (Paperback): 979-8-89881-215-7

Published by Bentham Science Publishers Pte. Ltd. Singapore, in collaboration with Eureka Conferences, USA.

First published in 2025.

Bentham Science Publishers Pte. Ltd.
No. 9 Raffles Place
Office No. 26-01
Singapore 048619
Singapore
Email: subscriptions@benthamscience.net

BENTHAM SCIENCE

CONTENTS

FOREWORD

The integration of Artificial Intelligence (AI) with Data Science, Cloud Computing, and the Internet of Things (IoT) is transforming the way organizations derive insights, drive innovation, and secure digital infrastructures. In this fourth volume, Applied Artificial Intelligence in Data Science, Cloud Computing, and IoT Frameworks: AI-Driven Competitive Intelligence and Next-Generation Security, the editors present a comprehensive exploration of AI's role in shaping competitive intelligence and enhancing cybersecurity.

AI-driven frameworks are redefining competitive intelligence by uncovering hidden patterns, predicting trends, and enabling strategic decision-making at unprecedented speed and scale. Simultaneously, the expansion of connected systems has introduced increasingly sophisticated cyber threats. This volume highlights how AI serves as both a proactive defense mechanism and an enabler of secure, adaptive digital ecosystems.

The chapters bring together cutting-edge research and practical applications, offering insights across business intelligence, cloud platforms, IoT networks, and security solutions. They provide readers with a clear understanding of AI's dual potential: driving innovation while fortifying next-generation security frameworks.

This volume serves as an essential resource for researchers, industry leaders, and policymakers aiming to harness AI in a responsible and strategic manner. By highlighting AI's profound influence on contemporary technologies, it provides a clear framework for building intelligent, secure, and sustainable digital ecosystems. I applaud the editors and contributors for assembling a forward-thinking collection that not only drives innovation but also enriches the understanding of AI's critical role in shaping the future of competitive intelligence and next-generation security.

Ming Yang
Kennesaw State University
USA

PREFACE

In today's hyper-connected and rapidly evolving global economy, the ability to harness artificial intelligence (AI) for competitive intelligence has become a cornerstone of strategic decision-making in business and finance. Organizations increasingly rely on advanced AI and machine learning (ML) techniques to not only analyze vast volumes of structured and unstructured data but also to anticipate market trends, optimize operations, and maintain a competitive edge. Equally critical is the next-generation security landscape, where sophisticated cyber threats challenge enterprises, financial institutions, and governments to adopt resilient, intelligent defense mechanisms.

This volume, **AI-Driven Competitive Intelligence and Next-Generation Security**, brings together a collection of research contributions, case studies, and applied frameworks that explore the convergence of AI, data analytics, and cybersecurity. The chapters cover a diverse range of topics, including predictive financial modeling, automated market analysis, fraud detection, risk assessment, and AI-enabled threat intelligence. By bridging the domains of business intelligence, financial analytics, and cybersecurity, the volume highlights innovative methodologies that not only enhance decision-making but also safeguard critical assets in an increasingly digital ecosystem.

We believe this volume will serve as a valuable resource for researchers, practitioners, and policymakers seeking to understand the transformative potential of AI in shaping competitive strategies while addressing emerging security challenges. The insights presented here reflect the collective expertise of leading scholars and industry professionals, providing readers with practical approaches and forward-looking perspectives that will drive sustainable growth and resilient security in the digital age.

Suneeta Satpathy
Center For Cybersecurity, SoA Deemed to be University
Bhubaneswar, Odisha, India

Sachi Nandan Mohanty
School of Computer Science & Engineering
VIT-AP University, Andhra Pradesh, India

&

Subhendu Kumar Pani
Computer Science & Engineering, Krupajal Engineering College BPUT
Odisha, India

List of Contributors

A. Ezil Sam Leni	Alliance School of Advanced Computing, Alliance University, Karnataka, India
Akhand Tiwari	Department of Commerce, CHRIST University, Lavasa Campus, Pune, India
Anjaiah Adepu	Department of CSE, IC Polytechnic, Maulana Azad National Urdu University, India
Amjan Shaik	Department of CSE, St. Peter's Engineering College, Hyderabad, Telangana, India
Akhil Singampalli	Department of Computer Science and Engineering, Vignan's Institute of Information Technology, India
Anil Pise	Cumulus Solutions, Johannesburg, South Africa
Arushi Sharma	Department of Commerce, CHRIST University, Lavasa Campus, Pune, India
Aryan Gupta	Department of Commerce, CHRIST University, Lavasa Campus, Pune, India
Bikash Chandra Naik	School of Computer Science and Engineering, Odisha University of Technology and Research, Bhubaneswar, India
Blesson Varghese James	Department of Commerce, CHRIST University, Lavasa Campus, Pune, India
D. Gousiya Begum	Department of CSE, BEST Innovation University (BESTIU), Andhra Pradesh, India
Dharma Teja Singampalli	Sagility, Bangalore, India
Gurpreet Singh Chhabra	Computer Science and Engineering, Gandhi Institute of Technology and Management, Vishakhapatnam, India
Jyotirmayee Rautaray	Department of Computer Science & Engineering, Odisha University of Technology and Research, Bhubaneswar, Odisha, India
Kavin Velavan G.	Department of Artificial Intelligence and Data Science, Karpagam College of Engineering, Coimbatore, India
K. Nagajyothi	R&D, BEST Innovation University (BESTIU), Andhra Pradesh, India
Lijo Thomas	Department of Management, CHRIST University, Pune Lavasa Campus, India
Lalmohan Pattnaik	Sri Sri University, Cuttack, Odisha, India
Meenakshi Kandpal	School of Computer Science and Engineering, Odisha University of Technology and Research, Bhubaneswar, India
Mano Paul P.	COE in iOS App Development, Dept of CSE, Alliance University, Bangalore, Karnataka, 562106, India
Manikandan S.	Department of Artificial Intelligence and Data Science, Karpagam College of Engineering, Coimbatore, India
Mukesh Chaudhary	Parul University Vadodara, Gujarat, India
Mary Analiya Babu	Department of Management, CHRIST University, Lavasa Campus, Pune, India

M. Shrahith	Alliance School of Advanced Computing, Alliance University, Karnataka, India
Purnamita Baral	Department of Computer Science & Engineering, Odisha University of Technology and Research, Bhubaneswar, Odisha, India
Pranati Mishra	Department of Computer Science & Engineering, Odisha University of Technology and Research, Bhubaneswar, Odisha, India
P. Uma Devi	Computer Science and Engineering, Gandhi Institute of Technology and Management, Vishakhapatnam, India
Preethi Nanjundan	Department of Data Science, CHRIST University, Lavasa Campus, Pune, India
R. Manik	Department of Computer Science & Engineering, Lovely Professional University, Jalandhar, India
Sruti Nayak	Department of Computer Science & Engineering, Odisha University of Technology and Research, Bhubaneswar, Odisha, India
Subhasmita Pradhan	School of Computer Science and Engineering, Odisha University of Technology and Research, Bhubaneswar, India
Sameer Khan	Alliance School of Advanced Computing, Alliance University, Karnataka, India
Shrishtee Khabra	Department of Commerce, CHRIST University, Lavasa Campus, Pune, India
S. Nonita	Department of Information Technology, Indira Gandhi Delhi Technical University for Women, Delhi, India
Sriram K.	Department of Artificial Intelligence and Data Science, Karpagam College of Engineering, Coimbatore, India
Surrenther I.	Department of Artificial Intelligence and Data Science, Karpagam College of Engineering, Coimbatore, India
Sathya K.	Department of Artificial Intelligence and Data Science, Karpagam College of Engineering, Coimbatore, India
Saswati Chatterjee	Parul University Vadodara, Gujarat, India
Suneeta Satpathy	Center For Cyber Security, SoA Deemed to be University, Bhubaneswar, Odisha, India
Tony Alosius S.	Department of Artificial Intelligence and Data Science, Karpagam College of Engineering, Coimbatore, India
Virendra Kumar Shrivastava	Centre of Excellence in Computer Vision, Department of Computer Science and Engineering, School of Advanced Computing, Alliance University, Bangalore, Karnataka, 562106, India
Vijaykumar Jayantibhai Solanki	Government Engineering College Bharuch, Gujarat, India
Vrushali Deshpande	D&M Tech, Pune, India
Y. Gokul	School of Computer Science and Engineering, VIT-AP University, Amaravati, India
Yogesh Khandokar	Beamline Scientist MX, Australia

Section 1
Competitive Intelligence in Business and Finance

CHAPTER 1

Revolutionizing Financial Futures: The AI Impact on Forecasting and Risk Management

Preethi Nanjundan[1,*], **Mary Analiya Babu**[2] and **Lijo Thomas**[2]

[1] *Department of Data Science, CHRIST University, Lavasa Campus, Pune, India*

[2] *Department of Management, CHRIST University, Lavasa Campus, Pune, India*

Abstract: For forecasting and risk management, the financial sector has historically depended on statistical models and historical data. Artificial intelligence (AI), on the other hand, is poised to completely transform traditional methods. This book examines how artificial intelligence (AI) can revolutionize risk management and financial forecasting. The book explores the ways in which artificial intelligence (AI) methods, such as machine learning and deep learning, may analyse enormous volumes of data from various sources to spot intricate patterns and relationships that conventional approaches might overlook. As a result, risk assessments and projections become more precise, empowering financial institutions to make more educated choices. The book also discusses the difficulties in integrating AI in finance, such as obstacles related to regulations, data quality, and model explainability. It offers suggestions on how to get past these obstacles and successfully incorporate AI into financial processes. Financial organizations can obtain a major competitive edge by utilizing AI. Anyone interested in the future of finance and the potentially disruptive power of artificial intelligence should read this book.

Keywords: Artificial intelligence (AI), Big data, Deep learning, Financial forecasting, Machine learning, Pattern recognition, Predictive analytics, Risk management, Regulatory challenges.

INTRODUCTION TO AI IN FINANCE

Artificial Intelligence (AI) has become a disruptive force in the financial industry, reshaping conventional procedures and transforming the way decisions are made. Artificial intelligence has become essential for risk management and financial forecasting because of its unparalleled speed at which it can analyse massive volumes of data and identify intricate patterns. Businesses need to get ready for the next wave of digital disruption that artificial intelligence is about to unleash. It

* **Corresponding author Preethi Nanjundan:** Department of Data Science, CHRIST University, Lavasa Campus Campus, Pune, India; E-mail: preethi.n@christuniversity.in

Suneeta Satpathy, Sachi Nandan Mohanty & Subhendu Kumar Pani (Eds.)

is now more important than ever for other businesses to speed up their digital transitions since we are witnessing tangible benefits for a select group of early adopting companies [1]. The evolution of financial forecasting has been marked by a shift from sophisticated artificial intelligence approaches to conventional statistical methodologies. Because machine learning models can learn from previous data and produce highly accurate predictions, they have become popular. Examples of these models are regression, decision trees, and random forests [2]. By identifying intricate links in data that produce deeper insights, deep learning techniques—such as neural networks—have further increased prediction potential. Furthermore, novel approaches to mine unstructured data sources—such as news articles, social media, and incoming calls—for insightful information have been made possible by natural language processing, or NLP. NLP-based algorithms can analyze text data to forecast market movements, gauge the impact of news events, and gauge market sentiment [3]. Artificial intelligence has not only greatly improved forecasting but also risk management procedures in the financial industry. Credit and market risks can be evaluated and reduced by institutions through the use of predictive analytics.

Additionally, investors can design diversified portfolios that are suited to their risk tolerance and financial objectives with the aid of AI-based portfolio optimization tools. The extensive application of AI in banking is not without difficulties, though. Data security, legal compliance, and ethical concerns all demand that AI technologies be used carefully and responsibly. Notwithstanding these obstacles, artificial intelligence has a bright future in banking, and more advancements could significantly alter the sector's structure.

The Evolution of Financial Forecasting

The practice of financial forecasting has changed dramatically throughout the years, moving from an intuitive to a technologically advanced era. In the beginning, traders made educated forecasts based on prior trends and market whispers by using their instincts and experience. Despite its shortcomings, this method cleared the path for more methodical approaches. The 20th century saw the advent of the data-driven age, in which analysts started to spot trends by looking back at previous price, volume, and economic indicator trends. Time series models were developed to better forecast by capturing the subtleties of financial data, and moving averages were used to reduce volatility and identify short-term patterns. The Monte Carlo simulations gained prominence in the 1960s and are still very important today. Risk could be evaluated and simulated by analysts.

The Role of AI in Modern Finance

Artificial Intelligence (AI) is being rapidly incorporated into the operations of the financial industry, resulting in a huge transformation. AI is having a wide range of effects on the sector, from bettering investor decisions to automating backend chores. Enhanced Efficiency and Risk Management: Artificial Intelligence (AI) frees up human specialists for more strategic work by automating repetitive processes like fraud detection and loan application processing. Large volumes of financial data may be analyzed by AI algorithms to find trends and forecast hazards related to investments, loans, and even money laundering. As a result, organizations are able to decide more quickly and intelligently. An organizational culture that welcomes human and machine collaboration is necessary to reap the long-term benefits of artificial intelligence. Here, trust is a crucial facilitator. The relationship between a machine's internal operations and the output it generates can become fairly hazy because of the interaction between training and inference in artificial intelligence [4].

AI gives financial experiences to clients and institutions a personalized touch. Banks can use artificial intelligence (AI) to comprehend client behaviour and provide individualized financial products or wealth management guidance. In a similar vein, AI-driven robo-advisors evaluate each client's risk tolerance and investing objectives before generating automated investment plans. To forecast future market movements, investment and artificial intelligence algorithms can examine social media data, news sentiment, and market patterns. This gives hedge funds and investment firms the ability to make data-driven judgments about their investments and maybe increase profits. AI-powered algorithmic trading has the ability to complete deals extremely quickly and take advantage of short-lived market opportunities. Financial services are becoming more widely available thanks to AI-powered financial solutions. For those without the funds to hire a traditional financial counsellor, robo-advisors offer investing advice.

Furthermore, AI can evaluate creditworthiness from non-traditional data sources, giving institutions access to populations that were previously unbanked. Even though artificial intelligence (AI) has a lot of promise, ethical issues and potential biases in algorithms must be addressed. In general, AI is bringing about a new era of intelligent finance that will be characterized by increased accessibility to financial services, efficiency, and personalization.

AI TECHNIQUES FOR FINANCIAL FORECASTING

For a very long time, financial forecasting has been an essential instrument for managing market volatility. These days, Artificial Intelligence (AI) is changing this area by providing strong methods that improve precision and reveal hidden patterns. Machine Learning (ML) is one of the main AI techniques. Large volumes of historical data, such as market patterns, economic indicators, and corporate financials, can be analyzed using machine learning algorithms. ML models are capable of forecasting future changes in stock prices, market movements, and even creditworthiness by seeing intricate links in this data.

Deep Learning is another effective technology. This branch of machine learning uses artificial neural networks to simulate the architecture of the human brain. Even more complicated data sets, such as social media trends, satellite images, and news sentiment, can be processed by deep learning models, which could result in more accurate projections.

Additionally, AI is able to comprehend and evaluate textual data such as financial reports, social media debates, and news articles thanks to Natural Language Processing, or NLP. NLP has the ability to extract sentiment and spot possible dangers or possibilities that conventional approaches could overlook. These AI methods provide a number of benefits. First off, compared to people, they are far faster and more capable of thorough data analysis. Second, although traditional analysis could miss subtle patterns and links, AI models are able to detect them. Moreover, lastly, over time, AI can learn new things and become more accurate at forecasting. However, it is crucial to keep in mind that AI is a tool, not a magic bullet. The caliber of the data utilized to train the models continues to influence the accuracy of the forecasts. Even the most advanced forecasts might be derailed by unanticipated circumstances. Thus, a cooperative approach is where financial forecasting is headed. Financial professionals can traverse the dynamic economic landscape and make better informed decisions by fusing artificial intelligence (AI) with human skill and judgment.

Machine Learning Models

The science (and art) of teaching computers to learn from data is known as machine learning [5]. Forecasting and risk management are being revolutionized by machine learning (ML) algorithms, which use massive datasets to find hidden patterns and make remarkably accurate predictions. Forecasting was formerly dependent on statistical models with predetermined assumptions. But machine learning models adopt a more adaptable strategy. ML algorithms are able to recognize intricate links and adjust to non-linear trends by directly learning from data. This makes it possible to make extremely detailed forecasts, which deepens our awareness of prospective hazards and opportunities [6].

ML models are used in finance to evaluate credit risk. These models are significantly more accurate than traditional credit scoring techniques at predicting the possibility of loan defaults by examining borrower data, transaction history, and even sentiment on social media. This gives lenders the ability to optimize loan portfolios, reduce bad debt, and make well-informed judgments. ML predictions are essential for supply chain management as well as financial services [7]. Through the examination of past sales data, meteorological trends, and social media tendencies, enterprises may anticipate shifts in demand and maximize stock levels. By being proactive, the likelihood of stockouts and overstocking is reduced, which boosts productivity and lowers expenses. It is crucial to remember that machine learning models are not perfect. The caliber of the data they are trained on determines the caliber of their predictions. Data biases can produce biased models, which could exacerbate already-existing disparities. Moreover, the inner workings of ML models can become opaque as they get more complicated, making it difficult to comprehend how they make their predictions. In many financial processes, such as option pricing, algorithmic execution, or risk monitoring, decisions must be made in accordance with predetermined guidelines. The majority of automation to date has occurred here, turning the financial markets into incredibly quick and highly connected networks for information sharing [8].

A strong toolkit for predicting and risk management is offered by machine learning. Through the use of data, machine learning models are able to discern patterns, forecast results, and facilitate enhanced decision-making. To ensure the proper and ethical application of this breakthrough technology, it is imperative to carefully assess data quality and model interpretability.

Deep Learning Approaches

The financial industry greatly depends on risk management and precise forecasting. Nevertheless, the ability to capture intricate relationships within data is limited by existing methods. Deep learning techniques are becoming more and more effective tools to tackle this problem. Deep learning algorithms are able to identify complex patterns from enormous volumes of data because they are modeled after the structure and operations of the human brain. As a result, their estimates become more accurate as they are able to unearth hidden secrets within financial markets.

Recurrent neural networks (RNNs), for example, can use historical patterns and dependencies to assess time-series data, like stock prices, and forecast future trends. Furthermore, by facilitating improved risk assessment, deep learning strengthens risk management. Convolutional neural networks (CNNs) are capable of analyzing unstructured data, including sentiment from social media or news articles, to predict future changes in the market and spot new dangers. This makes it possible to take preventative action to lessen losses [9]. Deep learning is not without its restrictions, though. It is challenging to comprehend how these algorithms create their predictions because of their "black box" design. Furthermore, the enormous volume of data needed to train these models can be a challenge, particularly for smaller organizations.

Deep learning has enormous potential to revolutionize risk management and financial forecasting, despite these obstacles. As data becomes more available and technology advances, we should anticipate the emergence of progressively more advanced applications. This will enable financial institutions to more accurately and confidently negotiate the market's complexity.

Natural Language Processing in Forecasting

Financial forecasting has always involved navigating the ever-changing markets while playing a game of odds. But with the development of Natural Language Processing (NLP), a new instrument has appeared to assist us in deciphering the always changing tides. NLP gives computers the ability to comprehend and evaluate enormous volumes of textual data, providing a distinctive viewpoint on the financial world. Forecasting used to be dependent on numerical data points. However, NLP can now extract sentiment and identify latent patterns from news stories, analyst reports, and social media discussions. This sentiment analysis can be used to determine the level of optimism or pessimism in the market, which is a useful tool for forecasting future price changes. NLP, for instance, can detect abrupt changes in consumer opinion about a certain industry based on conversations on social media, which could indicate a drop in stock prices [10].

NLP is not only capable of identifying sentiment, but also emerging topics. Through the examination of regulatory filings or corporate reports, NLP is able to identify changes in a business's approach or possible dangers concealed inside the letter of the law. Proactively adjusting investment decisions is made possible by the early recognition of these elements. But it's important to keep in mind that NLP is not a magical crystal ball. The quality and volume of data it processes have a major impact on how accurate its analysis is. Forecasts may get distorted as a result of data biases. Furthermore, NLP has trouble grasping irony and sarcasm, which are prevalent in financial conversations. When interpreting the subtleties of NLP's discoveries, human skill is still essential.

NLP is transforming financial forecasting by revealing text's hidden insights. It gives us the ability to make wiser decisions. It's crucial to remember that NLP is a tool, not a substitute for sound financial judgment. NLP and human knowledge work together to provide the key to navigating the ever-complex world of finance.

ENHANCING RISK MANAGEMENT WITH AI

Financial stability has always required effective risk management. Nevertheless, in the ever-changing world of finance today, conventional approaches frequently fall short. An additional line of defense against unanticipated threats is being provided by artificial intelligence (AI), which is becoming a more potent instrument.

Pattern recognition and data analysis are two critical components of risk management that AI excels at. Artificial intelligence (AI) systems can find subtle patterns and connections in financial data that may be challenging to find by hand. This makes it possible to provide a thorough risk assessment that takes into account both possible future events and historical trends. AI is widely used in fraud detection, where it can evaluate transaction patterns instantly and identify questionable activity that deviates from accepted norms. This can safeguard both individuals and institutions by drastically lowering financial losses brought on by fraudulent transactions. AI is also useful for stress testing, which is a vital procedure for determining how resilient an organization is to monetary shocks. AI can assist in identifying possible vulnerabilities and directing the creation of mitigation methods by simulating different economic scenarios. By being proactive, we can increase our financial resilience and protect against unanticipated catastrophes. The trifecta of modelling errors threatens all financial models, regardless of whether they are grounded in ML techniques or academic theories. These three flaws cannot be completely eradicated, but they can be lessened with the right tools, like probabilistic machine learning systems. Cognitive biases and information imbalance will always exist. Because human behaviour, capitalism, and technology innovation are dynamic, models of asset prices and hazards will also evolve over time.

The quality of AI algorithms depends on the data they are trained on. Risk evaluations can be tainted by biased data. Furthermore, AI finds it difficult to articulate the reasoning behind its decision-making, which makes it difficult to comprehend why a given danger is identified. Risk management has a revolutionary opportunity thanks to AI. Financial institutions are strengthened and individuals are protected by their capacity to analyze large datasets and uncover hidden patterns. However, a responsible application is essential. By maintaining data integrity and encouraging human-AI cooperation, we can harness AI's potential to create a more secure financial future.

Predictive Analytics for Risk Assessment

It has always been an intriguing desire to make future predictions. These days, artificial intelligence (AI)-powered predictive analytics is making this dream a reality. With the help of this potent mix, we can analyze enormous datasets and unearth hidden patterns, which help us predict future occurrences quite accurately.

Machine learning algorithms constitute the foundation of predictive analytics. Using historical data, these algorithms are trained to find patterns and relationships. They can then predict future events with a high degree of accuracy by providing them with fresh data points. For example, AI-powered predictive analytics can forecast client attrition to create customized retention strategies. Predictive analytics has many uses. It can evaluate patient data in the healthcare industry to forecast disease outbreaks or pinpoint those who are particularly vulnerable to particular ailments. Predicting demand for particular products helps improve inventory management in the retail industry. Another effective tool is predictive maintenance, which uses sensor data from equipment to anticipate breakdowns before they happen and save expensive downtime. Predictive analytics is not without its difficulties, though. The Skewed forecasts might result from missing or biased data. Furthermore, it's imperative to make sure that these potent instruments are used ethically. Discriminatory results may result from biases in the algorithms.

AI-powered predictive analytics is drastically changing the world. It gives us the ability to predict future trends and make data-driven decisions, which helps organizations to reduce risks, streamline operations, and customize experiences. Predictive analytics is expected to develop into an even more potent tool for constructing a more predictable future as artificial intelligence advances.

Portfolio Optimization using AI

The responsibility of a portfolio manager is to assign funds to a group of assets. It aims to accomplish two things. It seeks to balance minimizing risk with optimizing return on investment. It is possible to lower risk by diversifying. The first section of this chapter introduces the Markowitz model, a popular approach for estimating risks and returns. In the past, optimizing a portfolio has required a lot of effort due to the need to balance return and risk. However, a new era of automated portfolio management is beginning with the development of artificial intelligence (AI). Algorithms driven by AI are revolutionizing the construction and management of financial portfolios.

Portfolio optimization has always been based on predetermined models and historical data. AI, on the other hand, has the capacity to process enormous information and uncover intricate connections between various assets. This makes it possible to create extremely customized portfolios that are matched to each investor's particular risk tolerance and financial objectives. AI system can build a dynamically adjusted portfolio based on your age, income, and risk tolerance.

Machine learning is another tool that AI can use to find patterns and forecast trends. This gives the AI the ability to modify the portfolio in real-time, potentially maximizing profits while lowering risk. For example, based on news reports, an AI system may identify an asset class that is undervalued and automatically modify the weighting of your portfolio to take advantage of the opportunity. But there are restrictions with AI portfolio optimization. Because the algorithms are based on historical data, results in the past do not guarantee results in the future. Losses can still result from unforeseen market developments. Additionally, investors may find it challenging to comprehend the reasoning behind AI systems' decisions due to their complexity. Transparency is still a major issue.

The use of AI is transforming portfolio management. AI offers a potent tool for creating dynamic, tailored portfolios by utilizing its machine learning and analytical skills. But it's crucial to keep in mind that AI is a tool, not a financial panacea. For appropriate investing plans, human oversight and a thorough grasp of the AI's decision-making process are still necessary.

Fraud Detection and Prevention

As technology has advanced, financial fraud has emerged as a persistent problem. But our defenses have also advanced to address this issue. The two main strategies for combating fraud that are critical to securing financial systems in the digital age are prevention and detection, which are examined in this essay.

The first line of defense is prevention. Establishing robust internal controls is essential to preventing fraud. This entails assigning responsibilities to different people, following password regulations, and routinely checking money activity for odd trends. Furthermore, fostering an ethical culture within a company will deter dishonest behavior. The use of technology is essential in the fight against fraud. Large volumes of transaction data can be analyzed by machine learning algorithms, which can then spot irregularities that can point to fraud. For instance, an algorithm may detect credit card theft if it detects an abrupt increase in purchases coming from an unusual geographic area. However, detection on its own is insufficient. When suspicious conduct is discovered, a quick response is required. It is necessary to take a multi-layered approach, which can involve temporary account suspension, additional verification procedures, or even real-time transaction warnings.

Even with improvements in fraud detection and prevention, con artists still devise new plans. The secret is to always be vigilant. It's critical to identify fraud trends and modify detection systems appropriately. Additionally, regular fraud awareness training gives staff members the ability to recognize and report unusual activity. Fraud prevention calls for a proactive strategy. A strong defense against financial crime is created by combining preventive measures, cutting-edge technology, and quick action. We can maintain our competitive edge and guarantee the integrity of our financial systems by continuously refining our approach.

CHALLENGES AND FUTURE DIRECTIONS

Financial fraud is a recurring threat that is always changing its strategies to take advantage of weaknesses. Despite advancements in detection and prevention, there are still major obstacles to overcome. This essay looks at these obstacles as well as positive trends for financial security in the future.

A significant obstacle is the steadily rising amount and intricacy of financial transactions. The advent of digital payments and interlinked financial systems presents a broad terrain for deceivers to maneuver over. The intricacy of these techniques is often too much for conventional rule-based detection algorithms to handle. Fraudsters also take advantage of the rising popularity of false identities. Since these identities are produced by fusing genuine and phony data, it is challenging to discern between dishonest businesspeople and actual clients. Real-time identity verification is essential to preventing financial crimes such as account takeover. There are a few encouraging avenues to pursue in the future that give promise for increased security. The potential for combining machine learning and artificial intelligence (AI) is enormous. Artificial intelligence (AI) is able to identify abnormalities that older approaches might miss by analyzing large datasets and spotting minor trends. This makes it possible to take a more proactive stance, foreseeing and stopping fraud before it happens. The application of biometrics is another exciting avenue. When it comes to user authentication, fingerprint scanners and facial recognition software provide a more secure solution than passwords, which are frequently vulnerable to theft or hacking. Just like in our accustomed 3-dimensional environment, an ML algorithm may identify patterns in a 100-dimensional one. Even though it makes us all giggle when an algorithm makes a careless error, bear in mind that algorithms have only existed for a small portion of human history.

Cooperation is also very important. Financial institutions and law enforcement agencies can present a unified front against criminals by exchanging information on fraud trends and strategies. A more thorough defense strategy may be developed and new threats can be identified more quickly when there is open communication. There is a continuous arms race in the fight against financial fraud. The methods used by scammers will also change as technology does. Modern technologies like artificial intelligence (AI), biometrics, and information exchange can help us fortify our security and build a more secure financial environment that benefits everybody.

Ethical Considerations in AI-driven Finance

Artificial intelligence (AI) in finance has the ability to improve returns, speed up analysis, and provide individualized recommendations. However, in order to guarantee justice, openness, and responsible innovation, it is crucial to manage ethical issues.

Bias is one of the main issues. The quality of AI algorithms is contingent upon the quality of the training data. Biases in society may be reflected in historical financial data, which could result in unfair practices. To maintain financial inequality, an AI system might, for instance, reject loan applications to some people based on historical patterns. Diverse datasets and continual human supervision are necessary for bias mitigation in order to guarantee that everyone is treated fairly and equally. Transparency is yet another important factor. The "black box" aspect of AI prompts questions regarding the process of decision-making. Regulators and investors alike must comprehend how AI makes its decisions. By providing insight into the reasoning underlying financial suggestions, explainable AI solutions can promote accountability and confidence. Privacy is also very important. For AI systems to work well, enormous volumes of private financial information are needed. It is imperative that sensitive data be shielded from misuse or illegal access. To protect customer privacy, strong security measures and unambiguous data ownership standards are crucial.

It is impossible to overlook how AI automation in finance could result in job losses. Although AI can expedite procedures, human knowledge is still essential. Retraining the workforce to adjust to the evolving environment, facilitating a seamless transition, and optimizing the advantages of human-AI cooperation should be the main priorities. AI has the ability to completely transform financial innovation, but there are ethical issues that need to be resolved first. Fairness, transparency, data responsibility, and an emphasis on human-AI collaboration are all important ways to make sure that AI is used to drive responsible growth and financial inclusion.

Regulatory Implications

Artificial intelligence (AI) in finance has the ability to improve returns, speed up analysis, and provide individualized recommendations. However, in order to guarantee justice, openness, and responsible innovation, it is crucial to manage ethical issues.

Bias is one of the main issues. The quality of AI algorithms is contingent upon the quality of the training data. Biases in society may be reflected in historical financial data, which could result in unfair practices. To maintain financial inequality, an AI system might, for instance, reject loan applications to some people based on historical patterns. Diverse datasets and continual human supervision are necessary for bias mitigation in order to guarantee that everyone is treated fairly and equally. Transparency is yet another important factor. The "black box" aspect of AI prompts questions regarding the process of decision-making. Regulators and investors alike must comprehend how AI makes its decisions. By providing insight into the reasoning underlying financial suggestions, explainable AI solutions can promote accountability and confidence. Privacy is also very important. For AI systems to work well, enormous volumes of private financial information are needed. It is imperative that sensitive data be shielded from misuse or illegal access. To protect customer privacy, strong security measures and unambiguous data ownership policies are crucial. It is impossible to overlook how AI automation in finance could result in job losses. Although AI can expedite procedures, human knowledge is still essential. Retraining the workforce to adjust to the evolving environment, facilitating a seamless transition, and optimizing the advantages of human-AI cooperation should be the main priorities. AI has the ability to completely transform financial innovation, but there are ethical issues that need to be resolved first. We can make sure AI becomes a force for responsible growth and financial inclusion by encouraging justice, openness, data responsibility, and human-AI collaboration. Artificial intelligence's (AI) explosive rise in the financial industry has drawbacks. Although AI increases productivity and encourages creativity, it also presents new regulatory difficulties. The main areas where regulations must change to reflect the changing nature of AI-driven finance are examined in this essay. Explainability and transparency are two important issues. Because AI algorithms can be complicated "black boxes," it might be challenging to comprehend how they make judgments. The absence of clarity is a challenge for regulatory bodies that must evaluate the equity and efficiency of these algorithms. Imagine a loan approval system driven by AI that, for obscure reasons hidden in its intricate code, refuses loans to specific groups of people. To guarantee equity and avoid prejudice, regulations must require comprehensive justifications for AI-driven choices.

Security and privacy of data are crucial. Large volumes of private financial data are used by AI systems, which raises questions regarding misuse and illegal access. Clear data governance frameworks must be established by regulations to guarantee that data is gathered, maintained, and used appropriately. Consumers ought to be fully informed about their data rights and the ways in which AI systems use it. Accountability is still not clear-cut. Who is in charge if an AI system makes a mistake or malfunctions? Who is employing it—the financial institution, the developer, or the AI itself? To guarantee that someone can be held accountable for the conduct of AI systems in the financial sector, regulations must set up distinct lines of accountability. The field of cyber-risk management is dynamic and multifaceted. Executive management involvement, continuous governance, risk management strategies, threat correlation, cross-organizational cooperation, and the implementation of a new operating model are all necessary for staying ahead of the competition.

Finally, one must pay great attention to the possibility of algorithmic bias. Biases from the data used to train AI systems may be inherited by them. Discriminatory effects could result from this, including unreasonably low credit scores for some groups of people. Laws must address these prejudices and guarantee the moral and equitable operation of AI-driven financial systems. In conclusion, a careful strategy is needed to navigate the regulatory environment of AI-driven finance. Collaboration between financial institutions, regulators, and AI developers is necessary to strike a balance between promoting innovation and safeguarding consumers. Clear and flexible laws will guarantee that artificial intelligence (AI) is a valuable instrument for economic advancement rather than a cause of unanticipated dangers.

Emerging Trends and Opportunities

Artificial Intelligence (AI) is poised to revolutionize the banking sector. Beyond work automation, artificial intelligence (AI) opens up new possibilities that could transform the way we invest, manage our finances, and take calculated risks. We'll look at some of the most intriguing new developments and prospects in AI-driven finance in this essay.

One industry that is rapidly growing is highly tailored finance. Artificial Intelligence (AI) can assess large amounts of financial data, including a customer's spending habits, risk tolerance, and financial goals. This data can be used to create truly tailored financial planning and investment strategies. Imagine an AI system that automatically adjusts your investing portfolio based on fluctuations in the market and your evolving goals in life. Financial services democratization is another intriguing trend. Robo-advisors with AI capabilities are opening up sophisticated investing strategies to all investors, not just the wealthy. These automated platforms manage investments, lower fees, and provide an easy-to-use experience for all users through the application of AI algorithms. Additionally, AI is changing risk management. AI is better at predicting possible hazards by examining large databases of past transactions and market trends. This gives financial organizations the opportunity to decide with knowledge regarding lending, preventing fraud, and maintaining overall financial stability. Envision an artificial intelligence system that can identify possible loan defaults ahead of time, enabling lenders to reduce risk and safeguard their capital. In the future, even more disruption is anticipated from the combination of AI with other cutting-edge technologies like blockchain. Blockchain data may be analysed by AI to spot fraud and guarantee the security of financial transactions.

But ethical issues are still very important. Ensuring fairness and transparency is essential as artificial intelligence (AI) becomes more prevalent in financial decision-making. Discriminating results may result from bias in training data. To guarantee that AI functions properly and ethically, regulations must be put in place. Finance is about to change because of artificial intelligence. The potential is many and ranges from highly individualized financial services to sophisticated risk management. We can open the door to a future of financial inclusion, efficiency, and stability for everybody by adopting AI safely and ethically.

It is revolutionary to incorporate artificial intelligence (AI) into risk management and financial forecasting. Artificial Intelligence (AI) enables us to more accurately traverse the complexity of the financial world by utilizing its machine learning and analytical capabilities. The only foundation to rely on is no longer historical facts. AI mines massive amounts of textual data to reveal a deeper grasp of developing trends and market sentiment. This makes it possible to forecast more accurately, which helps us to identify possible hazards and take advantage of unanticipated possibilities. AI is hardly a magic wand, though. Both human oversight and trustworthy data are necessary for its efficacy. To interpret the insights that AI reveals, human skill and AI collaboration are essential. In summary, AI is revolutionizing risk management and financial forecasting. It offers a strong toolkit for decision-making, opening the door to a more profitable and secure financial future. There are countless opportunities for financial innovation as we continue to investigate AI's capabilities.

REFERENCES

[1] Edward Tsang (2020). AI for finance: Everything you need to know about how artificial intelligence is transforming the financial industry publisher. Apress.

[2] A. Géron, *Hands-on machine learning with Scikit-Learn, Keras, and TensorFlow: Concepts, tools, and techniques to build intelligent systems.* 2nd ed. O'Reilly Media, 2019.

[3] McKinsey Global Institute. (2017). Artificial intelligence: The next digital frontier? Retrieved from https://www.mckinsey.com/~/media/mckinsey/industries/advanced%20electronics/our%20insights/how%20artificial%20intelligence%20can%20deliver%20real%20value%20to%20companies/mgi-artificial-intelligence-discussion-paper.pdf

[4] PwC. (2017). Financial services technology 2020 and beyond: Embracing disruption. Retrieved from: https://www.pwc.com/gr/en/publications/financial-services/financial-services-technology-202--and-beyond-embracing-disruption.html

[5] S.J. Russell, and P. Norvig, *Artificial intelligence: A modern approach.* 3rd ed. Pearson, 2016.

[6] Y. Hilpisch, *Artificial intelligence in finance.* O'Reilly Media, 2020.

[7] M.L. De Prado, *Advances in financial machine learning.* John Wiley & Sons, 2018.

[8] S. Kaabar, *Deep Learning for Finance: Creating Machine & Deep Learning Models for Trading in Python.* O'Reilly Media, Inc., 2024.

[9] D.K. Kanungo, *Probabilistic Machine Learning for Finance and Investing.* O'Reilly Media, Inc., 2023.

[10] D. Silver, A. Huang, C.J. Maddison, A. Guez, L. Sifre, G. van den Driessche, J. Schrittwieser, I. Antonoglou, V. Panneershelvam, M. Lanctot, S. Dieleman, D. Grewe, J. Nham, N. Kalchbrenner, I. Sutskever, T. Lillicrap, M. Leach, K. Kavukcuoglu, T. Graepel, and D. Hassabis, "Mastering the game of Go with deep neural networks and tree search", *Nature,* vol. 529, no. 7587, pp. 484-489, 2016. [http://dx.doi.org/10.1038/nature16961] [PMID: 26819042]

CHAPTER 2

Forecasting Demand in Retail Supply Chain Management: A Comparison of Deep Learning and Machine Learning Methodologies

Sruti Nayak[1], **Purnamita Baral**[1], **Jyotirmayee Rautaray**[1,*], **Pranati Mishra**[1] and **Meenakshi Kandpal**[2]

[1] *Department of Computer Science & Engineering, Odisha University of Technology and Research, Bhubaneswar, Odisha, India*

[2] *Department of Computer Science & Engineering, KIIT, Bhubaneswar, India*

Abstract: The paper explores supply chain management, emphasizing the importance of accurate demand forecasting. The word supply chain refers to the product journey from supplier to consumer. Demand forecasting is the anticipation of the market's demand for a product. Various models that can be used for accurate prediction include ARIMA, LSTM, STL, Prophet, GBM, SVM, KNN, Neural Networks, *etc.*This paper compares five algorithms from the available algorithms pool: ARIMA, LSTM, FB-Prophet, XGBoost, and Decision Tree Regressor. Two datasets, sourced from Yahoo Finance, spanning a decade and including real-time sales data of Walmart and Amazon, are used for the study. The optical model for demand forecasting depends upon specific evaluation metrics and the nature of the dataset. Taking MAE (Walmart sales data: 0.036588, Amazon sales data: 0.066181) into account, FB-Prophet is a suitable model for both datasets. ARIMA can also be considered an appropriate model for linear data. Moreover, considering the diverse evaluation metrics, LSTM distinguishes itself as a formidable choice among other models for capturing complex relationships and predicting accurate demand.

Keywords: Demand forecast, Evaluation Metrics, LSTM, MSE, MAE, Retail, RMSE, Supply chain, Time Series.

INTRODUCTION

In the dynamic retail industry, precise demand forecasting is essential. Knowing the customer needs and preferences enables effective inventory management (low inventory cost throughout the entire supply chain), resource allocation, and strategic decision-making. Supply chain management is the method of managing a

* **Corresponding author Jyotirmayee Rautaray:** Department of Computer Science & Engineering, Odisha University of Technology and Research, Bhubaneswar, Odisha, India; E-mail: jyotirmayee.1990@gmail.com

Suneeta Satpathy, Sachi Nandan Mohanty & Subhendu Kumar Pani (Eds.)

service or product, from purchasing raw materials to efficiently distributing the finished product.

Supply chain management efficiently manages the movement of products and services on time and within budget [1]. A crucial aspect of supply chain management is demanding forecasting. Demand forecasting is the process that involves a set of activities for estimating the quantity of different kinds of goods and services for the future based on past data and present circumstances. There are two approaches used in demand forecasting: Qualitative method and Quantitative method. In the case of the Qualitative method, no mathematical computation is used. On the other hand, the Quantitative method is based on Mathematical Computations. The demand forecasting techniques include internal and external demand forecasting, long-term and short-term forecasting, and passive and active forecasting. Demand forecasting is helpful for long-term strategic planning and short-term decision-making. It is also beneficial in minimizing the effect of the *Bullwhip Effect*. Order variations are likely to increase as one progresses up the supply chain, a phenomenon known as the effect [2]. Various factors affect accurate demand forecasting, such as the existing condition of an organization, industry conditions, customer psychology, economic environment, and product life cycle. This work offers a thorough analysis of several machine learning and deep learning techniques, like Autoregressive integrated moving average (ARIMA), Long short-term memory (LSTM), FB Prophet, Extreme Gradient Boosting (XG Boost), and Decision Tree regressor, applied to retail sales data of Walmart and Amazon extracted from Yahoo. Finance. As shown in Fig. (**1**), our study's structure involves essential steps of data collection, preparation, and analysis, emphasizing the evaluation of different model performances.

The paper is organized in the following sequence: The literature assessment of several proposed models is presented in section 2. The suggested processes, which include flowcharts, are described in Section 3. Section 4 is subdivided into two parts, 4.1 and 4.2, where 4.1 demonstrates the implementation of the proposed model and section 4.2 represents the result analysis of the model. Finally, section 5 highlights key findings as the conclusion of this study.

LITERATURE REVIEW

Machine learning and deep learning for sales forecasting are gaining popularity due to their ability to predict future sales accurately. The purpose of this literature study is to clarify the various methods and models that have been put forth and used in this field, emphasizing their effectiveness and predicted accuracy [3].

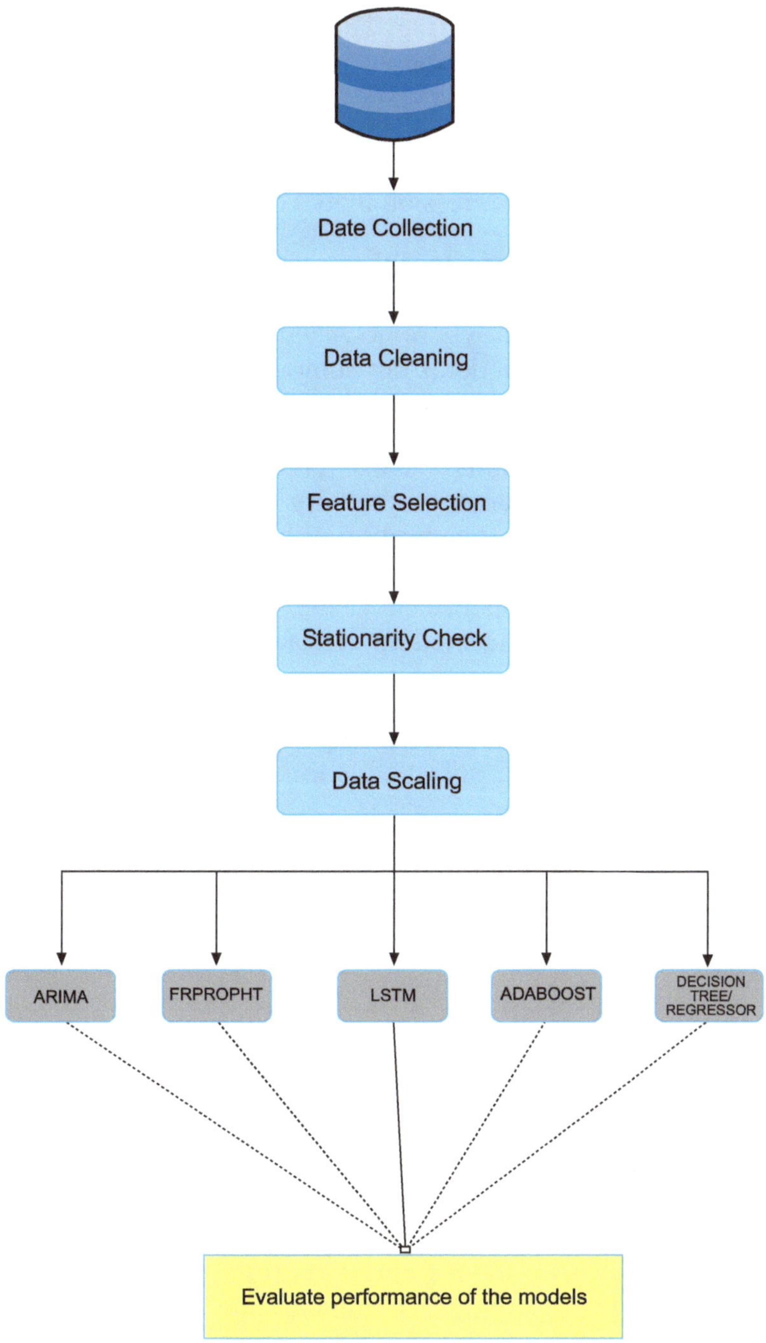

Fig. (1). Flowchart of proposed methodology for demand forecasting.

Farzana *et al.* [4] proposed a comparative study on different machine learning algorithms used for demand forecasting. They used a private dataset by applying algorithms like ARIMA regression-based methods, Regression-based methods, fuzzy-based approach, ANN, SVM, ELM (Extreme Learning machine), and Ensemble methods. This study concluded that LSTM provides the most trustworthy results. Still, the limitation is its computational time is higher than any other method, and the ARIMA regression model does not fit non-linear data.

Nicholas Ampazis [5] combined algorithms such as Artificial Neural Network (ANN) and support vector machine for a regressor to create a model for demand prediction for the Aggregator movie reviews dataset and a movie-focused social network (Flixster). While the model is not compatible with non-linear data, it can predict demand for one or more products in an uncertain environment.

Hassan *et al.* [6] used algorithms such as Auto-regressive integrated moving average (ARIMA) and long short-term memory (LSTM) to construct a model to estimate the demand for a dataset consisting of historical transaction records of a corporation. This model is agent-oriented and process-oriented, and it can suggest a way to address the Bullwhip effect. Using a single data set to assess the forecasting techniques limits the model's efficacy.

Zeynep *et al.* [7] created a decision-integrating technique for the supply chain and suggested an enhanced demand forecasting model utilizing a deep learning approach. However, the model is not suitable for seasonality or trend changes.

Asma *et al.* [8] developed a model by analyzing the data set from Corporacion Favorita grocery sales, incorporating algorithms like ANN, CNN, and LSTM, Python's deep learning Keras, and tensor flow packages. In this model, LSTM outperformed the other two approaches regarding performance.

Javad Feizabadi [9] proposed a model for demand forecasting and supply chain performance using Machine learning techniques like Neural networks and time series analysis on a dataset from Kaggle. ARIMAX Forecasting process articulation is the best finding of this paper, but the model is based on a single data set. As a result, it became less effective for multivariate data sets.

Wiyanti *et al.* [10] also contributed by applying deep learning algorithms like CNN and LSTM on DataCo Global with RapidMiner software. They found that Deep learning performs better than Random Forest, gradient-boosted trees, and SVM, and Deep learning has a minimum running time.

Carbonneau *et al.* [11] used data from chocolate manufacturers and toner cartridge manufacturers to develop a supply chain demand forecast model utilizing machine learning techniques such as SVM, Time Series Analysis, and Forecasting Method. In the Supply chain context, SVM forecasted distorted demand signals with a high noise-to-pattern ratio and generated the most accurate results, according to the study's key findings and complexity search's precision.

Shabani *et al.* [12] developed an improved model for demand forecasting utilizing a multilayer LSTM network and demand data from a manufacturing industry. They found that ETS and ARIMA perform poorly compared to SVM, ANN, and LSTM.

A model for predicting the demand for perishable farm products was given by Stephen *et al.* [13]. The use of algorithms such as SVM, Fuzzy Logic, Apriori, and Eclat aided in the identification of essential outcomes. Numerical experiments and a promising substitute for the RBF neural network demonstrate that the SVM and fuzzy theory forecasting system performs better than the RBF network when evaluated according to metrics such as absolute error and relative mean error.

The existing research on demand forecasting using machine learning techniques has shown promising results but also encountered several limitations. One standard limitation is the dependence on single datasets, which may fail to address the full complexity of real-world scenarios. Another challenge is the high computational cost of specific algorithms, such as SVM and LSTM. The effectiveness of some models is influenced by their inability to adapt to multivariate datasets. To address these limitations, future studies should focus on incorporating diverse datasets, developing models that can handle non-linear data and dynamic trends, developing hybrid models, increasing computational efficiency, and enhancing the adaptability of models to multivariate data sets so that accurate and reliable demand forecasting can be achieved.

PROPOSED METHODOLOGY

The objective of this study is to predict demand within the context of supply chain management using various machine learning algorithms and to evaluate and compare their effectiveness, which can provide the most accurate prediction of demand patterns in a supply chain. Fig. (**1**) diagrammatically explains how datasets are cleaned, scaled, trained, modeled, and tested. The diagram clearly shows how the datasets are processed and trained to produce a result that forecasts demand by evaluating the performance of various algorithms included in the paper, like ARIMA, FB-Prophet, LSTM, XGBoost, and Decision Tree Regressor.

The proposed methodology contains five steps and five algorithms. Each of the steps is important and is explained below:

Data Collection: Two datasets are extracted from Yahoo Finance. These two datasets are from Amazon and Walmart. The dataset contains - Date, Open, High, Low, Close Adj, Close, and Volume columns spanning 10 years for Amazon and Walmart. Volume refers to the quantity of product purchased on that particular day.

Data Cleaning: It is one of the most crucial steps. The missing values are handled and given an average value of their previous ten values.

Feature Selection: The aim is to predict the volume sold accurately according to the customers' demand to determine the correct demand in the future. Therefore, as feature selection, only the Volume column is considered as it is directly aligned with the quantities sold.

Stationarity Check: The dataset should be stationary for time series prediction to provide accurate results. So, a statistical test, the Dickey-Fuller test, first ensures the stationarity of the datasets.

Data Scaling: The sales data is not correctly scaled to fit the model. The Min-Max Standardization technique is applied to scale the sales data, typically from 0-1, to ensure uniformity in the whole dataset.

Diverse Algorithm

The data from both datasets are trained on five different algorithms. The five algorithms are - ARIMA, LSTM, FB-Prophet, XGBoost, and Decision Tree Regressor. A statistical model called ARIMA, or Autoregressive Integrated Moving Average, analyses historical data to look for trends. Further usage of these patterns is done to forecast future values. More precisely, the ARIMA model predicts the future value by combining the observations and the difference between these observations.

The general ARIMA model parameters are displayed below: Autoregressive integrated moving average, or ARIMA (l, m, n) (AR, I, MA)

- l, the autoregressive lags' order (AR Part)
- m, the differencing order (Part I of the integration)
- n, the moving average lags' order (MA Part)

A general formula for ARIMA is provided below (1).

$$F_t = L_t + \Omega_1 D_{t-1} + \ldots + \Omega_p D_{t-p} + \beta_1 E_{t-1} + \ldots + \beta_q E_{t-q} \quad \textbf{(1)}$$

Where F_t: forecasted value at time t, L_t: trend component at time t, D_{t-1} . . ., D_{t-p}: differenced values at times t − 1, . . ., t − p, capturing the autoregressive (AR) component of the model, E_{t-1}, . . ., E_{t-p}: error terms at times t−1, . . ., t−p, capturing the moving average (MA) component of the model, Ω_1, . . ., Ω_p and β_1, . . ., β_q: coefficients associated with the autoregressive and Moving average terms, respectively. In most cases, Prophet handles outliers well and is adaptable to missing data and trend changes.

Given below is a general equation of FB-Prophet (2):

$$y(t) = g(t) + s(t) + h(t) + e(t) \quad \textbf{(2)}$$

Where g(t) is the trend, or changes over a long period, s(t) seasonality, h(t): holiday effect on the forecasting process,

e(t): qualified modifications unique to a company, individual, or situation, y(t): estimation. In deep learning and AI, LSTMs are long, short-term memory networks that employ ANNs. Information added to, deleted, and output from the memory cell is governed by the input, forget, and output gates.

Given below is a general equation (3-8) of LSTM [16]–

$$f_t = \sigma g(W_f * X_t) + U_f * h_{t-1} + b_f \quad \textbf{(3)}$$

$$i_t = \sigma g(W_i * X_t + U_i * h_{t-1} + b_i) \quad \textbf{(4)}$$

$$o_t = \sigma g(W_o * X_t + U_o * h_{t-1} + b_o) \quad \textbf{(5)}$$

$$c_t = \sigma c(W_c * X_t + U_c * \tilde{h}_{t-1} + b_c) \quad \textbf{(6)}$$

$$c_t = f_t \odot c_{t-1} + i_t \odot c_t \quad \textbf{(7)}$$

$$h_t = o_t \odot \sigma h(c_t) \quad \textbf{(8)}$$

Where $c_0 = 0$ and $h_0 = 0$ are the starting values. The operator indicates the element-wise product ⊙. The subscript t indicates the time step. The input vector to the LSTM unit is $x_t \in R^d$ and $f_t \in (0, 1)_{r,\ \text{neglecting}}$ the activation vector of the gate. It lies between 0 and 1.

$I_t \in (0, 1)_r$ is the activation vector of the input/update gate.

$o_t \in (0, 1)_r$ denotes the activation vector for output gates.

$h_t \in (-1, 1)_r$ is the LSTM unit's hidden state vector

$c\sim_t \in (-1, 1)_r$ represents the activation vector for cell input

$c_t \in R^h$ denotes the cell state vector

$W \in R^h X^d$, $U \in R^h X^h$ and $b \in R^h$ The bias vector and weight matrix parameters must be learned during training using a popular machine-learning technique, XGBoost. Handling non-linear correlations, regularization, missing information, and outliers are some positive aspects of using XGBoost [17] for time-series forecasting. Another machine-learning approach that is used to solve regression and classification problems is the decision tree [18]. Averages of the training dataset's subsets make up Decision Tree predictions. The time-series measurements inside those intervals are then the arithmetic means of the projections (9).

$$f(t) = \frac{\sum_{i=1}^{N} 1}{|I_i|} \quad \sum_{s=1;..;T \cap I_i}^{T} \quad y_s \cdot I_t < \varepsilon \text{ and } s \in I_i < \varepsilon \text{ and } t \in I_i \qquad \textbf{(9)}$$

where $y_1, \ldots y_t$: training observations

$I_i = (l_i, u_i]$

$l_i, u_i \in \mathbb{R}^+; l_i < u_i; l_i = 0, u_N = \infty$

$I_i \cap I_j = \emptyset; U_{i=1}^{N} I_i = \mathbb{R}_0^+$

$I_s \in I_i = \{1 \text{ if } s \in I_i$

$0 \text{ else}\}$

Now, consider applying this model to forecast the time series in the future. As a result, the formula above becomes as follows (10) [19]:

$$\hat{}f(t) = \frac{1}{|\{y_s, s \in \{1;...;T\} \cap I_T\}|} \sum_{s=1}^{T} \quad y_s \cdot I_{s \in I_T} \qquad \textbf{(10)}$$

IMPLEMENTATION AND RESULT ANALYSIS

The paper's main objective lies in forecasting precise supply chain and logistics demand using accurate machine learning algorithms. Five algorithms and two distinct real-time datasets achieve the paper's mission. With the divergence of two datasets, the process becomes straightforward, and analyzing the performance becomes more effortless. Additionally, the performance of the algorithms is greatly influenced by the datasets used for analysis and training. Describing the steps of executing the algorithms taken and utilized proceeds as follows.

Implementation of ARIMA

The distinct datasets of Walmart Sales and Amazon Sales are picked. The datasets are cleaned using the null function. It generates a binary mask indicating if the value is present or absent in each dataset cell. The visual plot is seen to have various outliers. The data is scaled between 0 to 1, also called min-max scaling. After data pre-processing, the ARIMA model was initialized and called [20]. To begin, the model initializes a blank list to hold the predictions. To meet the requirements of the ARIMA model, the input data's dimensions are modified. Every time, a step in the dataset. The prediction list stores the values, providing a basis for training, testing, and validation. This approach enables accurate time forecasting using the ARIMA model.

Implementation of FB-Prophet

The distinct datasets of Walmart and Amazon sales are selected. With the help of the null function, the datasets are cleansed, generating a binary mask that indicates if the value is present or absent in each dataset cell. The single focus is placed on the sales volume column, deeming other features irrelevant for the research purpose, which aims at univariate forecasting. Over this, the FB-Prophet model is initialized and called. This parameter ensures that a subset of the dataset is trained and that the entire dataset is not trained to learn patterns and trends [21]. The cross-validation results provide insights into the model's performance over different time intervals. Implementing the FB-Prophet model helps with precise time series prediction for demand forecasting.

Implementation of LSTM

The separate datasets of Walmart Sales and Amazon Sales are picked. The datasets are purified utilizing the null function. It produces a binary mask signifying if the value is present or absent in each dataset cell. The missing values are recognized and replaced using the values of proximity. For regression tasks, a dense layer with a single unit is placed after the LSTM layer, with 50 units and a tan activation (tanh) function. Positive values remain unaltered, and all negative values are set to zero by the "tanh" activation [22]. The model is then assembled using the Adam optimizer and trained for ten iterations. Adam optimizer is an optimization algorithm that stands for Adaptive Moment Estimation, and it combines the concepts of momentum and RMSProp. This implementation of the LSTM model assists in precise time series prediction for demand forecasting.

Implementation of Xgboost

The distinct datasets of Walmart and Amazon sales are selected. With the help of the null function, the datasets are cleansed, generating a binary mask that indicates if the value is present or absent in each dataset cell. Data smoothing is applied to address them, and the data is scaled between 0-1. To train and test the dataset for XGBoost, the complete dataset has been divided into two parts: train, which contains 80% of the data for training, and test, which includes 20% of the data for testing. Next, time-related features like the day of the year are extracted for the datetime index, creating the feature matrices and target variables for training and testing [23]. XGBoost algorithm uses these features with specific hyperparameters like estimators, learning rate, and the maximum depth of trees.

Implementation of Decision Tree Regressor

The separate datasets of Walmart Sales and Amazon Sales are picked. The datasets are purified utilizing the null function. Scaling here helps bring all the features to the same scale for smooth prediction. Training uses 80% of the data, whereas testing uses 20%. The model of a decision tree regressor is initialized. Using the training data, the model is trained. The results are stored in a variable. This is the fundamental implementation for training and testing a decision tree regressor model for predicting demand.

Result Analysis

The principal objective of the paper is to employ machine learning techniques to forecast supply chain demand precisely. The goal is to compare the various algorithms and identify which performs better using advanced methodologies. Five different algorithms and two different real-time datasets are taken and compared for the same purpose. As two datasets are given, analyzing the algorithms is easier. Also, the accuracy of the algorithms depends on the dataset's nature. The accuracy of the various algorithms used depends upon several factors like RMSE (root mean squared error), MSE (mean squared error), and MAE (mean absolute error).

The square root of the average squared variances between the expected and observed outcomes is the root mean square error, or RMSE. The formula is as follows (11):

$$\text{RMSE} = \frac{\sqrt{\sum_{i=1}^{m} \quad (x_i - \hat{x}_i)^2}}{m} \tag{11}$$

Where: $\hat{x_i}$ = variable I, m = number of non-missing data points, xi = actual observations time series

MSE is calculated by measuring the average squared difference between estimated and actual data. The formula is shown below (12):

$$\text{MSE}=\frac{1}{m} * \sum_{i=1}^{m} (Y_i - \bar{Y}_i)^2 \quad \textbf{(12)}$$

where: *Yi* = observed values, Ȳi= predicted values

The extent of the difference between an observation's true value and its prediction is the MAE. The formula is as follows (13):

$$\text{MAE} = \frac{\sum_{i=1}^{m} |y_i - x_i|}{m} \quad \textbf{(13)}$$

Where: *yi* = observed value, xi = actual value and m = total number of data points.

The table below is an enhanced version that examines five algorithms and two datasets. The algorithms considered for evaluation encompass ARIMA, FB-Prophet, LSTM, XGBoost, and Decision Tree Regressor. The datasets taken are Dataset 1, which entails Walmart's real-time sales data, and Dataset 2, which entails Amazon's real-time sales data. This tabular analysis in Table **1** provides excellent insights into the performance of each algorithm across each dataset, offering an integrated view of their performance in demand prediction.

Table 1. Evaluation metrics for algorithms on amazon and walmart datasets.

	WALMART			AMAZON		
Model	**RMSE**	**MSE**	**MAE**	**RMSE**	**MSE**	**MAE**
ARIMA	0.04165406	0.0017350	0.0236814	0.04531028	0.00205302	0.0234937
FB-Prophet	0.053943	0.002910	0.036588	0.091557	0.008383	0.066181
LSTM	0.0418714773	0.001753221	0.02611676	0.045218875	0.00204475	0.03302872
XGBoost	0.0557017322	0.003102683	0.039425591	0.116141925	0.01348895	0.08770922
Decision Tree Regressor	0.05313950	0.0028238	0.0303540	0.066497	0.00442190	0.0423229

After the examination of each algorithm, the following findings have been acquired. The ARIMA model achieved the lowest RMSE (Walmart Sales Data: 0.04, Amazon Sales Data: 0.04) in both datasets. FB-Prophet has the highest RMSE (Walmart Sales Data: 0.05, Amazon Sales Data: 0.09) and MSE (Walmart

Sales Data: 0.002910, Amazon Sales Data: 0.008383) on both datasets, but records a lower MAE (Walmart Sales Data: 0.03, Amazon Sales Date: 0.06) than ARIMA and XGBoost in most cases. LSTM achieved the second lowest RMSE (Walmart Sales Data: 0.0027328, Amazon Sales Date: 0.06) AND MAE (Walmart Sales Data: 0.02, Amazon Sales Date: 0.04) in both datasets but received the lowest MAE (Walmart Sales Data: 0.02, Amazon Sales Date: 0.04) in the Amazon sales dataset. XGBoost neither excelled nor failed behind, thus giving an average performance in most cases. XGBoost is not an outstanding performer, but it is also not ranked last. Based on the evaluation metrics, the Decision Tree Regressor appears less suited for demand forecasting.

Graphical Analysis

ARIMA

Figs. (**2a** and **2b**) show the ARIMA implementation for the Walmart and Amazon datasets, respectively, showing plot deviation values for training, testing, and validation data points. The green line denotes the deviation of values of validation data. The red line denotes the deviation of values of the testing data. Overall, the plot provides insights into deviation across values of different datasets, that is, training, testing, and validation.

FB-Prophet

Regression and confidence intervals are superimposed on a scatter plot in Figs. (**3a** and **3b**), respectively, illustrating the FB-Prophet implementation for the Walmart and Amazon datasets. The blue line shows the regression lines that fit the data. To show the confidence intervals, the blue color is darkened. Overall, the plot provides insights into actual data, regression lines fitted to data, and the confidence interval.

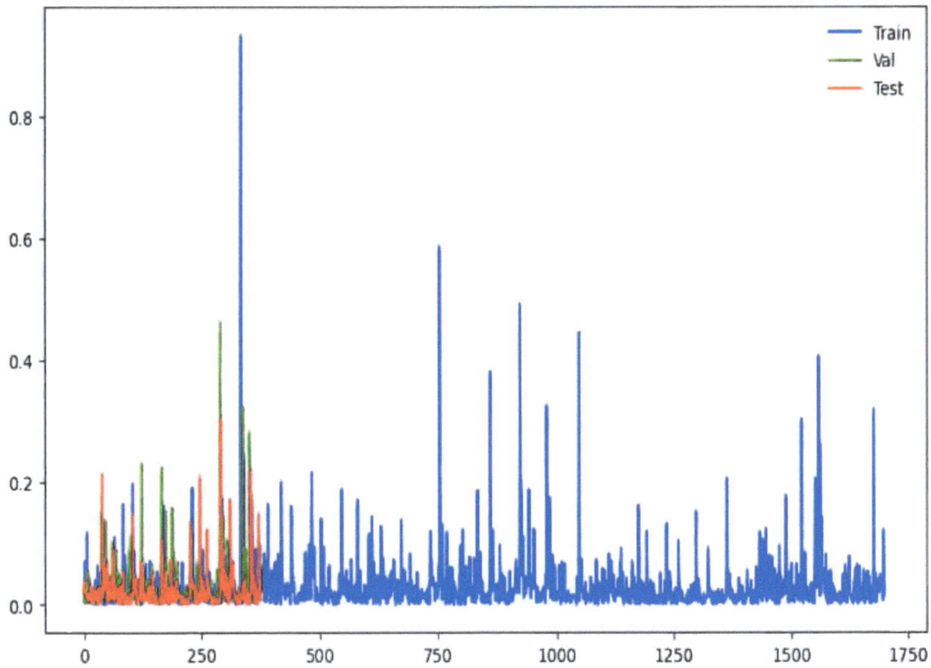

Fig. (2a). Walmart data.

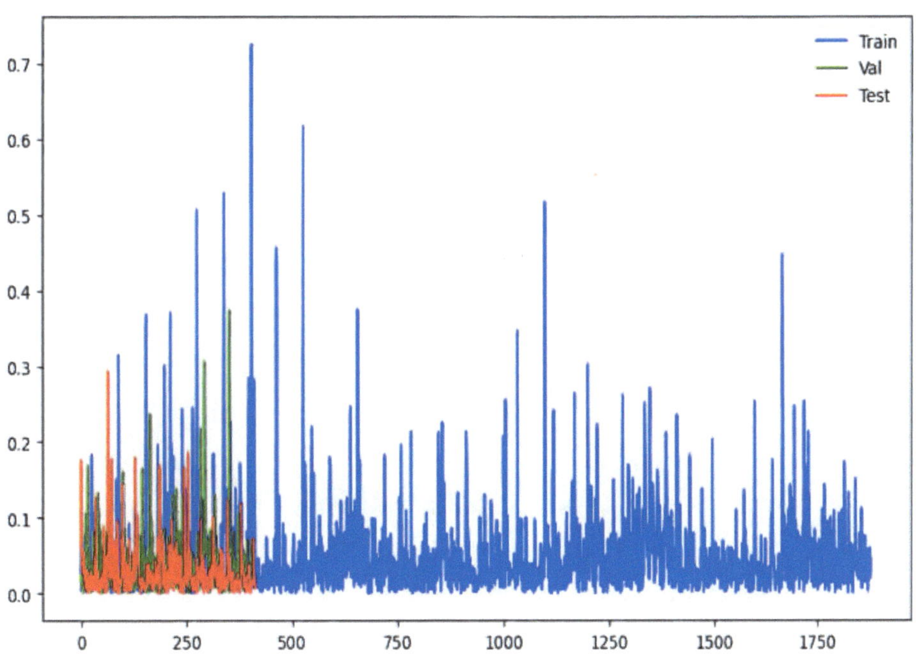

Fig. (2b). Amazon data.

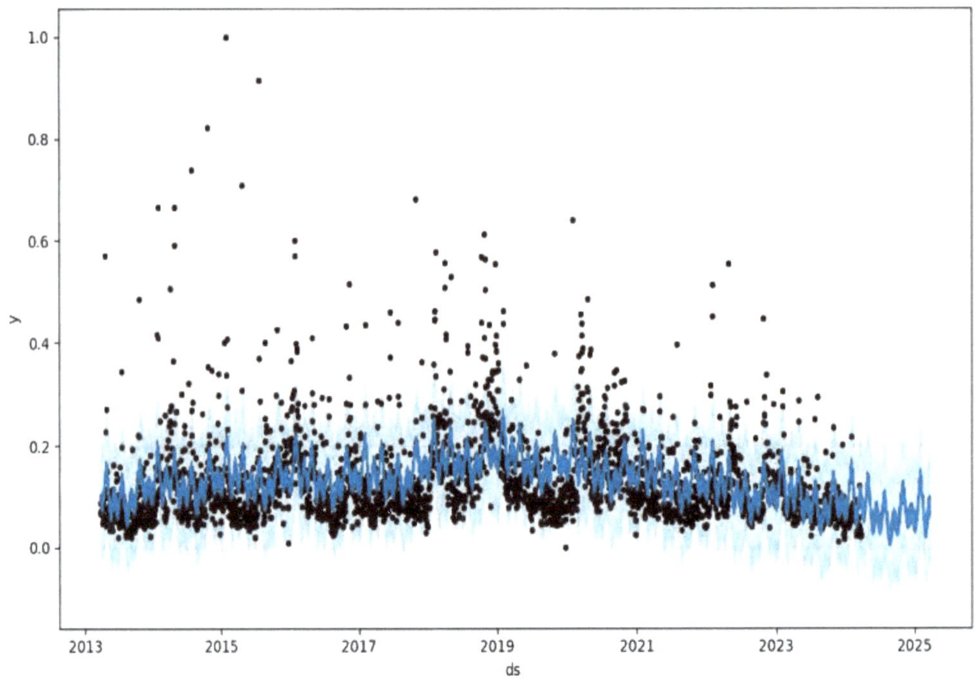

Fig. (3a). Walmart data.

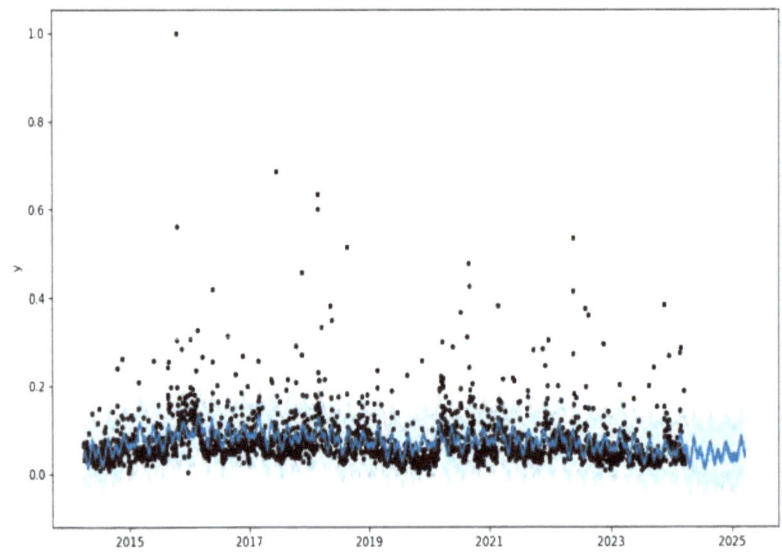

Fig. (3b). Amazon data.

LSTM

The below Figs. (**4a** and **4b**) show the LSTM implementation for the Walmart and Amazon datasets, respectively, comparing actual and predicted sales over time. Overall, the plot provides insights into actual and predicted data in the given time interval, showing the visual comparison.

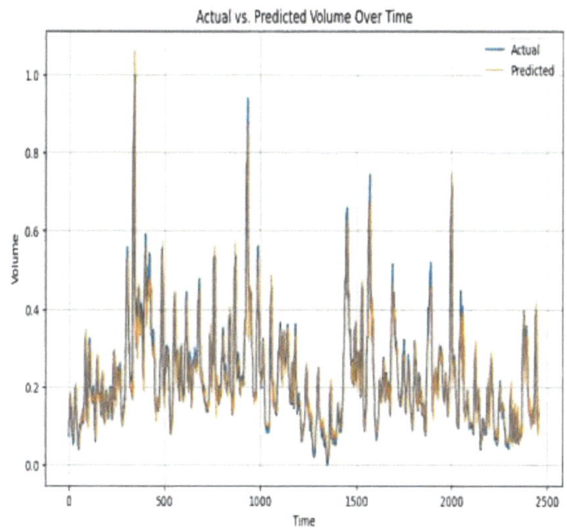

Fig. (4a). Walmart data.

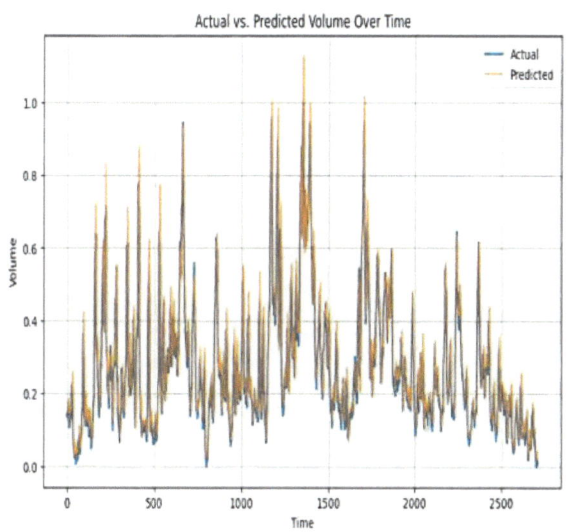

Fig. (4b). Amazon data.

XGBoost

The below Figs. (**5a** and **5b**) show the XGBoost implementation for the Walmart and Amazon datasets, respectively, comparing actual and predicted sales over time. Overall, the plot provides insights into actual and predicted data in the given time interval, showing the visual comparison.

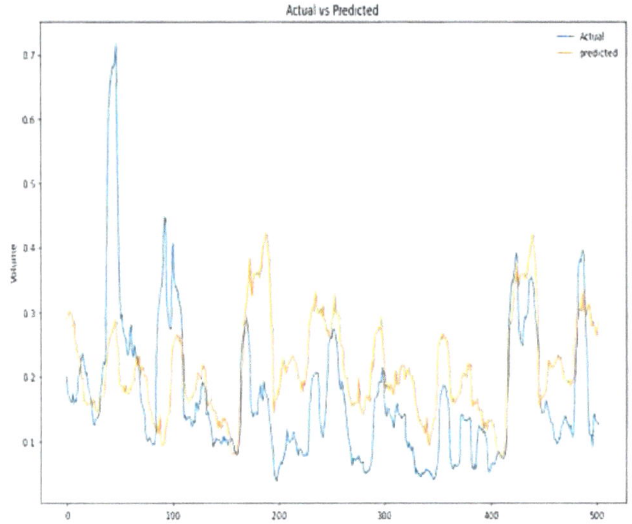

Fig. (5a). Walmart data.

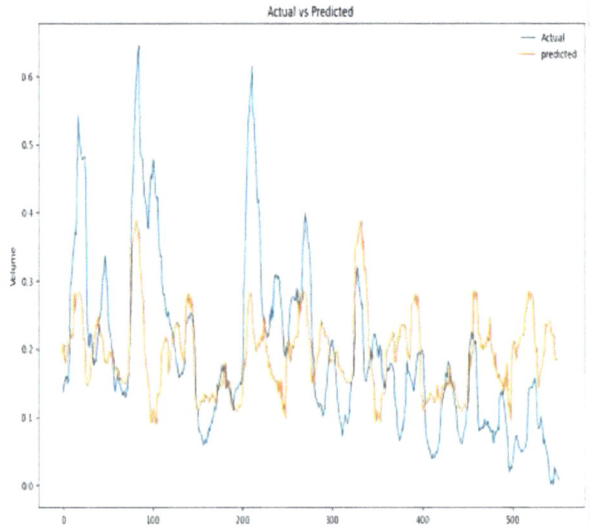

Fig. (5b). Amazon data.

Decision Tree Regressor

The above Figs. (**6a** and **6b**) show the Decision Tree Regressor implementation for the Walmart and Amazon datasets, which compares actual and predicted sales over time.

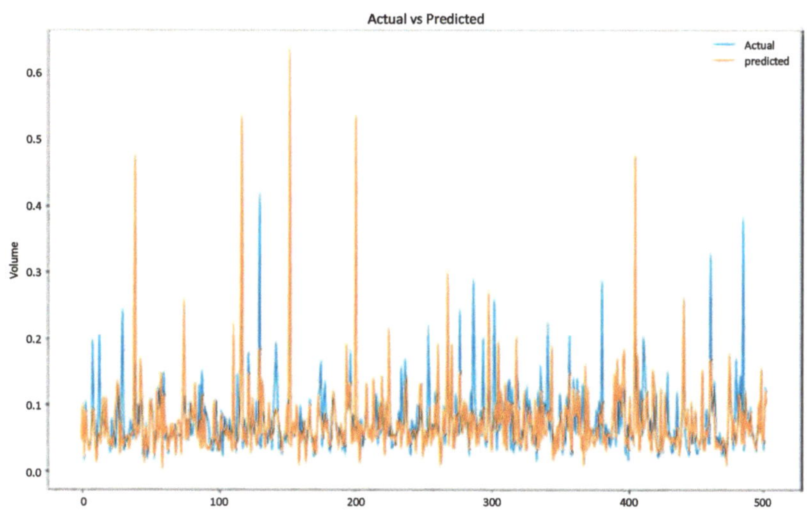

Fig. (6a). Walmart data.

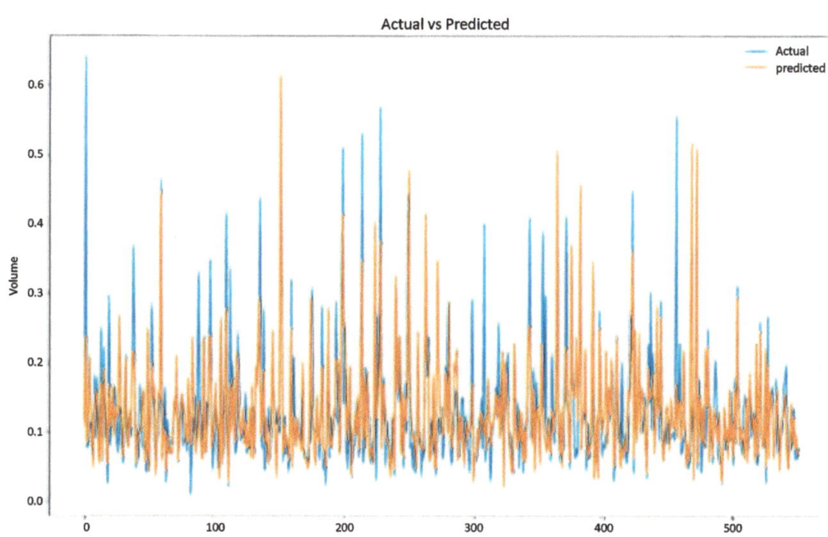

Fig. (6b). Amazon data.

CONCLUSION

This study comprehensively evaluated five distinct machine learning and deep learning algorithms—ARIMA, FB-Prophet, LSTM, XGBoost, and Decision Tree Regressor—for demand forecasting in retail supply chain management. By utilizing real-time sales data from two major retailers, Walmart and Amazon, our research offers valuable insights into the performance and applicability of these algorithms in practical scenarios.

Key Findings

1. FB-Prophet's Efficiency: FB-Prophet emerged as a strong contender, particularly in minimizing Mean Absolute Error (MAE) for both datasets (Walmart: 0.036588, Amazon: 0.066181). This suggests its potential utility in scenarios where minimizing absolute prediction errors is crucial.
2. LSTM's Robustness: LSTM showed consistent performance across multiple metrics, indicating its capability to capture complex temporal relationships in the data. This makes it a versatile choice for demand forecasting, especially when dealing with non-linear patterns.
3. ARIMA's Reliability: ARIMA demonstrated a good balance between performance and interpretability for datasets exhibiting linear trends. Its low RMSE scores (Walmart: 0.04165406, Amazon: 0.04531028) highlight its effectiveness in capturing overall trend patterns.
4. XGBoost and Decision Tree Limitations: While XGBoost showed average performance, the Decision Tree Regressor appeared less suited for this demand forecasting task. This emphasizes the need for algorithm selection based on the specific characteristics of the forecasting problem.

In conclusion, this comparative study provides valuable guidance for practitioners in selecting appropriate demand forecasting models in retail supply chain management. It also lays the groundwork for further research into improving the accuracy and reliability of demand forecasts, ultimately contributing to more efficient and responsive supply chain operations.

REFERENCES

[1] L. Terrada, A. Alloubane, J. Bakkoury, and M. El Khaili, "IoT contribution in supply chain management for enhancing performance indicators", *International Conference on Electronics, Control, Optimization and Computer Science (ICECOCS),* pp. 1-5, 2018. [http://dx.doi.org/10.1109/ICECOCS.2018.8610517]

[2] A.R.S. Parmezan, V.M.A. Souza, and G.E.A.P.A. Batista, "Evaluation of statistical and machine learning models for time series prediction: Identifying the state-of-the-art and the best conditions for the use of each model", *Inf. Sci.,* vol. 484, pp. 302-337, 2019. [http://dx.doi.org/10.1016/j.ins.2019.01.076]

[3] P. Malviya, and V. Bhandari, "A systematic study on effective demand prediction using machine

learning", *Journal of Integrated Science and Technology,* vol. 12, no. 1, pp. 711-711, 2024.

[4] S.F. Ga, and N. Prakashb, "Machine learning in demand forecasting-a review", *Proceedings of the 2nd International Conference on IoT, Social, Mobile, Analytics & Cloud in Computational Vision & Bio-Engineering,* 2020.

[5] N. Ampazis, "Forecasting demand in supply chain using machine learning algorithms", *Int. J. Artif. Life Res.,* vol. 5, no. 1, pp. 56-73, 2015. [http://dx.doi.org/10.4018/IJALR.2015010104]

[6] L. Terrada, M.E. Khaili, and H. Ouajji, "Demand forecasting model using deep learning methods for supply chain management 4.0", *Int. J. Adv. Comput. Sci. Appl.,* vol. 13, no. 5, 2022. [http://dx.doi.org/10.14569/IJACSA.2022.0130581]

[7] Z.H. Kilimci, A.O. Akyuz, M. Uysal, S. Akyokus, M.O. Uysal, B. Atak Bulbul, and M.A. Ekmis, "An improved demand forecasting model using deep learning approach and proposed decision integration strategy for supply chain", *Complexity,* vol. 2019, no. 1, p. 9067367, 2019. [http://dx.doi.org/10.1155/2019/9067367]

[8] A. Husna, S.H. Amin, and B. Shah, "Demand forecasting in supply chain management using different deep learning methods", In: *Demand forecasting and order planning in supply chains and humanitarian logistics.* IGI Global, 2021, pp. 140-170. [http://dx.doi.org/10.4018/978-1-7998-3805-0.ch005]

[9] J. Feizabadi, "Machine learning demand forecasting and supply chain performance", *Int. J. Logist.,* vol. 25, no. 2, pp. 119-142, 2022. [http://dx.doi.org/10.1080/13675567.2020.1803246]

[10] D.T. Wiyanti, I. Kharisudin, A.B. Setiawan, and A.K. Nugroho, "Machine-learning algorithm for demand forecasting problem", *J. Phys. Conf. Ser.,* vol. 1918, no. 4, p. 042012, 2021. [http://dx.doi.org/10.1088/1742-6596/1918/4/042012]

[11] Carbonneau, R., Vahidov, R., & Laframboise, K. (2009). Forecasting supply chain demand using machine learning algorithms. In Distributed Artificial Intelligence, Agent Technology, and Collaborative Applications (pp. 328-365). IGI Global. [http://dx.doi.org/10.4018/978-1-60566-144-5.ch018]

[12] X.F. Du, S.C.H. Leung, J.L. Zhang, and K.K. Lai, "Demand forecasting of perishable farm products using support vector machine", *Int. J. Syst. Sci.,* vol. 44, no. 3, pp. 556-567, 2013. [http://dx.doi.org/10.1080/00207721.2011.617888]

[13] H. Abbasimehr, M. Shabani, and M. Yousefi, "An optimized model using LSTM network for demand forecasting", *Comput. Ind. Eng.,* vol. 143, p. 106435, 2020. [http://dx.doi.org/10.1016/j.cie.2020.106435]

[14] Available from: https://blogs.cisco.com/analytics-automation/arima2

[15] Available from: https://www.geeksforgeeks.org/time-series-analysis-using-facebook-prophet/

[16] Available from: https://en.wikipedia.org/wiki/Long_short-term_memory

[17] Available from: https://en.wikipedia.org/wiki/XGBoost

[18] H. Min, "Artificial intelligence in supply chain management: theory and applications", *Int. J. Logist.,* vol. 13, no. 1, pp. 13-39, 2010. [http://dx.doi.org/10.1080/13675560902736537]

[19] Available from: https://sarem-seitz.com/posts/forecasting-with-decision-trees-and-random-forests/

[20] K. Gilbert, "An ARIMA supply chain model", *Manage. Sci.,* vol. 51, no. 2, pp. 305-310, 2005. [http://dx.doi.org/10.1287/mnsc.1040.0308]

[21] L. Terrada, J. Bakkoury, M. El Khaili, and A. Khiat, "Collaborative and communicative logistics flows management using the internet of things", In: *Lecture Notes in Real-Time Intelligent Systems.* Springer

International Publishing, 2019, pp. 216-224.
[http://dx.doi.org/10.1007/978-3-319-91337-7_21]

[22] Y. Issaoui, A. Khiat, A. Bahnasse, and H. Ouajji, "An advanced LSTM model for optimal scheduling in smart logistic environment: E-commerce case", *IEEE Access,* vol. 9, pp. 126337-126356, 2021. [http://dx.doi.org/10.1109/ACCESS.2021.3111306]

[23] S. Hochreiter, and J. Schmidhuber, "Long short-term memory", *Neural Comput.,* vol. 9, no. 8, pp. 1735-1780, 1997.
[http://dx.doi.org/10.1162/neco.1997.9.8.1735] [PMID: 9377276]

CHAPTER 3

Assessing the Optimal Deep Learning Model for Predicting Financial Insolvency

Bikash Chandra Naik[1], **Meenakshi Kandpal**[1,*], **Jyotirmayee Routray**[1], **Pranati Mishra**[1] and **Subhasmita Pradhan**[1]

[1] *School of Computer Science and Engineering, Odisha University of Technology and Research, Bhubaneswar, India*

Abstract: This research presents a groundbreaking Deep Learning-Based Model for Financial Distress Prediction, leveraging advanced neural network architectures to enhance the accuracy and reliability of forecasting financial distress. The model is designed to autonomously learn intricate patterns and relationships within extensive financial datasets, addressing the limitations of traditional methods in capturing complex, non-linear dependencies. Key to its efficacy is the incorporation of different deep learning models like CNN, ANN, LSTM, BiLSTM and XGBoost, enabling the model to grasp sequential dependencies within financial time series data. This temporal awareness is crucial for understanding the evolving nature of financial indicators over time, providing a more nuanced perspective on potential distress signals. The model's strength lies in its ability to automatically extract relevant features, eliminating the need for manual feature engineering, which is a common challenge in traditional models. As financial markets continue to grow in complexity, the Deep Learning-Based Model offers a proactive and innovative response to the evolving challenges of risk management.

Keywords: ANN, BiLSTM, CNN, Financial distress, LSTM, Neural network architecture, XGBoost.

INTRODUCTION

Bankruptcy is a situation of liquidation where the original company is unable to repay its loan amount to creditors. When a company's debt is higher than average and the situation remains unchanged for a long time; as a result, the company is not able to pay back the obligation, this situation is called as Bankruptcy. In other instances, businesses go bankrupt right after experiencing a problem, such as significant fraud. The company which is announced bankruptcy is taken as a failed company. Bankruptcy affects the company's reputation as well as the profit

* **Corresponding author Meenakshi Kandpal:** School of Computer Science and Engineering, Odisha University of Technology and Research, Bhubaneswar, India; E-mail: meenakshikandpal14@gmail.com

Suneeta Satpathy, Sachi Nandan Mohanty & Subhendu Kumar Pani (Eds.)

made by individual stakeholders, and as a result, it further affects the economic expansion of the business.

Therefore, bankruptcy prediction is taken as a global-level issue. Such forecasting helps banks avoid providing financial support to companies that have a higher probability of going bankrupt in the near future. Additionally, investors can protect themselves from financial loss by avoiding investments in such companies. The failure of a company does not come overnight; it gradually arrives through several stages slowly. Prediction of this bankruptcy will help to warn the company about the danger knocking on their door and take actions accordingly, modifying their course of action. Therefore, bankruptcy prediction (BP) has been the subject of much research for the past fifty years.

This paper presents novel Deep Learning-Based Models for Financial Distress Prediction, leveraging advanced neural network architectures to analyze extensive datasets with a focus on capturing nonlinear relationships and temporal dependencies. The key strength of deep learning lies in its ability to autonomously extract relevant elements, eliminating the need for manual feature engineering, which is a common challenge in traditional models. The deep learning-based approach is designed to adapt and evolve as market conditions change, making it inherently more robust in capturing the dynamic nature of financial markets.

Moreover, the model's incorporated include *ANN, CNN LSTM, BiLSTM* and *XGBoost* networks. The accuracy of all the given models was then compared to identify the most accurate model, which was found to be the most successful in predicting bankruptcy.

As financial markets continue to grow in complexity and interconnectivity, the deployment of a Deep Learning-Based Model for Financial Distress Prediction represents a proactive and innovative response to the evolving challenges of risk management. This paper explores the methodology, performance, and implications of such a model, aiming to contribute to thc advancement of predictive analytics in finance and fortify the financial industry's resilience against uncertainties.

RELATED WORK

Abror *et al.* [3] implemented a data set compiled by the Taiwan Economic Journal that trained an estimated 6,819 machines using machine learning algorithms and methods for classification. In this paper, the author found a categorization technique that provided the best accuracy outcomes. The author focused simply on forecasting the occurrence of bankruptcy and did not take into account the socio-economic ramifications of the traditional bankruptcy prediction models [2].

As a result, the motive of the research was to incorporate the viewpoints through the machine-learning (ML) modeling technique in order to account for the various costs associated with bankruptcy [6]. An approach for processing small-sample domestic company financial data was also presented [3]. To solve the problem of getting the prediction accuracy of companies, the author explored instance of random sampling of companies through an approximate entropy and an optimization threshold based on AUC [4].

Adisa *et al.* [2] implemented self-learning and multi-learning strategies to develop the cognitive and social learning parts of the PSO algorithm. Moreover, the algorithm used by PSO identified the best LSTM settings. The author's final method for bankruptcy prediction combined optimal feature selection with the LSTM model. As a result, an improved feature selection approach for the LSTM model was devised [4, 5, 7]. Five feature selection strategies to produce datasets with fewer duplicate characteristics in order to determine which feature selection methods perform most effectively in bankruptcy prediction were evaluated and employed [5].

The author investigated the Taiwanese Bankruptcy dataset from the Taiwan Economic Journal. Then, for dealing with imbalanced datasets, the author employed an artificial minority oversampling strategy that used GA-SVM to select the best feature, then the classifier was stacked and extreme gradient boosting was applied as a meta-learner. As a result, it was demonstrated that the proposed strategy could forecast bankruptcy with high accuracy [6, 14]. The author also proposed a transfer learning-based model and the test was using a self-collected and cautiously labelled dataset [7]. The LSTM model assumptions were used to generate machine learning models on both the primary and K-Means SMOTE balanced datasets.

Valaskova *et al.* [8] focused on developing a model for forecasting bankruptcy data from 20,693 firms from all sectors that functioned in Visegrad group countries over time (2020-2021), also to find key predictors of bankruptcy. Further, the author stated that to avoid losses caused by an enterprise's economic crisis, multiple discriminatory evaluations could be used to create individual prediction models for every Visegrad and an intricate individual model for overall Visegrad group [8, 9]. The author implemented the Black-Scholes asset pricing model for combining conceptual and professional evaluation to pinpoint the financial ratios and macroeconomic variables impacting bankruptcy [9].

The evaluation of multilayer artificial neural networks to examine the trustworthiness of the outcome in determining and prioritizing the factors influencing the prediction of bankruptcy revealed that the least significant variable was the company's capital to net profit ratio, and its most significant factor was the company's profit prior to interest and taxes relative to its overall assets [12]. The author analyzed EBP models for MiSEs in the construction sectors [10].

Denis *et al.* [11] presented a mathematical framework that could forecast the insolvency of Serbian enterprises one year before the bankruptcy proceedings begin. A system for computing the unseen parameters behind the main parametric model of bankruptcy prediction at the same time was created [12]. In particular, undetectable parameters, including asset value and asset volatility by means of learning by embedding a neural network in the structural models that maps the neural network's input space to the undetectable parameter space were computed [8, 9]. The author used a super efficiency model in the European Union to identify insolvent and actively manufactured enterprises [13].

The goal of the research was to create a novel bankruptcy prediction framework that takes into account aspects other than traditional financial proportions and to increase the performance and consistency of bankruptcy prediction models of the Indian ecosystem [15]. Papik *et al.* [16] aimed to examine the influence of the financial crisis on the productivity of bankruptcy prediction models. Data for over 90,000 SMEs was collected from 2015 to 2019 in order to construct prediction models for three periods - two non-crisis periods and one crisis period. CatBoost, LightGBM, and XGBoost techniques were used to make one-year, two-year, and three-year predictions for the three time periods.

An adaptive whale optimization algorithm along with Deep learning (AWOA-DL) technique, was employed in a financial distress prediction study to develop a novel financial distress prediction model [17]. The AWOA-DL technique's purpose was to identify whether or not a company is in financial trouble. Jabeur *et al.* [18] focused on finding the model specification with the best clarity for bankruptcy prediction. Based on this foundation, an enhanced XGBoost algorithm (FS-XGBoost) based on feature importance selection was proposed. FS- XGBoost was pitted against seven machine learning algorithms using three widely used feature selection approaches from Bankruptcy prediction PLS-DA [17, 18]. Harroua *et al.* [19] provided an effective technique for knowing daily and hourly visitors at an emergency department using the Variational AutoEncoder (VAE) algorithm.

The VAE model, as a deep learning-based model, has received significant attention in feature extraction and modeling [19]. In such a fast-evolving and competitive industry, providing customers with the information they need to choose a proper deposit takes more than simply following one's passion [20].

RESEARCH METHODOLOGY

Data Collection: The dataset collected from Kaggle was loaded into the model, which consisted of 21 attributes and 78682 instances. Then, the dataset was checked for any existing missing values. The value counts for bankrupt and non-bankrupt companies in the dataset were inconsistent, resulting in a class imbalance in most of the datasets. Therefore, it was necessary to perform a balancing technique.

Data Preprocessing: Data preprocessing technique involved the major operations of the various testing models *i.e.*, feature scaling, over-sampling the data and splitting the data. Feature scaling is a process of range normalization of data elements or independent variables. This technique was preferred to scale the features to a range of 0-1; however, some features still have values greater than 2, while most of them range between 0-1. For the balancing technique, the dataset is reshaped to identify bankrupt and non-bankrupt individuals and mainly balance the dataset for easy training of the model. For this, we used the SMOTE (Synthetic Minority Oversampling Technique) to balance the dataset using an oversampling method. Splitting the data involves dividing the dataset as testing and learning dataset in the proportion of 80% training dataset and 20% testing dataset.

Data Prediction: After completion of data preprocessing, the dataset is trained through different deep learning models like ANN, CNN, LSTM, BiLSTM and XGBoost. After the model is trained, the model is tested and analyzed based on the precision, recall, f1-score and accuracy of the given model. After finding out the accuracy of all the given models, the most accurate model is identified to be the most successful in predicting the bankruptcy of the financial sector, as described in Fig. (**1**).

Missing Values: Missing values were checked and handled from the given set of data and the following statement is generated for the absence of missing values: 'There are no missing values, therefore we can proceed'

Label Encoding: Label encoding serves primarily to turn category data into numerical values. It requires providing a distinct integer label for every designated variable. In this case, the status label of the company is converted from 'alive' and 'failed' to 1 and 0, respectively, representing non-bankruptcy and bankruptcy.

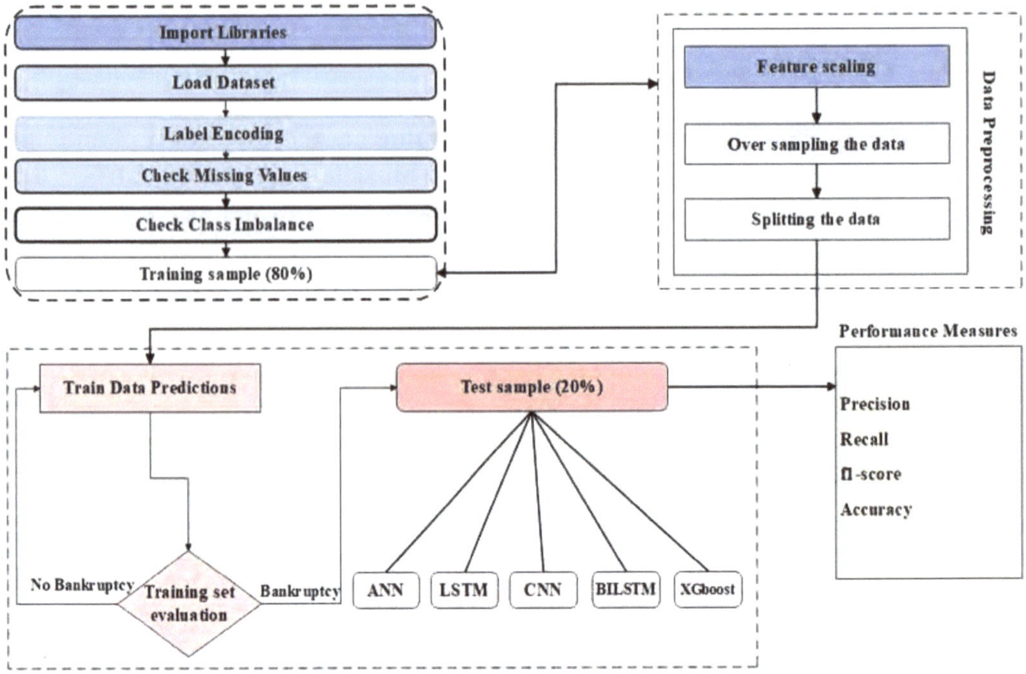

Fig. (1). Block diagram of an optimal deep learning system.

Checking for Class Imbalance: Class imbalance of the data was checked and the following observations were recorded:(Financially Stable: 96.77%, Financially Unstable: 3.23%). It was seen that the class imbalance was too high therefore it's necessary to perform under or over sampling techniques to balance the dataset. 'There are no missing values, therefore we can proceed'

A. Feature Scaling: For the model, it was preferable to scale the features in the range between 0-1. Some features have values more than 2 while most of them range between 0-1.

B. Balancing the data (Oversampling): First of all, NaN (Not a Number) values were checked in the 'status label'. Further, the NaaN values were replaced using the simple imputer, which mainly used the median. Then, the SMOTE oversampling technique was applied to resample the target variable, under which the under-sampled data "Non-Bankrupt Company" was oversampled to match the number of companies that went bankrupt.

C. Splitting the Data: The bankrupt dataset was further separated as testing and learning datasets to the ratio of 80% training dataset and 20% testing dataset. The training dataset is mainly used to train, whereas the testing dataset is mainly used for testing the model accuracy, precision and other parameters to identify the best model for bankruptcy prediction.

D. Model Implementation: Multiple models were implemented, such as ANN, LSTM, CNN, BiLSTM and XGBoost models to predict bankruptcy of different companies.

RESULT AND ANALYSIS

First of all, a dataset was extracted from Kaggle and applied onto the following given models. Then, the missing values were identified. If missing values were present, then the next step was interrupted and if there were no missing values, then it would proceed to the next step. The inconsistent value counts in the datasets led to class imbalance, making an over-sampling technique necessary. Data preprocessing technique involved the major operations of the various testing models *i.e.* feature scaling, over sampling the data and splitting the data. Feature scaling technique was preferred to scale the features in the range between 0-1 but still some features have values more than 2 while most of them range between 0-1. In the over sampling technique, the dataset was reshaped to identify bankrupt and non-bankrupt individuals. Splitting the data involved a confusion matrix to generate the classification report with 4 digits after the decimal point. After the completion of data preprocessing, the dataset was trained. If the bankruptcy was identified then, the test data was predicted to find the weighted average of precision, weighted average of recall, f1-score, and accuracy of the given model and if the dataset showed bankruptcy, then the dataset was again moved to train data prediction. After finding out the accuracy of all the given models, the most accurate model was identified to be the most successful in predicting bankruptcy.

Accuracy, Precision, Recall, Fl-score

a. **Accuracy:** In this paper, the accuracy score is a metric of evaluation that compares the number of right predictions generated to the total number of predictions. It is calculated by dividing the total numbers of the forecast by the number of correct guesses. For example, the precision of the Artificial Neural Network framework was 0.6181, which shows that the model correctly predicted the bankrupt or non-bankrupt class for approximately 61.81% of all instances.
b. **F1 Score:** F1-Score evaluates a model's predictive abilities by focusing on the performance of each class unlike accuracy which considers the overall performance.
c. **Precision:** Precision, in the realm of machine learning, acts as a yardstick for a model's accuracy in positive predictions. Essentially, it gauges how well the model nails down the true positives among all the positive predictions,

expressed as the ratio of true positives to the total positive predictions.

d. **Recall:** Recall represents the proportion of precisely predicted positive data relative to the entirety of data within the actual class. It is a measure that signifies the model's ability to capture and correctly figure out all data of the positive class, estimated as a proportion of true positives to the sum of! true Positives and false negatives.
e. **Weighted Average:** The weighted average calculates the mean precision, recall, and F1-score, taking into consideration the class imbalance. For example, in the ANN model, the weighted-average precision was 0.6850, recall was 0.6181, and F1-score was 0.5803 according to the given test predictions.

According to Table **1**, XGBoost model was identified as the most accurately predicting model among all of the above models *i.e.* 91.00% while LSTM model was identified as the second most accurately predicting model with an accuracy of 88.02% and it was preceded by CNN, BiLSTM and ANN model. The same goes with the weighted average of precision as well, where ANN model gave the least precision and XGBoost model produced the highest precision.

Table 1. Test data of applied model accuracy.

-	ANN	CNN	LSTM	BILSTM	XGBOOST
Accuracy	61.81%	78.95%	88.02%	78.15%	91.00%
Weighted avg of Precision	68.50%	79.42%	88.46%	80.40%	91.00%
F1-score	58.03%	78.88%	87.99%	77.73%	91.00%
Weighted avg of Recall	61.81%	78.95%	88.02%	7815%	91.00%

In all of the above cases, *i.e.* F1-score, weighted avg of recall, the XGBoost model produced the best result while ANN model resulted in the weakest accuracy among all of the above bankruptcy prediction models. Hence, with the given results, it was found that the XGBoost model was the best model for predicting bankruptcy or financial insolvency of an individual or an organization.

Confusion Matrix

A Confusion Matrix is essential for evaluating how well a model performs. These matrices divide the model's predictions into several groups according to actual results, giving a clear visual representation of the predictive power. A table that classifies model predictions into four groups is called a confusion matrix. True Positives (TP) are scenarios in which the framework accurately predicts a class that is positive (bankruptcy). True Negatives (TN) are instances in which the system correctly predicts an undesirable class, such as non-bankruptcy. False

Positives (FP) are events whereby the model mistakenly predicts a favourable class—for example, bankruptcy when it should not be. False Negatives (FN) occur when the simulation anticipates a class that is negative instead of a non-bankruptcy class.

Based on Table **2** and Fig. (**2**), test data prediction of ANN model had the accuracy of 0.6181, which was the least among all of the above models. Its weighted mean accuracy was 0.6850; weighted mean recall was 0.6181 and F1-score was 0.5803, which was the least among all of the above bankruptcy or financial insolvency prediction models.

Table 2. Test data of ANN model accuracy.

-	Precision	Precision	Precision
0	0.5735	0.5735	0.5735
1	0.9185	0.9185	0.9185
Accuracy	0.7061	0.7061	0.7061
Macro avg.	0.7963	0.7963	0.7963
Weighted avg.	0.3182	0.3182	0.3182

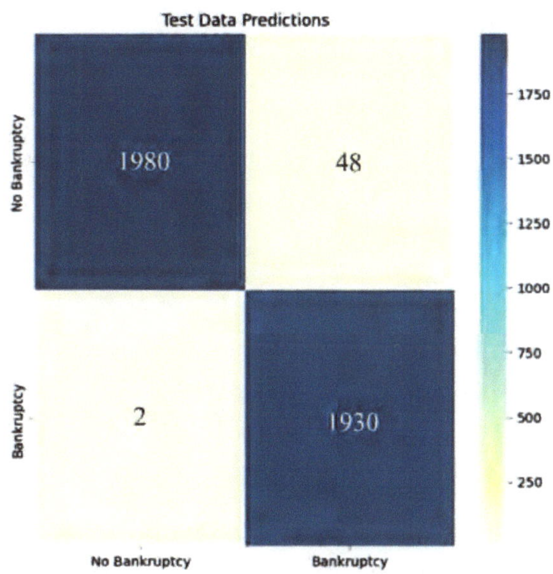

Fig. (2). Confusion matrix of artificial neural network.

According to Table **3** and Fig. (**3**), test data prediction of CNN model had the accuracy of 0.7895 which was the third highest among all of the above models. Its weighted average precision was 0.7942, weighted average recall was 0.7895 and f1-score was 0.7888, which was the third highest among all of the above bankruptcy or financial insolvency prediction models.

Table 3. Test data of CNN model accuracy.

-	Precision	Precision	Precision
0	0.7565	0.7565	0.7565
1	0.8515	0.8515	0.8515
Accuracy	0.8012	0.8012	0.8012
Macro avg.	0.8317	0.8317	0.8317
Weighted avg.	0.7280	0.7280	0.7280

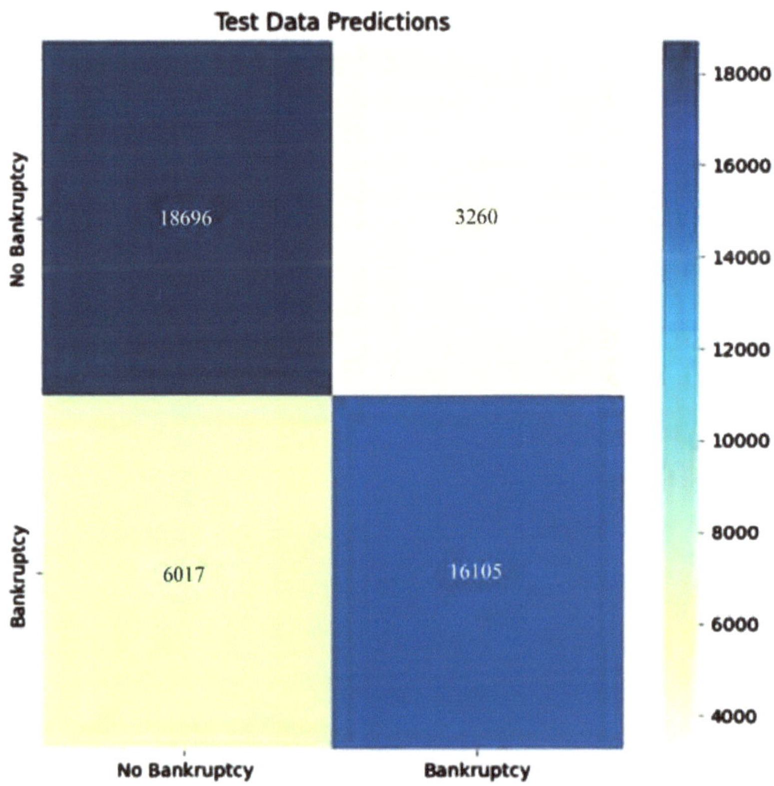

Fig. (3). Confusion matrix of convolutional neural network.

According to Table **4** and Fig. (**4**), test data prediction of the LSTM model had an accuracy of 0.8802 which was the second highest among all of the above models. Its weighted average precision was 0.8846, weighted average recall was 0.8802 and F1-score was 0.8799, which was the second highest among all of the above bankruptcy or financial insolvency prediction models.

Table 4. Test data of LSTM model accuracy.

-	Precision	Precision	Precision
0	0.8436	0.8436	0.8436
1	0.9338	0.9338	0.9338
Accuracy	0.8864	0.8864	0.8864
Macro avg.	0.9257	0.9257	0.9257
Weighted avg.	0.8265	0.8265	0.8265

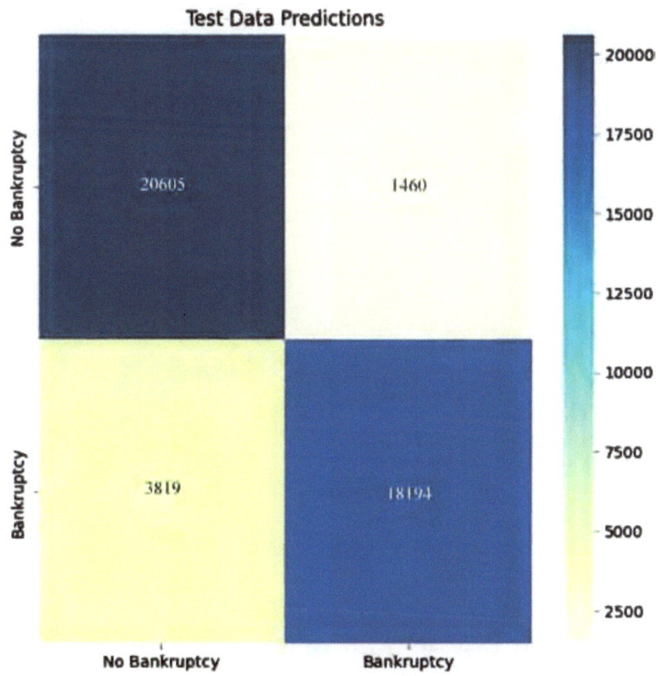

Fig. (4). Confusion matrix of long short-term memory.

According to Table **5** and Fig. (**5**), test data prediction of the BiLSTM model had an accuracy of 0.7815, which was the second least among all of the above models. Its weighted mean precision was 0.8040; weighted mean recall was 0.7815 and F1- score was 0.7773, which was the second least among all of the above bankruptcy or financial insolvency prediction models.

Table 5. Test data of BiLSTM model accuracy.

-	Precision	Precision	Precision
0	0.7217	0.7217	0.7217
1	0.9180	0.9180	0.9180
Accuracy	0.8081	0.8081	0.8081
Macro avg.	0.8867	0.8867	0.8867
Weighted avg.	0.6444	0.6444	0.6444

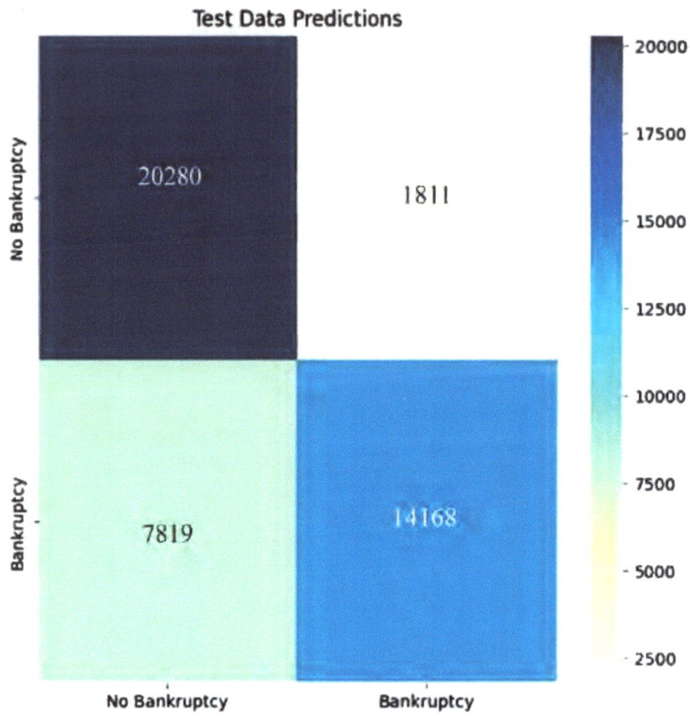

Fig. (5). Confusion matrix of bidirectional long short-term memory.

According to Table **6** and Fig. (**6**), test data prediction of the XGBoost model had an accuracy of 0.91 which was the highest among all of the above models. Its weighted mean accuracy was 0.91, weighted mean recall was 0.91 and F1-score was 0.91, which was the highest among all of the above bankruptcy or financial insolvency prediction models.

Table 6. Test data of XGBoost model accuracy.

-	Precision	Precision	Precision
0	0.89	0.89	0.89
1	0.94	0.94	0.94
Accuracy	0.91	0.91	0.91
Macro avg.	0.94	0.94	0.94
Weighted avg.	0.88	0.88	0.88

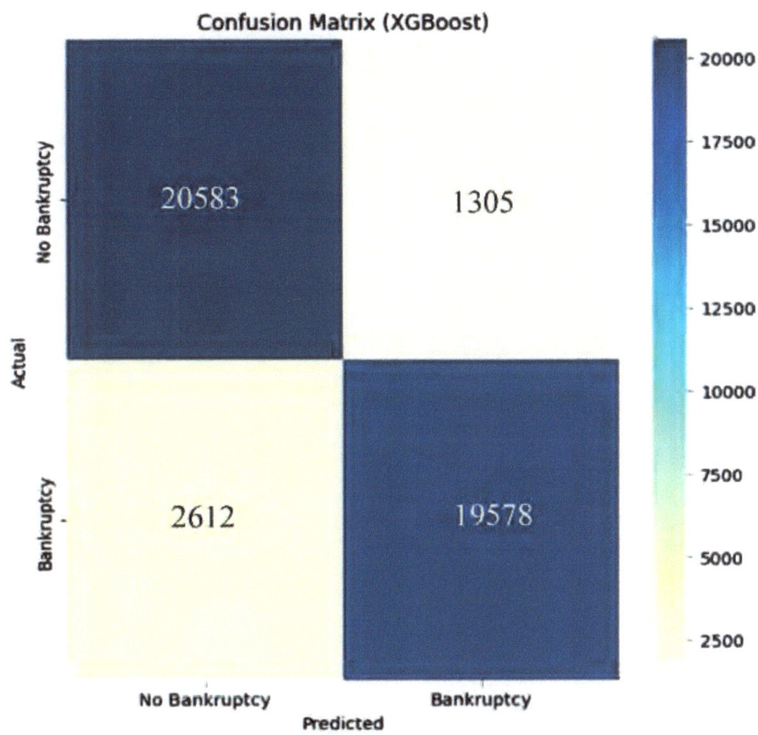

Fig. (6). Confusion matrix of extreme gradient boost.

CONCLUSION

In summary, our research endeavors have made substantial strides in tackling a pivotal financial dilemma. A thorough examination of pertinent literature, problem definition, and the establishment of a holistic methodology involving data collection, preprocessing, and model selection have been integral to our project.

The application of XGBoost for bankruptcy prediction in financial analysis stands out, demonstrating the highest accuracy and reinforcing risk assessment capabilities. The sophistication of XGBoost's ensemble learning approach excels in capturing intricate financial patterns, providing enhanced perspectives for investors and creditors. While challenges persist, our ongoing commitment to research assures the refinement of models, promising valuable contributions to informed decision-making and resilient risk management within the financial sector. The future scope of this work can be global market analysis, early warning systems and risk assessment for lenders.

REFERENCES

[1] S.H. Noh, "Comparing the Performance of Corporate Bankruptcy Prediction Models Based on Imbalanced Financial Data", *Sustainability (Basel),* vol. 15, no. 6, p. 4794, 2023. [http://dx.doi.org/10.3390/su15064794]

[2] J.A. Adisa, S. Ojo, P.A. Owolawi, A. Pretorius, and S.O. Ojo, "Application of an Improved Optimization Using Learning Strategies and Long Short Term-Memory for Bankruptcy Prediction", *IAENG Int. J. Comput. Sci.,* vol. 50, no. 2, 2023.

[3] W.F. Abror, A. Alamsyah, and M. Aziz, "Bankruptcy prediction using genetic algorithm-support vector machine (GA-SVM) feature selection and stacking", *Journal of Information System Exploration and Research,* vol. 1, no. 2, 2023. [http://dx.doi.org/10.52465/joiser.v1i2.180]

[4] J. Radovanovic, and C. Haas, "The evaluation of bankruptcy prediction models based on socio-economic costs", *Expert Syst. Appl.,* vol. 227, p. 120275, 2023. [http://dx.doi.org/10.1016/j.eswa.2023.120275]

[5] Carlsson, E. *Evaluating a LSTM model for bankruptcy prediction with feature selection*, 2023.

[6] Muslim, M. A., Dasril, Y., Javed, H., Abror, W. F., Pertiwi, D. A. A., & Mustaqim, T. "An Ensemble Stacking Algorithm to Improve Model Accuracy in Bankruptcy Prediction". *Journal of Data Science and Intelligent Systems*, 2023.

[7] H.U.R. Siddiqui, B.S. Abajo, I.T. Díez, F. Rustam, A. Raza, S. Atta, and I. Ashraf, "Predicting bankruptcy of firms using earnings call data and transfer learning", *PeerJ Comput. Sci.,* vol. 9, p. e1134, 2023. [http://dx.doi.org/10.7717/peerj-cs.1134] [PMID: 37346732]

[8] K. Valaskova, D. Gajdosikova, and J. Belas, "Bankruptcy prediction in the post-pandemic period: A case study of Visegrad Group countries", *Oeconomia Copernicana,* vol. 14, no. 1, pp. 253-293, 2023. [http://dx.doi.org/10.24136/oc.2023.007]

[9] Sahraei, F., Jamali, J., Vakilifard, H. R., Zare, A., & Zeraatkish, S. Y. "Bankruptcy prediction using the Black-Scholes asset pricing model (Experimental evidence: Tehran Stock Exchange)". *International Journal of Nonlinear Analysis and Applications*, 2023.

[10] R. Kanapickienė, T. Kanapickas, and A. Nečiūnas, "Bankruptcy prediction for micro and small enterprises using financial, non-financial, business sector and macroeconomic variables: the case of the Lithuanian construction sector", *Risks,* vol. 11, no. 5, p. 97, 2023. [http://dx.doi.org/10.3390/risks11050097]

[11] Kušter, D. "Construction of bankruptcy prediction model using discriminant analysis and financial ratios". *Ekonomija: teorija i praksa*, 16(1), 1-22, 2023.

[12] C. Charalambous, S.H. Martzoukos, and Z. Taoushianis, "A neuro-structural framework for bankruptcy prediction", *Quant. Finance,* pp. 1-20, 2023.

[13] Staňková, M., & Hampel, D. "Optimal threshold of data envelopment analysis in bankruptcy prediction". *SORT-Statistics and Operations Research Transactions*, 129-150, 2023.

[14] B. Beauvais, Z. Ramamonjiarivelo, J. Betancourt, J. Cruz, and L. Fulton, "The Predictive Factors of Hospital Bankruptcy—An Exploratory Study", *Healthcare (Basel),* vol. 11, no. 2, p. 165, 2023. [http://dx.doi.org/10.3390/healthcare11020165] [PMID: 36673533]

[15] M.I. Bonelli, "Beyond Financial Ratios: A Novel Approach to Bankruptcy Predictions for Indian Firms", *Indian Journal of Finance,* 2023.

[16] M. Papík, and L. Papíková, "Impacts of crisis on SME bankruptcy prediction models' performance", *Expert Syst. Appl.,* vol. 214, p. 119072, 2023. [http://dx.doi.org/10.1016/j.eswa.2022.119072]

[17] M. Elhoseny, N. Metawa, G. Sztano, and I.M. El-Hasnony, "Deep learning-based model for financial distress prediction", *Ann. Oper. Res.,* pp. 1-23, 2022. [PMID: 35645445]

[18] S. Ben Jabeur, N. Stef, and P. Carmona, "Bankruptcy prediction using the XGBoost algorithm and variable importance feature engineering", *Comput. Econ.,* vol. 61, no. 2, pp. 715-741, 2023. [http://dx.doi.org/10.1007/s10614-021-10227-1]

[19] F. Harrou, A. Dairi, F. Kadri, and Y. Sun, "Forecasting emergency department overcrowding: A deep learning framework", *Chaos Solitons Fractals,* vol. 139, p. 110247, 2020. [http://dx.doi.org/10.1016/j.chaos.2020.110247] [PMID: 32982079]

[20] N. M. Tuan, "Machine Learning Performance on Predicting Banking Term Deposit," in *Proceedings of the International Conference on Enterprise Information Systems (ICEIS)*, vol. 1, 2022, pp. 267–272. [http://dx.doi.org/10.5220/0011096600003179]

CHAPTER 4

An Enhanced Bank Loan Approval Prediction using Machine Learning Approach

Virendra Kumar Shrivastava[1,*], **Mano Paul P.**[2], **A. Ezil Sam Leni**[3], **M. Shrahith**[3] and **Sameer Khan**[3]

[1] *Centre of Excellence in Computer Vision, Department of Computer Science and Engineering, School of Advanced Computing, Alliance University, Bangalore, Karnataka 562106, India*

[2] *COE in iOS App Development, Dept of CSE, Alliance University, Bangalore, Karnataka 562106, India*

[3] *Alliance School of Advanced Computing, Alliance University, Karnataka, India*

Abstract: Bank loans are essential finance tools that enable individuals to capitalize on investments, purchase, or improve the family's economy by covering unseen expenses. Nowadays, banks are actively offering loans to support business growth through various investment strategies—ranging from low to high risk—with the aim of improving individuals' lifestyles and social status. Transactions play an essential role in processing debit, credit, internet banking, and other modes of payment and play a vital role in today's processing either in bank or gold transfer or online transfer and even in digital currencies and market trends to predict share market business stocks. The number of loan applications is increasing daily for loan processing to verify the customer base for loan approval. Bank policies are also stringent in selecting genuine or fake applicants by selecting various parameters for loan approval. Based on a few parameters about eligibility and the Cibil score, the bankers must decide whether they are eligible for loan approval. In this study, machine learning algorithms were applied to predict whether an individual is eligible or ineligible for a loan based on previous related records of the person on whom the loan was previously accredited and initiated by the naive Bayes classifier and supported Support Vector classifier. This study employed further classification using an extreme gradient classifier algorithm and proceeded by boosting this classifier using XGB boosting methods for the prediction with maximum choices with ensemble learning. Finally, text analysis methods are used to identify the accuracy, false positive rates, true favorable, and F1 scores. The proposed prediction model provides 98.5% accuracy for bank loan approval with the educated level, namely graduated and un-graduated levels.

Keywords: Artificial neural network, Credibility limits, Loan approval, Loan prediction, Machine learning.

* **Corresponding author Virendra Kumar Shrivastava:** Centre of Excellence in Computer Vision, Department of Computer Science and Engineering, School of Advanced Computing, Alliance University, Bangalore, Karnataka 562106, India; E-mail: Virendra.shrivastava@alliance.edu.in

Suneeta Satpathy, Sachi Nandan Mohanty & Subhendu Kumar Pani (Eds.)

INTRODUCTION

In today's dynamic financial landscape, the ability to accurately predict loan approvals is crucial for lenders and borrowers. Our system harnesses the power of advanced ML techniques and algorithms to analyze vast datasets of diverse profiles, financial histories, and market trends. By leveraging sophisticated predictive models, our system can assess applicants' creditworthiness with unprecedented precision, providing lenders with invaluable insights to make decisions effectively. Whether it is assessing risk, streamlining approval processes, or enhancing customer experience, our Loan Approval Prediction System offers a comprehensive solution tailored to meet the evolving needs of the lending industry. The loan system allows us to jump on the application that deserves approval on a priority basis, whether the candidate is educated or uneducated, based on their graduation status. With today's evolving trends in the bank loan approval process, several key parameters are typically used for prediction. These include loan ID, loan amount, loan terms, credit history, property area, applicant income, employer details, educational qualifications, marital status, number of dependents, gender, and other features. Loan approval decisions are often supported by predictive models and further validated using a credit score—such as the CIBIL score—which represents an individual's standard creditworthiness

LITERATURE SURVEY

To perform a prediction, technical machine learning algorithms exceptionally work and will assert the prediction about the approval or disapproval shortly; we impose the machine learning strategy for predictions made frequently by people with many of these conjectures, while some are highly serious and calculated and based on scientific calculations. In many ways, prediction aids our ability to calculate what will transpire in the future, whether a year from now or so. Here, a methodology called predictive analytics is used, which is a subset of advanced analytics that analyses current data and generates forecasts using a variety of methods from data mining, exploratory analysis, statistics, and modeling, which is used with the algorithms for learning and used in artificial intelligence—Arun Kumar *et al.* [1] engaged in the task of predicting housing prices. They employ PSO (particle swarm optimization) and regression analysis to forecast property prices. Through loan default prediction, banks can lower their non-performing assets. This emphasizes the importance of investigating this issue. Previous studies have demonstrated that reduced loan defaults may be studied using various methodologies. However, because accurate forecasting is crucial for optimizing earnings, it is critical to examine the characteristics of the project.

The data collection process was accomplished using the Kaggle dataset for analysis and forecasting purposes to predict approval. The application of Logistic Regression models calculated various performance metrics. There are test and training datasets in the bank customer dataset. Compared to the test crop yield dataset, which has 250 or more rows and 10 or more columns but lacks the target variable, the training dataset has about 600 more rows and 12 more columns. Because the datasets are already tiny, the mean, mode, and median fill the missing, null, and vacant values in the rows rather than eliminating the rows. Both datasets contained vacant values in their rows. The project was advanced to exploratory data analysis using feature engineering methodologies.

This project's primary goal is to forecast the safety of granting a loan to an individual. This is structured into four parts: gathering data, comparing predictive models on the data, training the system using the most promising model, and testing. In this study, we employ machine learning techniques, including gradient boosting, decision trees, classification, and logic regression, to forecast the loan data. The bank must work hard to analyze and predict whether the customer (defaulter or non-defaulter) can repay the loan balance within the allotted time. This paper aims to find out about the client's past, character, and loan application. Our method for addressing the issue of accepting or denying a loan request, or, more succinctly, loan prediction, is exploratory data analysis.

This paper's primary goal is to decide whether to authorize a loan provided to a specific individual or organization. Adyan Nur *et al.* [2] focus on the modeling of house prediction, which follows a machine learning algorithm, and Rao R *et al.* [3] focus on anomaly detection *via* a machine learning algorithm, which describes the removal of duplicate data from the rows, which is a record. Quinlan, J. Ross, *et al.* [4] used a regression analysis approach to create a prediction for supervised learning methods. Sentimental analysis was shown by S. Liao *et al.* [5], which provides the convolution neural network to understand the semantics *via* sentimental analysis Singhal *et al.* [6] described medical data and Jingle *et al.* [7] focused on the prevention of attacks in networks and to develop high-performance systems. In machine learning, supervised learning approaches were given with optimization imposed by Mohamed EI *et al.* [8], who stated that supervised learning schemes, Saha *et al.* [9] focus on text analysis by reducing false positives. Supriya P *et al.* [10] process datasets and classify with decision tree algorithms stated by Quinlan *et al.* [11] describes the decision tree approach in the classification prediction models; Rahmani *et al.* [12] state the efficient indexing algorithms which transform the data for the quick access with the help of keys. Madane *et al.* [13] focused on the decision tree for loan prediction and didn't classify the result as boosting its performance at output levels. Kumar *et al.* [14] provide AI techniques for predictive analysis, which inculcate the features of classification techniques. M. M Rao *et al.* [11] classified strategies with decisions in forecasting business strategies. Shrivastava *et al.* [16] focus on predicting COVID-19 datasets, whereas Lalli *et al.* [18] focus on anomaly detection to remove duplicates with machine-learning approaches. Shrivastav *et al.* [19 - 21] focus on deep learning approaches to impact disease prediction analysis by diagnosing the trained datasets using boosting and bagging algorithms. An optical network with deep learning in nonlinear prediction with exploratory data analysis was also submitted using deep learning methodology. In Mano Paul *et al.* [22, 23], cooperative and collaborative methods were used to filter the data for protection in wireless networks and were focused on a formulated prediction algorithm. Selvaraj *et al.* [24] deal with the prediction data, which formulates reliability and mitigates attacks in cloud networks on a large scale.

PROPOSED METHODOLOGY

The dataset was collected from a Kaggle source that offers datasets with bank application data for the study and analysis of object types. Ensuring that datasets are sourced from Kaggle is crucial for preserving data accuracy and integrity, as shown in Table **1**, which has more than 600 records.

Table 1. Bank loan dataset.

Loan_ID	Gender	Married	Dependents	Education	Self_Employed	Applicant Income	Coapplicant Income	LoanAmount	Loan_Amount_ Term	Credit_History	Property_Area	Loan_Status
LP001	Male	No	0	Graduate	No	5849	0	0	360	1	Urban	Y
LP001	Male	Yes	1	Graduate	No	4583	1508	128	360	1	Rural	N
LP001	Male	Yes	0	Graduate	Yes	3000	0	66	360	1	Urban	Y
LP001	Male	Yes	0	Not Graduate	No	2583	2358	120	360	1	Urban	Y
LP001	Male	No	0	Graduate	No	6000	0	141	360	1	Urban	Y
LP001	Male	Yes	2	Graduate	No	5417	4196	267	360	1	Urban	Y
LP001	Male	Yes	0	Not Graduate	No	2333	1516	95	360	1	Urban	Y
LP001	Male	Yes	3+	Graduate	No	3036	2504	158	360	0	Semiurban	N
LP001	Male	Yes	2	Graduate	No	4006	1526	168	360	1	Urban	Y
LP001	Male	Yes	1	Graduate	No	12841	10968	349	360	1	Semiurban	N
LP001	Male	Yes	2	Graduate	No	3200	700	70	360	1	Urban	Y
LP001	Male	Yes	2	Graduate	No	2500	1840	109	360	1	Urban	Y
LP001	Male	Yes	2	Graduate	No	3073	8106	200	360	1	Urban	Y
LP001	Male	No	0	Graduate	No	1853	2840	114	360	1	Rural	N
LP001	Male	Yes	2	Graduate	No	1299	1086	17	120	1	Urban	Y
LP001	Male	No	0	Graduate	No	4950	0	125	360	1	Urban	Y
LP001	Male	No	1	Not Graduate	No	3596	0	100	240	1	Urban	Y

Each row in the dataset belongs to a unique individual; its details are given in Table **2**. Here, data include parameters like Loan ID, Gender, marriage, Loan Amount Term, amount, Property Area, Credit History, employment, Education, customer Income, Loan Status, Dependents, Co-applicant Income with dependents, *etc.*Table **1** focuses on sample data, which will be available in our loan prediction datasets.

Table 2. Dataset pre-processing.

Sl. No	Column	Not Null (NN) Count	Datatype
1	Loan ID	601 NN	Object
2	Gender	614 NN	Object
3	Loan Amount Term	614 NN	Object
4	Credit history	570 NN	Object
5	Property Area	604 NN	Object
6	Loan Status	603 NN	object
7	Married	607 NN	Object
8	Dependents	587 NN	Object
10	Education	600 NN	Object
11	Self Employed	614 NN	Object
12	Applicant Income	614 NN	Object
13	Co-Applicant Income	614 NN	Object

Proposed Model

Future event data is predicted using predictive analytics imposed for a bank loan application, as shown in Fig. (**1**). Here, different process stages were given and initiated with data preprocessing to clean and process data. After processing, it will undergo splitting and processing as training data with 75% quantity and testing data with 25% quantified for the prediction through history. After modeling, the dataset was processed for prediction by preparing a confusion matrix and read to adopt algorithms to encompass a wide range of methods, including modeling, data mining, and exploratory data analytics algorithms. Artificial intelligence, deep learning, and various machine learning algorithms enable software to learn from data and improve its prediction accuracy using algorithms without human interactions. Here, a computer statistic that automatically learns and anticipates the data and circumstances may be designed and developed with machine learning techniques or deep learning techniques. Machine learning is frequently separated into many groups based on the types of challenges that are encountered. ML types include two levels of learning methods: supervised learning and unsupervised learning techniques. Supervised learning is the process of constructing a model using a labeled dataset, which is referred to as supervised learning. Datasets are labeled in this type of instruction, assessment, training, and testing. The output is always 1 or 0. In unsupervised learning techniques, we process the algorithm with assumed data to label unsupervised usages, which involve unlabeled input data without prior knowledge about the data. In this case, the machine uses cluster analysis to extract the hidden pattern from the data. Because the dataset was labeled, we could apply supervised learning in this instance. We employed a supervised learning strategy in our work in Fig. (**1**).

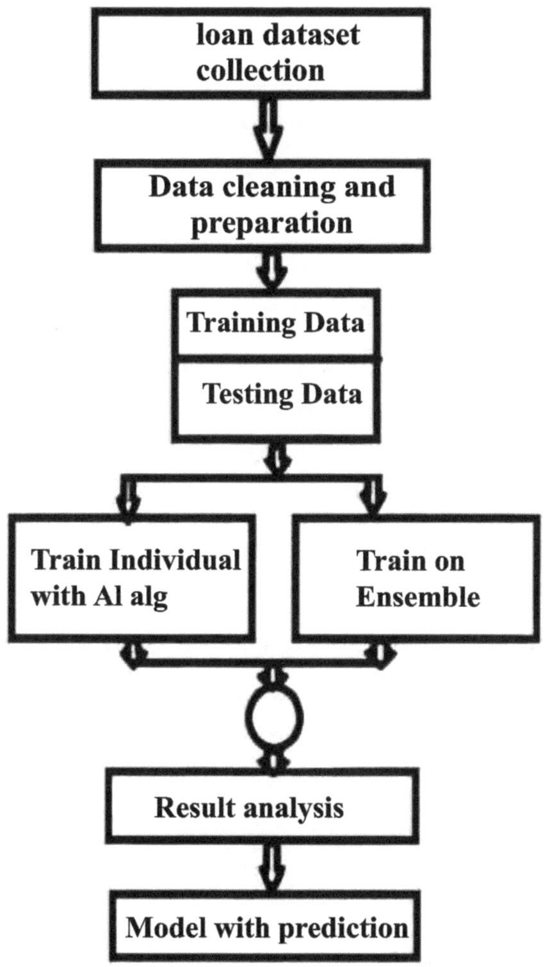

Fig. (1). Proposed loan approval prediction model.

Algorithms Used for Prediction

In these algorithmic approaches, a logistic regression modeling method is used to identify the inputs over the discrete results states *via* logistic regression. As a result, with the binary classifier, we need to produce the result as 1 or 0, which is yes or no, which will be presented to the logistic regression and prediction models. The probability that it will perform binary logistical regression is by finding the connection between the predictor and the answer by entering this into the equation for θ above, while setting X (1) identical to X (2) save in a single position (*i.e.*, just one prediction varies by one unit). Another approach is identifying the probabilistic approach used to determine the classification using a conditional probabilistic naïve Bayes Classifier. This naive Bayes classifier assumes that a feature's presence in a class is independent of any additional characteristics. Here, the model of the supervised learning metrics for statistical data is based on Bayes theorem, which is represented as a conditional probability that can be written as P(p) and P(W), the marginals. In contrast, P(w,p) represents the joint probability. The source of Sunil's explanation of the Bayes rule is shown in formula (1), which is

$$P(w, p) = P(w \cap p) / P(p) \tag{1}$$

SVC is a support vector classifier in machine learning techniques created with classification problems; SVC is a classification-specific SVM that looks for the hyperplane that divides the information points into several classes the best. Otherwise, the SVC is a classification-specific SVM. The hyperplane that divides the information points into several courses is the best. This study uses different methodologies in classification and regression techniques and other algorithms used in these datasets for bank loan predictions. The decision tree encoder generates the classification model by constructing a decision tree. In classification by decision trees, every tree has a root and two child nodes, namely the left and right nodes, which will potentially descend with the other branch or denote another root that frames a parent node. A function to perform training and testing data for the prediction samples is given in Python programming in sections D and E. In the next section, how does the XGB classifier work with the split datasets with different predictors?

Function to fit the model with XgbClassifier

```
def modelfit(alg, dtrain, predictors,useTrainCV = True, cv_folds
            = 5, early_stopping_rounds = 50):

   if useTrainCV:

      xgb_param = alg.get_xgb_params()

      xgtrain = xgb.DMatrix(dtrain[predictors].values, label = dtrain[target].values)

      cvresult = xgb.cv(xgb_param, xgtrain, num_boost_round
                = alg.get_params()['n_estimators'],

                nfold = cv_folds,metrics = 'auc', early_stopping_rounds
                = early_stopping_rounds)

      alg.set_params(n_estimators = cvresult.shape[0])

   #Fit the algorithm on the data

   alg.fit(dtrain[predictors], dtrain['Loan_Status']

,eval_metric = 'auc')

   #Predict training set:

   dtrain_predictions = alg.predict(dtrain[predictors])

   dtrain_predprob = alg.predict_proba(dtrain[predictors])[:,1]

   print ("\nModel Report")

   print ("Accuracy : %.4g" % metrics.accuracy_score(dtrain

['Loan_Status'].values, dtrain_predictions))

   print ("AUC Score (Train): %f" % metrics

.roc_auc_score(dtrain['Loan_Status'], dtrain_predprob))

   featimp = pd.Series(alg.booster().getfscore())

.sort_values(ascending = False)

   feat_imp.plot(kind = 'bar', title = 'Feature Importances')

   plt.ylabel('Feature Importance Score')

predictors = [x for x in train.columns if x not in [target, IDcol]]

xgb2 = XGBClassifier(learning_rate = 0.1, n_estimators = 1000, max_depth
            = 5, min_child_weight = 1, gamma = 0, subsample
            = 0.8, colsample_bytree = 0.8, objective = 'binary:logistic', nthread
            = 4, scale_pos_weight = 1, seed = 27)

modelfit(xgb2, train, predictors)
```

Model Report

Accuracy: 0.9186

AUC Score (Train): 0.984918

Function to Perform XGB Classifier

```
param_test1 = {'max _depth':list(range(3,10,2)),

'min_child_weight':list(range(1,6,2))}

gsearch1 = GridSearchCV(estimator = XGBClassifier( learning_rate
                = 0.1, n_estimators
                = 140, max_depth = 5, min_child_weight = 1, gamma = 0, subsample
                = 0.8, colsample_bytree = 0.8,

objective
                = 'binary:logistic', nthread = 4, scale_pos_weight = 1, seed = 27), Param grid
                = param_test1, scoring = 'roc_auc',n_jobs = 4,iid = False, cv = 5)

gsearch1.fit(train[predictors],train[target])

gsearch1.gridscores,gsearch1.bestparams

gsearch1.best_score_

predictors = [x for x in train.columns if x not in [target, IDcol]]

xgb2 = XGBClassifier(learning_rate = 0.1, n_estimators = 1000, max_depth
                = 8, min_child_weight = 6, gamma = 0.1, subsample = 0.9,

colsample_bytree = 0.95,reg_alpha = 2, objective = 'binary:logistic', nthread
                = 4, scale_pos_weight = 1, seed = 27)

modelfit(xgb2, train, predictors)
```

Model Report

Accuracy: 0.8632

AUC Score (Train): 0.944152

In decision trees, a distinctive standard form is used in all branches to identify the root node, left node, and right node, which formulates a combination of the sum of products to translate it to a conjunctive norm form with larger values. Branches that finish in different classes combine to generate a disjunction (sum).

One approach to tuning the data for the prediction is ensemble learning, a machine learning approach that combines multiple models called Gradient Boosting. Here, a type of neural network boosting is gradient boosting. Based on the values, combining the best subsequent model with earlier models minimizes the total prediction error. The primary objective is to reduce the error by setting the desired results for the following model. Here, assume that input and target have N samples, respectively, X and Y. Finding a function called f(x) that translates the given input features X into the desired parameters Y is our aim—the total number of strengthened trees. The variation between actual and anticipated variables is known as the loss function.

Random forest learning, or decision forests, is a popular ensemble learning technique for classification, regression, and other problems. It works by building many decision trees during the training phase. After selecting observations randomly, the random forest algorithm creates a decision tree, and the average outcome is determined. It does not make use of a formulary set. Therefore, we conclude that, provided the trees are suitable and diverse, random forests outperform decision trees in terms of success.

RESULTS AND DISCUSSION

One strategy cannot be overfitted or underfitted by evaluating these prediction models. Instead, the model's performance is assessed based on certain limitations. There are several ways to determine the model's performance, including the F1 score, accuracy, precision, recall, and confusion measures confusion matrices:

Typically, the disorientation of the matrix is displayed in tabular form, with the actual classes represented by the rows and the predicted classes by the columns. By highlighting the model's successes (opposite components, TP and TN) and failures (off-diagonal components, FP and FN), it becomes easier to see how well the model performed. To determine accuracy, we must identify the metrics used to gauge the model's accuracy. A balanced model exhibits greater clarity than the overall model.

$$\text{Accuracy} = TP + TN / TP + TN + FP + FN \tag{2}$$

The precision value is calculated as a proportion of positive instances to all projected positive instances. We achieved good precision in the data collection.

$$\text{Precision} = \text{True positive (True positive +False positive)} \tag{3}$$

Here are the metrics for the confusion matrix, which will be discussed in Fig. (**2**) with graduate and non-graduate education metrics. Fig. (**3**) corresponds to the false positive rate and its value, as given in formulas 2 & 3. Fig. (**4**), the analysis of loan prediction concerning educated, such as graduate and non-graduate values, succeeded with 98.5% accuracy.

Actual Education	Predicted Rate Graduate	Not Graduate
Graduate	0.998	0.002
Not Graduate	0.022	0.978

Fig. (2). Confusion matrix of datasets.

Prob	1-Specificity	Sensitivity	Sens-(1-Spec)	True Pos	True Neg	False Pos	False Neg
	0.0000	0.0000	0.0000	0	383	0	97
1.0000	0.0000	1.0000	1.0000 *	97	383	0	0
0.0000	1.0000	1.0000	0.0000	97	0	383	0
0.0000	1.0000	1.0000	0.0000	97	0	383	0

Fig. (3). The false positive rate for text analysis in education prediction.

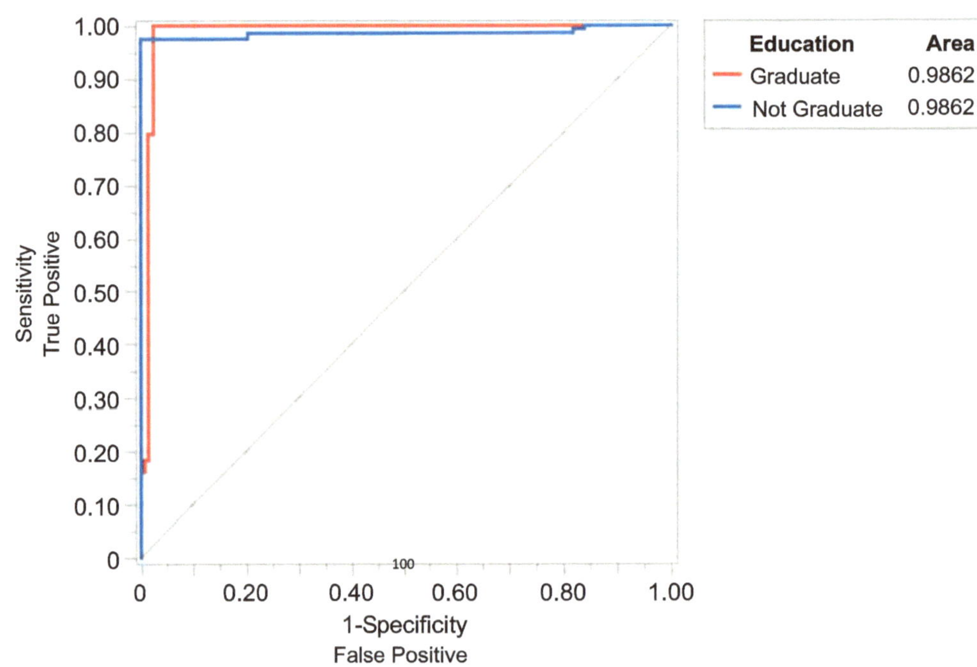

Fig. (4). Analysis of prediction rate in terms of education concerning loan dataset.

Fig. (**5**) gives the heat map of the efficiency of the given calibrations. This talks about the density and intensity of the data concerning the datasets. F formula (4) calculates recall as the percentage of positive cases compared to the total number of positive instances. The total number of positive cases over the entire dataset is displayed by the numerator (TP + FN), which is the value in this case. Consequently, "how much value will be provided in the simulation will give up if it displays maximum right ones" is what it acquired.

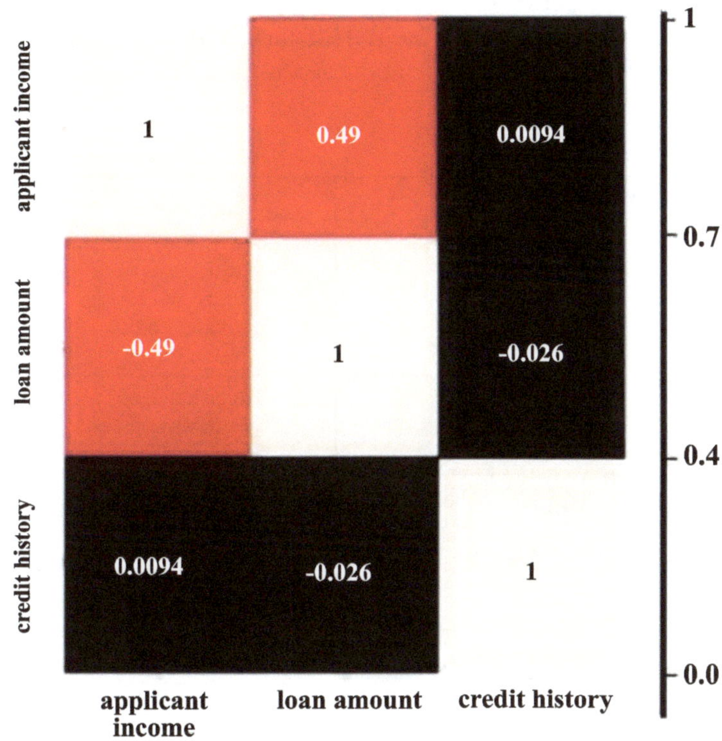

Fig. (5). Heap Map.

$$\text{Recall} = \text{True Positive (TP)} / (\text{True Positive (TP)} + \text{False Negative (FN)}) \quad (4)$$

The F1 Score in formula (5) is said to be the harmonic average (HM) of the recall and precision values. If the model achieves the highest F1 Score, it will perform better; its final value will be considered, as this F1 score decreases dramatically if either precision or memory is low. The numerator displays the product in terms of both recall and precision. Therefore, if a model predicts positives with a positive value (precision) and does not overlook positives and predicts them negatively (recall), it does well in the F1 score.

$$\text{F1 score} = 2 * \text{proportion\_of\_positive\_class} / (1 + \text{proportion\_of\_positive\_class}) \quad (5)$$

In F1 scores, we focus on improving prediction accuracy. This method is also used to predict the indirect features by prioritizing credit scores. Here, the heat map identifies the value with the credit history, loan amount, and income based on the applicant so that they will be granted a loan. This process banks are developing using Cibil score estimation and then process for approval by the authority of banks. Table **3** presents the performance of approval with its accuracy for various models, with the reference accuracy as shown in Table **3**.

Table 3. Model performance of loan approval.

Reference / Algorithm	Models	Accuracy(%)
Usage of Prediction with low risk	Logistic Regression	78.5
	Decision Tree	66.2
	SVM	65
	Random Forest	77.3
	Naïve Bayes	77.9
Usage of Prediction with medium risk	Decision Tree	69
	SVM	70
	Random Forest	72
Usage of Prediction with high risk	Logistic Regression	82.17
	Decision Tree	82.17
	SVM	70
	Random Forest	82.17
	Naïve Bayes	80.65

CONCLUSION

Thus, the rapid proliferation of the increase in wealth and sophisticated life in cities includes new technology and modern lifestyles and also boosts productivity *via* a financial system, which is highly demanding. Evidently, to further improve the life system, we need to attain external support through banks and other financial services. The bank will raise funds and provide loans to support its citizens in improving society's lifestyle. It helps people by approving loans, providing resources, and so on. One such mechanism in this manuscript is based on the loan prediction process. Here, the loan amount, customer dependencies, and existing scores are needed to identify the prediction of bank loans, whether the customer is educated or not. To verify the graduate status, we can frame our application to predict it using different learning mechanisms, namely SVM, decision tree, and ensemble-based learning, which indicate the future retrieval of the loan amount. Many fraudulent sources will provide wrong predictions about credit scores and other parameters to verify their unique identities. Thus, in this process, we filtered data in the preprocessing stage; at the next level, we did a splitting with training and testing datasets for the prediction and, in the further steps, processed it by decision tree algorithm for the classification approach and also proceed by the ensemble learning methods to boost the algorithm using XGB boosting methods for the accurate prediction. Finally, text analytics was used to identify the accuracy, false positive rates, true positives, and F1 score. Our prediction provides 98.5% accuracy for bank loan approval.

REFERENCES

[1] K. Arun, I. Garg, and S. Kaur, "Loan approval prediction based on machine learning approach", *Proceedings of the 2023 International Conference on Artificial Intelligence and Data Science (ICAIDS),* pp. 1-6, 2023.

[2] A. Nur, R. Ema, H. Taufiq, and W. Firdaus, "Modeling house price prediction using regression analysis and particle swarm optimization case study: Malang, East Java, Indonesia", *Int. J. Adv. Comput. Sci. Appl.,* vol. 8, no. 10, 2017. [http://dx.doi.org/10.14569/IJACSA.2017.081042]

[3] K. Rao, G. Srinivas, A. Damodhar, and M. Krishna, "Implementation of anomaly detection technique using machine learning algorithms", *Int. J.,* vol. 2, no. 3, 2011.

[4] J.R. Quinlan, "Induction of decision trees", *Mach. Learn.,* vol. 1, no. 1, pp. 81-106, 1986. [http://dx.doi.org/10.1023/A:1022643204877]

[5] S. Liao, J. Wang, R. Yu, K. Sato, and Z. Cheng, "CNN for situations understanding based on sentiment analysis of twitter data", *Procedia Comput. Sci.,* vol. 111, pp. 376-381, 2017. [http://dx.doi.org/10.1016/j.procs.2017.06.037]

[6] A. Singhal, M. Phogat, D. Kumar, A. Kumar, M. Dahiya, and V.K. Shrivastava, "Study of deep learning techniques for medical image analysis: A review", *Mater. Today Proc.,* vol. 56, pp. 209-214, 2022. [http://dx.doi.org/10.1016/j.matpr.2022.01.071]

[7] I.D.J. Jingle, and P.M. Paul, "A collaborative defense protocol against collaborative attacks in wireless mesh networks", *Int. J. Enterp. Netw. Manag.,* vol. 12, no. 3, p. 199, 2021. [http://dx.doi.org/10.1504/IJENM.2021.118055]

[8] M. El Mohadab, B. Bouikhalene, and S. Safi, "Predicting rank for scientific research papers using supervised learning", *Applied Computing and Informatics,* vol. 15, no. 2, pp. 182-190, 2019. [http://dx.doi.org/10.1016/j.aci.2018.02.002]

[9] A. Saha, T. Denning, V. Srikumar, and S.K. Kasera, "Secrets in source code: Reducing false positives using machine learning", *International Conference on Communication Systems and Networks, Comsnets,* 2020. [http://dx.doi.org/10.1109/COMSNETS48256.2020.9027350]

[10] P. Supriya, M. Pavani, and N. Saisushma, "Loan prediction by using machine learning models", *International Journal of Engineering and Techniques,* vol. 5, no. 2, 2019.

[11] T. Sarkar, M. Rakhra, V. Sharma, and A. Singh, "An empirical comparison of machine learning techniques for bank loan approval prediction", In: *2024 international conference on communication, computer sciences and engineering (IC3SE)* IEEE, 2024, pp. 137-143. [http://dx.doi.org/10.1109/IC3SE62002.2024.10593355]

[12] M.K.I. Rahmani, M.A. Ansari, and A.K. Goel, "An Efficient Indexing Algorithm for CBIR", *2015*

IEEE International Conference on Computational Intelligence & Communication Technology, pp. 73-77, 2015.Ghaziabad, India.
[http://dx.doi.org/10.1109/CICT.2015.165]

[13] N. Madane, and N. Siddharth, "Loan prediction analysis using decision tree", *Journal of the Gujarat Research Society,* vol. 21, no. 14, 2019.

[14] A. Kumar, V.K. Shrivastava, P. Kumar, A. Kumar, and V. Gulati, "Predictive and experimental analysis of forces in die-less forming using artificial intelligence techniques", *Proceedings of the Institution of Mechanical Engineers, Part E: Journal of Process Mechanical Engineering,* 2024.
[http://dx.doi.org/10.1177/09544089241235473]

[15] M.M. Rao, and V.K. Shrivastava, "Predicting probable product swaps in customer behaviour: An in-depth analysis of forecasting techniques, factors influencing decisions, and implications for business strategies", *ICST Transactions on Scalable Information Systems,* vol. 10, no. 6, 2023.
[http://dx.doi.org/10.4108/eetsis.4049]

[16] V.K. Shrivastava, A. Kumar, A. Shrivastava, A. Tiwari, K. Thiru, and R. Batra, "Study and Trend Prediction of Covid-19 cases in India using Deep Learning Techniques", *J. Phys. Conf. Ser.,* vol. 1950, no. 1, p. 012084, 2021.
[http://dx.doi.org/10.1088/1742-6596/1950/1/012084]

[17] R. Batra, V. K. Shrivastava, and A. K. Goel, "Anomaly Detection over SDN Using Machine Learning and Deep Learning for Securing Smart City", *Green Internet of Things for Smart Cities,* 2021.
[http://dx.doi.org/10.1201/9781003032397-13]

[18] K. Lalli, V.K. Shrivastava, and R. Shekhar, "Detecting copy move image forgery using a deep learning model: A review", *International Conference on Artificial Intelligence and Applications (ICAIA), Alliance Technology Conference (ATCON-1),* 2023.
[http://dx.doi.org/10.1109/ICAIA57370.2023.10169568]

[19] V.K. Shrivastava, A. Shrivastava, N. Sharma, S.N. Mohanty, and C.R. Pattanaik, "Deep learning model for temperature prediction: A case study in New Delhi", *J. Forecast.,* vol. 42, no. 6, pp. 1445-1460, 2023.
[http://dx.doi.org/10.1002/for.2966]

[20] V.K. Shrivastava, A. Shrivastava, N. Sharma, S.N. Mohanty, and C.R. Pattanaik, "Deep learning model for temperature prediction: an empirical study", *Model. Earth Syst. Environ.,* vol. 9, no. 2, pp. 2067-2080, 2023.
[http://dx.doi.org/10.1007/s40808-022-01609-x]

[21] V.K. Shrivastava, C.J. Shelke, A. Shrivastava, S.N. Mohanty, and N. Sharma, "Optimized deep learning model for disease prediction in potato leaves", *EAI Endorsed Trans. Pervasive Health Technol.,* vol. 9, no. 1, 2023.
[http://dx.doi.org/10.4108/eetpht.9.4001]

[22] P. Mano Paul, and R. Ravi, "Cooperative Vector Based Reactive System for Protecting Email Against Spammers in Wireless Networks", *Journal of Electrical Engineering,* vol. 18, pp. 54-61, 2018.

[23] P.M. Paul, and R. Ravi, "A collaborative reputation-based vector space model for email spam filtering", *J. Comput. Theor. Nanosci.,* vol. 15, no. 2, pp. 474-479, 2018.
[http://dx.doi.org/10.1166/jctn.2018.7128]

[24] J.D. Selvaraj, I.D. Jingle, and P.M. Paul, "EShield: an effective detection and mitigation of flooding in DDoS attacks over large scale networks", *Networks,* vol. 23, p. 24, 2019.

CHAPTER 5

Exploring Consumer Awareness within Electronic Payment Systems

Blesson Varghese James[1], **Preethi Nanjundan**[2,*], **Akhand Tiwari**[1] and **Shrishtee Khabra**[1]

[1] *Department of Commerce, CHRIST University, Bengaluru, India*

[2] *Department of Data Science, CHRIST University, Bengaluru, India*

Abstract: This paper presents a comprehensive review of the literature on the adoption of electronic payment (E-Payment) systems in the Indian context. Through an extensive examination of existing studies, the paper explores the various factors influencing E-Payment adoption, including perceived usefulness, ease of use, facilitating conditions, and system credibility. Moreover, their study investigates the role of demographic factors—such as gender, education, employment status, age, and technological literacy—as moderators influencing individuals' attitudes toward e-payment. A key finding is the need for targeted interventions to enhance digital payment literacy among young consumers, suggesting opportunities for educational initiatives and user experience enhancements. The paper concludes with recommendations for policy makers, businesses, and researchers to address the identified gaps and foster wider adoption of E -Payment solutions in India's evolving digital economy. The findings highlight the significance of addressing trust, security concerns, and technological literacy to foster greater acceptance of E-Payment systems. Moving forward, further research is recommended to explore emerging trends and innovations in the digital payment landscape, ensuring the continued relevance and effectiveness of interventions aimed at driving E-Payment adoption in India.

Keywords: Consumer awareness, Digital payment, E-Payment adoption, India, Technology acceptance.

INTRODUCTION

"E-payment" denotes payment methods facilitated through the Internet. It encompasses a collection of elements and processes that enable two or more parties to conduct financial transactions exclusively over the web. Examples of electronic payment systems include online credit card transactions, electronic wallets (e-wallets), electronic cash (e-cash), and digital currencies [1]. With this

* **Corresponding author Preethi Nanjundan:** Department of Data Science, CHRIST University, Bengaluru, India; E-mail: preethi.n@christuniversity.in

Suneeta Satpathy, Sachi Nandan Mohanty & Subhendu Kumar Pani (Eds.)

shift, the currency is no longer constrained in its usage, and appropriate procedures are employed to diminish the reliance on physical cash. The significance of digital transactions is heightened, offering the population an alternative solution from various perspectives [2]. The latest stage reflects a notable transformation in how payments are made and received. Ongoing changes in daily infrastructural activities indicate a shift in policies. Everyone must recognize that India's future is moving towards a "cashless economy" for the overall welfare of society [3].

The Digital India program stands as a flagship initiative of the Government of India, aiming to metamorphose the country into a digitally empowered society and knowledge economy. One of the proclaimed objectives of Digital India is to make processes "Faceless, Paperless, Cashless." This implies a transition toward administrative processes that eliminate physical interactions, reduce paperwork, and minimize reliance on bank visits and ATM withdrawals. The emphasis is on replacing physical wallets with digital alternatives, making transactions more convenient and reducing reliance on cash. E-payment apps play a pivotal role in this transition, enabling individuals to send money and make purchases at shops seamlessly. A notable trend in India is the rapid introduction and widespread acceptance of various mobile wallets (m-wallets). This shift is pushing the payment trend away from traditional Cash on Delivery (COD) models to "Payment on Delivery" or "Payment On Order," with mobile phones serving as the primary medium for these transactions. This signifies a significant paradigm shift towards the mobile wallet space in recent times, highlighting the increasing preference for digital payment solutions [4]. The provided text discusses the current landscape of payment methods in Vietnam, emphasizing the predominant use of cash in transactions. The State Bank of Vietnam's data from 2008 indicates that cash remains the primary method of payment, especially among individuals, constituting over 90 percent of retail payments. The text also highlights that a significant portion of the population, less than 15 percent, uses bank services regularly, and less than 30 percent have savings in banks [5].

The global trends of liberalization, globalization, and Vietnam's integration into the World Trade Organization (WTO) are acknowledged, presenting both opportunities and threats to the country's economy and banking sector. To participate more actively in the global economy, there is a need for a shift in payment transaction habits among Vietnamese citizens. The text notes the emergence of new business models like e-commerce and e-business, requiring the integration of information technology (IT) into banking systems to enhance service quality [6].

Various modern banking applications, including online transactions, ATMs, POS systems, payment cards, and Internet banking, are now present in Vietnam. Efforts by the State Bank of Vietnam to reduce cash transactions are mentioned, with a project spanning 2006-2009 aimed at increasing the issuance of non-cash transactions. Despite progress in e-payment, the text notes that the preference for cash persists, with concerns about security, lack of information on e-payment methods, and hesitancy to shift from traditional to electronic methods. The public's attitude towards e-payment has improved in recent years, encouraged by the increase in bank card users and the expansion of ATM and POS networks, particularly in major cities like Hanoi and Ho Chi Minh. However, challenges remain as the public grapples with the security implications and unfamiliarity associated with electronic payment methods [7].

This study aims to explore the variables impacting the uptake of electronic payments in the Indian setting. Its objectives are to determine how much consumer knowledge there is about using electronic payment systems and to investigate security issues related to online financial transactions. Through an examination of these aspects, the research aims to offer a significant understanding into the complex dynamics of electronic payment uptake in India. These insights will be instrumental for policymakers, businesses, and financial institutions in developing tailored strategies to foster increased acceptance of digital financial services while addressing institutions in developing tailored strategies to foster increased acceptance of digital financial services while addressing security concerns and enhancing consumer awareness.

Literature Review

In the Information Systems (IS) literature, examinations of Mobile Payments (M-Payment) usage predominantly centre around three key factors: behavioural beliefs, social influence, and personal traits [8]. Study delves into the implementation of enterprise integration to promote a cashless revolution in Pakistan [9]. The study likely explores the technical aspects and potential benefits of enterprise integration in transitioning towards a cashless economy. Notably, a limited number of studies have explored the impact of awareness regarding mandatory payments as a significant driver in the context of M-Payment adoption, and yet, only a few studies have delved into its influence [10]. While the study explores users' intentions, a potential research gap lies in explicitly addressing the awareness levels and preferences of young consumers [11].

INFLUENCE OF GENDER IN UNDERSTANDING E-PAYMENT

In a seminal work that explores consumer awareness among young minds in e-payment, it is essential to examine potential gender-related variations in the factors influencing adoption and the overall awareness landscape [12]. The study primarily focuses on how young consumers' attitudes and perceptions toward digital payment methods can be influenced by gender-specific factors [13]. Existing literature suggests that gender differences may exist in technology acceptance and usage patterns, with studies indicating variations in perceptions of technology usefulness and ease of use. Therefore, a research gap arises in understanding how gender may moderate the impact of these determinants on awareness and adoption among young consumers in the e-payment domain. Moreover, the study may not explicitly investigate whether gender-related factors play a role in shaping trust perceptions. Young consumers, particularly in the context of emerging technologies, might exhibit distinct trust concerns influenced by their gender identities. Exploring how trust considerations differ between male and female users could contribute to a more comprehensive understanding of the factors impacting gender-specific acceptance of mobile payment services.

Influence of Education in E-Payment

A study on users' perception and awareness towards digital payment security threats among youngsters in Chennai contributes significantly to understanding the nuanced dynamics of digital payment security concerns [14]. The research addresses a crucial aspect of consumer behaviour, particularly among the younger demographic, in the context of a rapidly evolving digital payment landscape. The study likely delves into factors shaping perception, providing insights into the specific security threats that concern young users in Chennai, Tamil Nadu and India. However, the scope of the paper might be limited to security aspects, leaving potential research gaps in comprehensively understanding other facets of consumer awareness among young minds in e-payment.

Prior research underscores the significance of technological familiarity, ease of use, and perceived benefits in shaping consumer awareness of e-payment methods among the youth. University settings, being hubs of technological advancement and diversity, serve as unique environments for studying the dynamics of e-wallet adoption. Educational interventions and financial literacy programs have also been explored in the literature as influential factors in enhancing young individuals understanding and awareness of cashless transactions. However, the studycontributes to this literature by offering a focused examination of e - wallet usage within the specific demographic of university students [15]. By delving into the factors influencing cashless transactions in this context, the research bridges gaps in our understanding of the nuanced elements that contribute to consumer awareness among young minds. This study provides a timely exploration of the attitudes, preferences, and challenges faced by university students in adopting e-wallets, shedding light on potential strategies to enhance financial literacy and promote responsible usage of digital payment technologies in this dynamic demographic [16].

Influence of Employment Status

The paper explores the factors influencing the intention to adopt e-wallets among Micro, Small, and Medium Enterprises (MSMEs), although the paper focuses on MSMEs, it contributes valuable insights that can be contextualized within the broader research on consumer awareness among young minds in the context of e-payment [17]. The literature on e-payment adoption has extensively examined various determinants, including perceived ease of use, perceived usefulness, trust, and extensively examined various specific considerations and challenges faces by MSMEs, an investigated in this study, often intersect with the concerns of young consumers. The research gap addressed in this study lies in the nuanced exploration of e-wallet adoption intentions within the MSME sector [18]. This sector's experiences and challenges may have parallels with the dynamics of young consumers, such as limited resources, technological familiarity, and a need for streamlined financial solutions.

The paper investigates the impact of payment technology adoption on the financial behaviour of Small and Medium Enterprises (SMEs) [19]. Existing literature on electronic payment adoption often explores factors such as perceived ease of use, perceived security, and the influence of external factors on adoption decisions. However, the study introduces a unique angle by examining the effects of payment technology adoption on the financial practices of SMEs. This study gap is important because it emphasizes how important it is to comprehend adoption factors as well as how they affect financial behaviour afterward. The study addresses a research gap by delving into the consequences of payment technology adoption for SMEs, providing nuanced perspective that can contribute to a more comprehensive understanding of electronic payments dynamics. This understanding, in turn, has implications for fostering awareness and adoption among young minds in the evolving landscape of digital transactions.

The study explores the factors influencing the adoption of e-payment systems in the public sector [20]. While the primary focus is on government budget disbursement, this study holds relevance for understanding the broader landscape of e-payment adoption, particularly concerning consumer awareness among young minds. The literature on e-payment adoption often centres on individual and organizational factors influencing the acceptance and usage of electronic payment methods.

A study explores the factors influencing the intention to adopt e-wallets among Micro, Small, and Medium Enterprises (MSMEs). Although the paper focuses on

MSMEs, it contribute valuable insights that can be contextualized within the broader research on consumer awareness among young minds in the context of e-payment. The literature on e-payment adoption has extensively examined various determinants, including perceived ease of use and perceived usefulness, which often intersect with the concerns of young consumers. The research gap addressed in this study lies in the nuanced exploration of e-wallet adoption intentions within the MSME sector [21]. This sector's experience and challenges may have parallels with the dynamics of young consumers, such as limited resources, technological familiarity, and a need for streamlined financial solutions.

The paper investigates the impact of payment technology adoption on the financial behaviour of Small and Medium Enterprises (SMEs) [22]. Existing literature on electronic payment adoption often explores factors such as perceived ease of use, perceived security, and the influence of external factors on adoption decisions This research gap is significant, as it highlights the need to understand not only the determinants of adoption but also the subsequent impact on financial behaviour. The study addresses a research gap by delving into the consequences of payment technology adoption for SMEs, providing a nuanced perspective that can contribute to a more comprehensive understanding of electronic payment dynamics. This understanding, in turn, has implications for fostering awareness and adoption among young minds in the evolving landscape of digital transactions.

The study explores the factors influencing the adoption of e-payment systems in the public sector. While the primary focus is on government budget disbursement, this study holds relevance for understanding the broader landscape of e-payment adoption, particularly concerning consumer awareness among young minds [23]. The literature on e-payment adoption often centres on individual and organizational factors influencing the acceptance and usage of electronic payment methods.

Influence of Age

The research conducted, titled "Moderation effect of demographic factors in the adoption of electronic payments," explores the nuanced influence of demographic factors on the adoption of electronic payment methods [24]. While the primary focus is on understanding how factors such as age, education, and income moderate the relationship between awareness and adoption, the findings can inform targeted strategies to enhance digital payment literacy among young consumers, thereby addressing potential gaps in existing research. As the study considers the moderation effect of Demographic factors may contribute to a more tailored understanding of the unique challenges and opportunities faced by young individuals in adopting e-payment methods. Thus, research holds the potential to advance our understanding of the complex interplay between demographic factors and consumer awareness, providing insights that can inform educational initiatives and awareness campaigns targeted at the youth demographic in the rapidly evolving landscape of electronic payments [25].

The study conducted titled “Influencing Factors on the Adoption of Online Payment Systems among the Elderly and Middle-Aged People,” investigates the factors shaping the adoption of online payment systems in the context of older age groups [26]. While the primary focus is on the elderly and middle-aged population, this research contributes valuable insights that can be considered in the broader discussion of e-payment adoption, particularly concerning consumer awareness among young minds. Study introduces a distinctive perspective by examining these factors within the context of an older demographic [26]. This research gap is notable, as it raises questions about potential differences in adoption factors across age groups, indirectly highlighting the need for nuanced strategies to enhance awareness and adoption, even among younger individuals. The results may offer valuable perspectives on the wider patterns of electronic payment acceptance among various age groups [26].

The study “Influencing factors of young consumers' e-payment behavior: an empirical study of Macao's Y and Z generations” explores the variables influencing the younger generations' e-payment behavior [27]. This study is especially pertinent to filling the knowledge gap around youth e-payment consumer awareness. Research is useful when it focuses on Macao's Y and Z generations in particular. This focused study is crucial because it sheds light on the particular variables that motivate young customers' e-payment behavior and gives a more detailed knowledge of the dynamics affecting adoption. Additionally, the study may address the context-specific subtleties of e-payment acceptance, which might lead to a more focused knowledge of the variables affecting behavior in the Y and Z generations [28]. Since young people frequently have unique preferences and behaviors when it comes to adopting technology, this study can be a useful tool for educators, businesses, and politicians that want to raise youth knowledge of e-payments. By providing empirical insights into the influencing elements of e-payment behavior among the Y and Z generations in Macao, the study closes a large research gap [29]. This focused study can provide useful benchmarks for understanding and addressing youth consumer awareness in the specific context of e-payment uptake.

Influence of Technological Literacy

Furthermore, it would be valuable to explore whether the study addresses the potential barriers faced by young consumers, such as technological literacy, security concerns, or the perceived benefits of digital payment systems. A comprehensive understanding of these aspects is essential in designing targeted interventions to enhance consumer awareness and adoption among the youth. In the study, they consider the technological literacy of young consumers and how it influences their understanding of privacy risks associated with M-payment services. Assessing the impact of technological literacy on awareness levels can lead to the development of user-friendly interfaces and educational materials tailored to the specific needs of the younger demographic. A study on the limitations to the rapid adoption of mobile payment (M-payment) services, specifically addressing the impact of privacy risk, contributes significantly to understanding the complexities associated with the adoption of digital financial services [30]. Young users, often early adopters of technology, may have distinct attitudes towards privacy, necessitating a more focused investigation into their perceptions and awareness in the context of M-payment services. Also, a study [31] made an investigation of adopting low e-payment systems in cities where majority of the people prefer cash on delivery due to lack of awareness and operational constraint.

Systematic literature review on technological factors of mobile payment makes a valuable contribution by synthesizing existing knowledge in this domain. The study comprehensively reviews the technological dimensions influencing mobile payment systems. However, when contextualizing this review within the broader theme of consumer awareness among young minds in e-payment, certain research gaps become apparent. Furthermore, the study may not extensively cover the role of educational initiatives and marketing strategies in fostering technological literacy and awareness among young consumers. Investigating the effectiveness of educational programs and communication strategies in improving technological understanding could offer actionable insights for industry stakeholders seeking to bridge the awareness gap among young users.

CONCEPTUAL FRAMEWORK

The following diagram, as shown in Fig. (**1**), demonstrates the conceptual framework of the research.

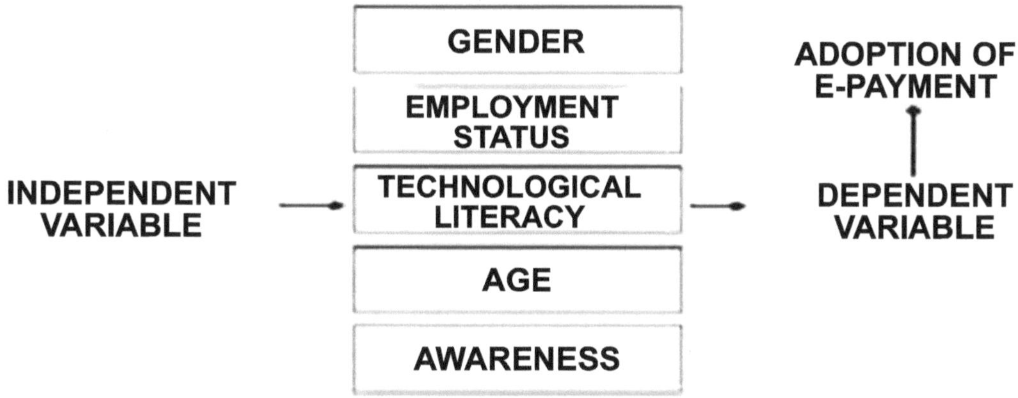

Fig. (1). Conceptual framework exploring consumer awareness within electronic payment systems.

This study defines major constraints in adoption of E-Payment system are Perceived Usefulness, Perceived Ease of Use, Facilitating Conditions and system credibility. The first three reasons or constraints are identified from UTAUT and TAM model and last constraint System creditability is another constraint that affects customer's adoption of E-Payment system. This study has dependent as well as independent variables, whereas Users adoption of E-Payment system is a dependent variable.

Hypothesis

H1: Perceived usefulness has a positive and moderate relationship with User's adoption of E-Payment system.

H2: Perceived usefulness has a positive and significant relationship with User's adoption of E-Payment system.

H3: Facilitating conditions have a positive and moderate relationship with User's adoption of E-Payment system.

H4: System credibility has a positive and significant relationship with User's adoption of E-Payment system.

RESEARCH METHODOLOGY

The research methodology for this study involves a quantitative approach utilizing a structured questionnaire to collect data from users of E-Payment systems. A representative sample will be selected using a cross-sectional design, considering demographic factors like age, gender, education, and employment status. Analysing the data and testing the suggested hypotheses will include the use of statistical techniques, including structural equation modelling, regression analysis, and correlation analysis. The entire study procedure will be conducted with ethical issues in mind. The study's overall goal is to offer insightful information on the variables affecting the uptake of electronic payment methods.

Nature of the Study

The research is quantitative in nature, with the goal of gathering numerical data and using statistical analysis to examine particular hypotheses. Participants' opinions, attitudes, and actions about the implementation of electronic payment systems are gathered for the study using a standardized questionnaire. The data is analyzed and conclusions are drawn using statistical techniques including regression analysis, correlation analysis, and structural equation modeling. In order to comprehend the relationship between variables and successfully test the suggested hypotheses, the emphasis is on objective measurement and interpretation of data.

Population

The people in India who could utilize electronic payment systems make up the study's population. This encompasses a wide spectrum of people from many demographic categories, including age, gender, education level, work position, and amount of experience with technology. Given that various parts of India have differing degrees of access to digital infrastructure and financial services, the population includes both urban and rural areas. To guarantee a thorough grasp of the adoption of electronic payments in the Indian context, the population may also include users of various E-Payment systems, such as digital payment platforms, online banking, and mobile wallets.

Tools and Techniques

This study uses both quantitative and qualitative methodologies. Surveys arc used to collect quantitative data from a large sample of individuals. To find trends, patterns, and connections pertaining to the adoption of electronic payments, statistical analysis is performed using methods such as descriptive statistics, regression analysis, and correlation analysis. Additionally, qualitative techniques such as interviews or focus group discussions are utilized to gain in-depth insights into participants' attitudes and perceptions regarding E-Payment systems. Thematic analysis is employed to analyze qualitative data. Advanced statistical software, such as SPSS or R, is utilized for data analysis to ensure the accuracy and reliability of findings.

RESULT AND DISCUSSION

Demographic Statistics

The provided data delineates the distribution of individuals across different gender categories, along with their respective frequencies. It seems to capture the gender demographics within a surveyed population. The majority of respondents are identified as male, comprising 62 individuals, which constitutes the largest portion of the dataset. Following closely behind, 49 respondents are identified as female, indicating a significant representation of women in the surveyed group. Additionally, there are only two individuals who were identified as non-binary, suggesting a smaller but still present gender identify within the dataset.

Moreover, there are seven respondents who prefer not to disclose their gender, which is a notable aspect indicating a preference for privacy or a reluctance to specify. This gender breakdown is summarized in Table **1**.

Table 1. Gender groups of the population.

Gender	Gender Scale	No. of Gender Count
Male	1	62
Female	2	49
Non- binary	3	2
Prefer not to say	4	7

The data represents the distribution of individuals across different age groups, along with their corresponding frequencies (Table **2**). To provide a clearer understanding, I've calculated the percentages for each group based on the total number of individuals surveyed. The 18-21 age bracket, comprising 42 individuals, represents approximately 42% of the total population. Similarly, the 21-25 age group, with 28 individuals, constitutes roughly 28% of the surveyed population. Moving forward, individuals aged 26 -30 account for approximately 15% of the total, followed by the 31-35 age bracket at around 8%. The 36-40 age group and individuals above 40 make up approximately 9% and 11% of the population, respectively. This breakdown offers a clearer perspective on the proportion of individuals within each category relative to the overall surveyed population.

Table 2. Age groups of the population.

Age	Age Scale	No. of count as per the scale
<18	1	7
18-21	2	42
21-25	3	28
26-30	4	15
31-35	5	8
36-40	6	9
>40	7	11

Ethical Considerations in AI-driven Finance

Artificial intelligence (AI) in finance has the ability to improve returns, speed up analysis, and provide individualized recommendations. However, in order to guarantee justice, openness, and responsible innovation, it is crucial to manage ethical issues.

Bias is one of the main issues. The quality of AI algorithms is contingent upon the quality of the training data. Biases in society may be reflected in historical financial data, which could result in unfair practices. To maintain financial inequality, an AI system might, for instance, reject loan applications to some people based on historical patterns. Diverse datasets and continual human supervision are necessary for bias mitigation in order to guarantee that everyone is treated fairly and equally. Transparency is yet another important factor. The "black box" aspect of AI prompts questions regarding the process of decision-making. Regulators and investors alike must comprehend how AI makes its decisions. By providing insight into the reasoning underlying financial suggestions, explainable AI solutions can promote accountability and confidence. Privacy is also very important. For AI systems to work well, enormous volumes of private financial information are needed. It is imperative that sensitive data be shielded from misuse or illegal access. To protect customer privacy, strong security measures and unambiguous data ownership standards are crucial.

It is impossible to overlook how AI automation in finance could result in job losses. Although AI can expedite procedures, human knowledge is still essential. Retraining the workforce to adjust to the evolving environment, facilitating a seamless transition, and optimizing the advantages of human-AI cooperation should be the main priorities. AI has the ability to completely transform financial innovation, but there are ethical issues that need to be resolved first. Fairness, transparency, data responsibility, and an emphasis on human-AI collaboration are all important ways to make sure that AI is used to drive responsible growth and financial inclusion.

The data provided illustrates the distribution of individuals based on their highest level of education attained, along with the corresponding frequencies (Table **3**). It appears to offer insights into the educational background of a surveyed population. Among the respondents, 15 individuals have achieved a higher secondary education level, representing a foundational stage of education. Moving forward, the majority of respondents, comprising 65 individuals, have attained a graduation degree, indicating a significant portion of the surveyed population has completed an undergraduate level. Additionally, 12 respondents have obtained master's degrees, reflecting a higher level of academic achievement and specialization. Lastly, there are 10 individuals who have reached the pinnacle of academic attainment by obtaining a doctorate degree, denoting a significant expertise and dedication to their field of study.

Table 3. Qualification statistics of the population.

Level of Education	Education Scale	Count According to Scale
Higher Secondary	1	15
Graduation	2	65
Professional Degree	3	16
Masters	4	12
Doctorate	5	10

The data provided offers insights into the employment status of individuals within a surveyed population, along with corresponding frequencies (Table **4**). Among the respondents, 23 individuals are engaged in full-time employment, indicating a substantial portion of the surveyed group is actively working on a full-time basis. Additionally, there are 17 individuals who are employed on a part-time basis, reflecting the presence of individuals balancing work commitments with other responsibilities. Furthermore, seven respondents identify as self-employed, showcasing a smaller but still notable representation of individuals managing their own businesses or freelance work. Notably, a significant portion of the surveyed population, comprising 70 individuals, is students, indicating a focus on education and skill development. Lastly, eight individuals are currently unemployed, which may represent a segment of the population actively seeking employment opportunities.

Table 4. Employment status of the population.

Employment Status	Employment Scale	No. of count according to the scale
Full Time	1	23
Part-Time	2	17
Self-Employed	3	7
Student	4	70
Unemployed	5	8

Customer Awareness of E-Payment System

Based on the collected data by questionnaire and after applying descriptive statistics, we found the following results:

The pie chart illustrates, as shown in Fig. (**2**), the familiarity of respondents with various e-payment systems, with mobile wallets being the most familiar, followed by debit/credit cards, net banking, cryptocurrency, and other systems according to their age group.

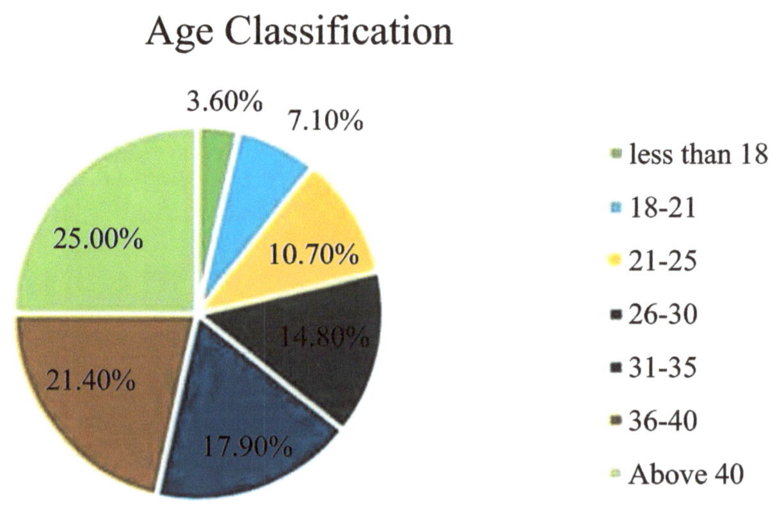

Fig. (2). Understanding of the concept of e-payment.

The pie chart illustrates, as shown in Fig. (**3**), the varying levels of confidence in understanding e-payment systems, with the majority feeling very confident followed by moderately confident, extremely confident, slightly confident, and the least number feeling not confident at all.

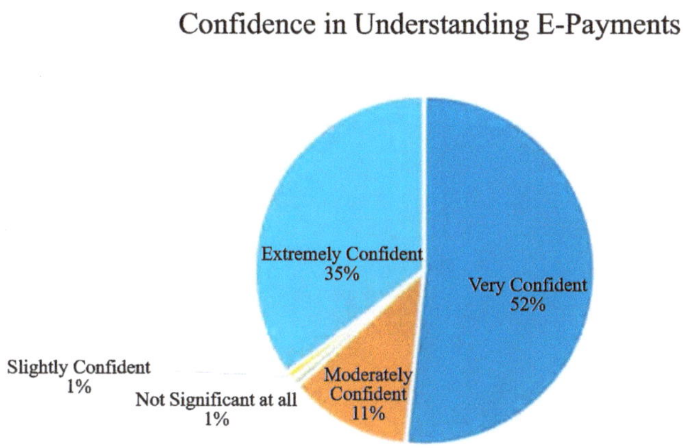

Fig. (3). Confidence in understanding e-payment systems.

The pie chart, as shown in Fig. (**4**), illustrates the comfort levels of respondents in utilizing e-payment systems for various transactions, with money payments being the most comfortable, followed by bill payments, online shopping, in-store purchases, and no respondents choosing "Other."

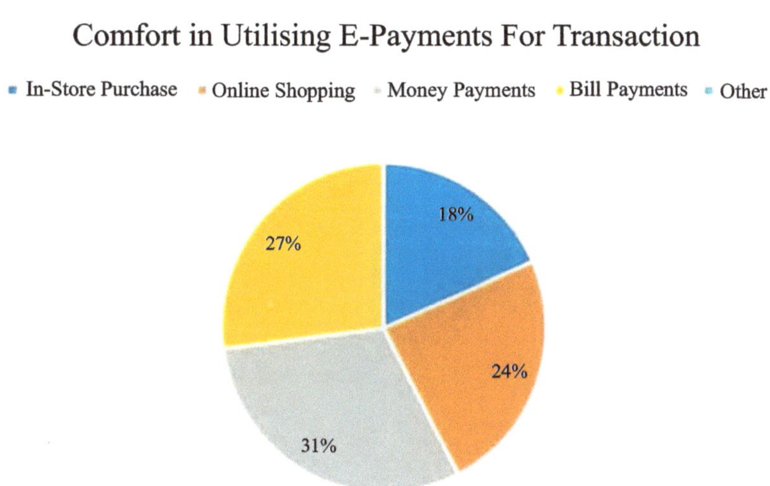

Fig. (4). Comfort in utilizing e-payment systems.

The pie chart, as shown in Fig. (**5**), illustrates the frequency of using e-payment systems on a daily basis, with the majority using them frequently or always, followed by sometimes, rarely, and no respondents selecting never.

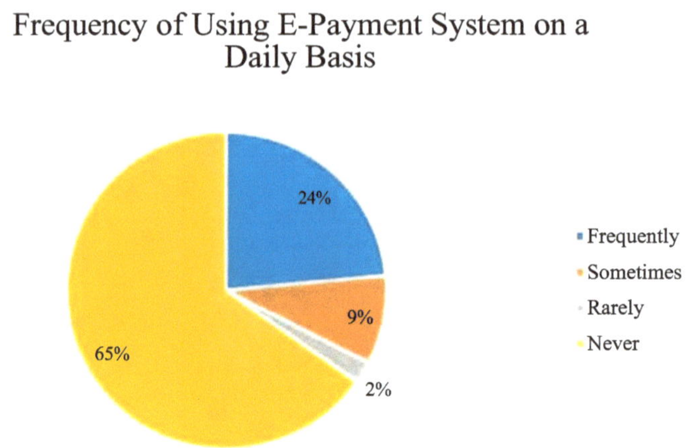

Fig. (5). Frequency of using e-payment on a daily basis.

The pie chart, as shown in Fig. (**6**), illustrates that the majority of respondents' primary method for online transactions is mobile wallets, followed by net banking, debit/credit cards, and crypto currency, with no respondents selecting "Others."

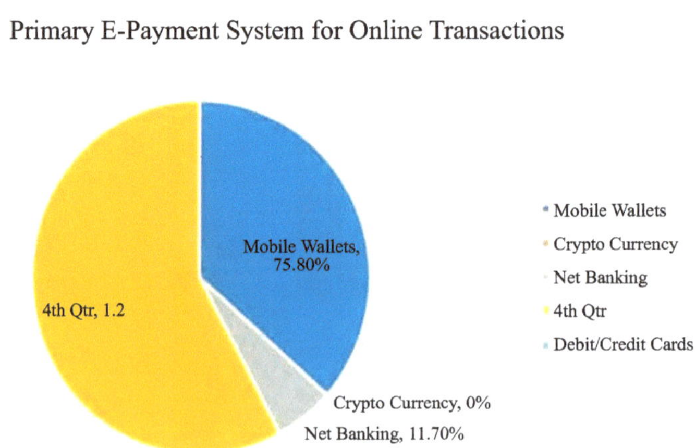

Fig. (6). Primary e-payment systems.

The pie chart, as shown in Fig. (**7**), illustrates that the main sources of information for learning about e-payment systems are bank/financial institution websites, followed by government websites, technology news websites, friends and family, social media influencers, and others.

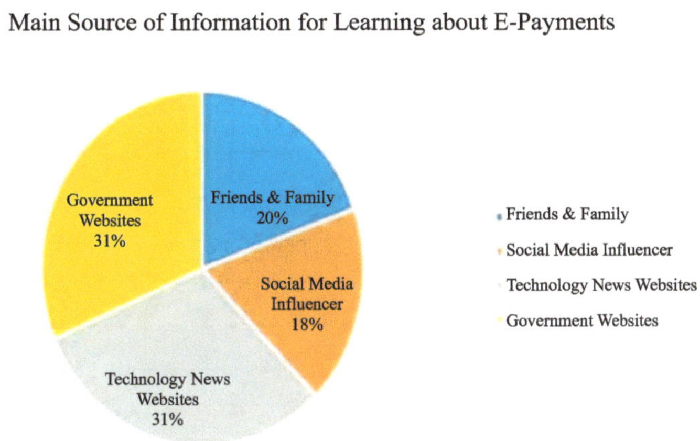

Fig. (7). Main sources of information about learning e-payment systems.

The pie chart, as shown in Fig. (**8**), illustrates that the main reasons for choosing e-payment systems are convenience, speed, rewards and discounts, security, and others.

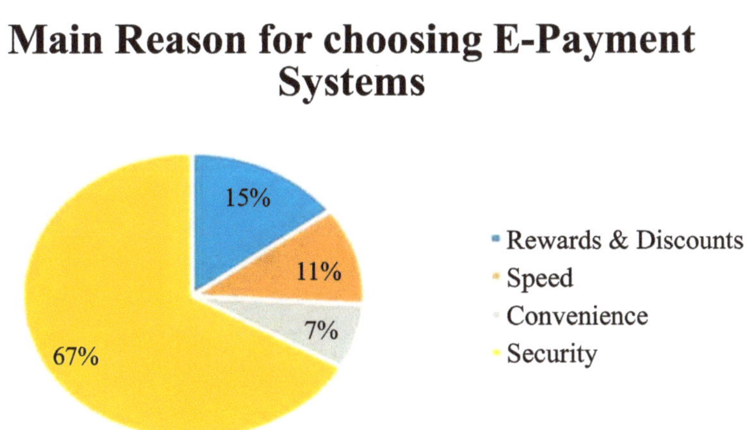

Fig. (8). Main reasons for choosing e-payment systems.

Descriptive Statistics

These results of the analysis of the variables are shown in Table **5**. The number of observations is the total of N and the number of missing values. The total number of respondents is 306, who were asked to fill out the questionnaire. The table shows the descriptive statistics of the data. A Likert scale was used to answer the questions.

Table 5. Descriptive statistics of e-payment data.

	Number of Observations (N)	Mean	Standard. Deviation
System Credibility	254	2.1891	0.66542
Perceived Ease of Use	254	2.0394	0.74847
Facilitating Conditions	254	2.3241	0.72949
Perceived Usefulness	282	2.0523	0.75997
User Adoption	282	2.1371	0.83429
Valid N(list wise)	254	-	-

The mean statistic identifies the answer of most of the respondents on average. The mean answer for System Credibility is 2.1891, for Perceived Ease of Use is 2.0394, for Facilitating Conditions is 2.3241, for Perceived Usefulness is 2.0523, and for User Adoption is 2.1371. The answer for all variables was almost 2.3. This means that most of the answers were "Average" on the like scale.

The standard deviation statistic measures the spread of the data. A greater number in the Standard Deviation means more widespread data. The lowest standard deviation is for System Credibility of 0.66542and the highest standard deviation is for User Adoption of 0.83429. The standard deviation for Perceived Ease of Use, facilitating condition and Perceived Usefulness is 0.74847, 0.72949 and 0.75997, respectively. The standard deviation on average is manageable since it is close to "0" for all the variables.

Correlation Analysis

The output is a heatmap visualizing the correlation matrix of the numeric columns in the dataset (Table **6**). Each cell in the heatmap represents the correlation coefficient between two variables, with warmer colors indicating positive correlations, cooler colors indicating negative correlations, and white indicating no correlation. This visualization helps to identify relationships between different variables in the dataset. The generated heatmap offers a graphical representation of the correlation matrix, as shown in Fig. **(9)**, which contains correlation coefficients between pairs of numerical variables in the dataset. Each square in the heatmap corresponds to the correlation coefficient between two variables: the darker the shade, the stronger the correlation. Positive correlations, where an increase in one variable corresponds to an increase in the other, are depicted in warmer colors (closer to red). In contrast, negative correlations, where an increase in one variable corresponds to a decrease in the other, are shown in cooler colors (closer to blue). Conversely, white or lighter shades signify little to no correlation between variables. By interpreting this visualization, one can discern which variables tend to move together or in opposite directions. Identifying such relationships can be crucial for understanding patterns and dependencies within the dataset, aiding in subsequent analysis and decision-making processes.

Table 6. Model summary of the e-payment data collected.

Model	R	R Square	Adjusted R square	Std. Error of the Estimate
1	652a	0.425	0.416	0.65036

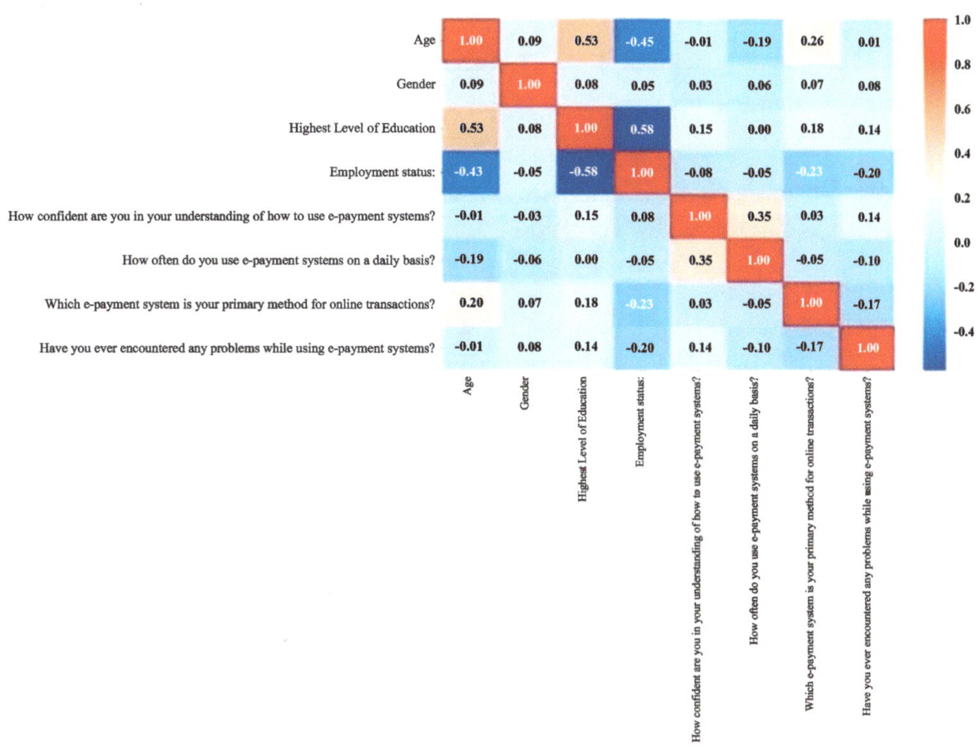

Fig. (9). Correlation of the system credibility, perceived ease of use, facilitating conditions, perceived usefulness.

Regression Analysis

The model summary table shows an R-square of 0.425, which is 42.5% and adjusted R-square of 0.416, which is 41.6% (Table 7). This means that there is a probability of almost 41.6% that changes in the dependent variable are because of the independent variables and the rest 59% are because of unexplained factors.

Table 7. Coefficients of the e-payment data collected.

Model	B	Std. Error	Beta	T	Sig.
(Constant)	0.074	0.162	-	0.46	0.646
System Credibility	0.336	0.086	0.263	3.917	0
Perceived Ease of Use	0.262	0.076	0.231	3.464	0.001
Facilitating Conditions	0.208	0.067	0.178	3.089	0.002
Perceived Usefulness	0.15	0.075	0.134	2	0.047

a. Dependent Variable: User Adoption
b. Predictors: (Constant), Perceived Usefulness, Facilitating Conditions, Perceived Ease of Use, System Credibility

The result shows that most of the people are aware about E-Payment system in Hyderabad. Moreover, by reviewing the literature and applying UTAUT theory and the TAM Model, it is possible to identify the reasons for the lack of adoption of the E-Payment system as Perceived Usefulness, Perceived Ease of Use, Facilitating Conditions, and System Credibility. The correlation shows that if the system is credible then customers have no worries to adopt E-Payment system and according to results, Perceived Ease of Use, Facilitating Conditions and System Credibility has an impact on Adoption of E-Payment system but Perceived usefulness has less impact on it.

RECOMMENDATION AND FUTURE WORK

In light of the study's findings, several recommendations emerge to bolster the adoption and utilization of E-Payment systems. Firstly, there is a pressing need for comprehensive educational programs targeting various demographic segments to raise awareness about the advantages, ease of use, and security features of E-Payment platforms. Improving the user interface and overall experience of these systems can mitigate perceived barriers to adoption. Furthermore, it is essential to make investments in strong security mechanisms, such as encryption protocols and multi-factor authentication, in order to provide users, trust in transaction security. Encouraging adoption *via* incentives or prizes can encourage wider acceptance among the public. Working together, financial institutions, government agencies, and technology companies may create interoperable solutions that meet a range of user demands. Adoption rates, user happiness, and security events should all be tracked *via* systems for ongoing review and monitoring in order to make preventative adjustments. Longitudinal studies monitoring the effect of e-payments on financial inclusion and investigating the integration of developing technologies might yield insightful information for future study, in addition to sector-specific adoption dynamics studies.

CONCLUSION

In summary, our research has illuminated the complex terrain of e-payment acceptance, identifying critical factors and obstacles that consumers encounter while adopting digital financial services. Numerous adoption-influencing aspects, such as perceived utility, simplicity of use, enabling circumstances, and system legitimacy, have been found and investigated through a thorough examination of the literature. Age, gender, education, work level, and technology literacy have all been shown to be important moderators in determining how people feel and act with regard to e-payment systems. In order to address these results, recommendations have been made that place a strong emphasis on the value of cooperation, education, improving user experiences, and security measures. Looking ahead, to further enhance our understanding and encourage greater acceptance of E-Payment solutions in the changing digital world, future research initiatives should concentrate on longitudinal studies, sector-specific investigations, and developing technological integrations.

REFERENCES

[1] A. Mohamad, M.M.M. Mohd Mazinun, and S. Idris, "The influencing factors on the acceptance of digital payment among universiti malaysia kelantan students", *Journal of Entrepreneurship and Business,* vol. 10, no. 1, pp. 130-171, 2022. [http://dx.doi.org/10.17687/jeb.v10i1.865]

[2] S.S. Chaurasia, S. Verma, and V. Singh, "Exploring the intention to use M-payment in India", *Transforming Gov.,* vol. 13, no. 3/4, pp. 276-305, 2019. [http://dx.doi.org/10.1108/TG-09-2018-0060]

[3] P. Upadhyay, and S. Jahanyan, "Analyzing user perspective on the factors affecting use intention of mobile based transfer payment", *Internet Res.,* vol. 26, no. 1, pp. 38-56, 2016. [http://dx.doi.org/10.1108/IntR-05-2014-0143]

[4] S. Zafar, S. Riaz, and W. Mahmood, "Conducing the Cashless Revolution in Pakistan Using Enterprise Integration", *International Journal of Education and Management Engineering,* vol. 11, no. 4, pp. 12-25, 2021.

[http://dx.doi.org/10.5815/ijeme.2021.04.02]

[5] M. Karsen, Y.U. Chandra, and H. Juwitasary, "Technological factors of mobile payment: A systematic literature review", *Procedia Comput. Sci.,* vol. 157, pp. 489-498, 2019. [http://dx.doi.org/10.1016/j.procs.2019.09.004]

[6] V.L. Johnson, A. Kiser, R. Washington, and R. Torres, "Limitations to the rapid adoption of M-payment services: Understanding the impact of privacy risk on M-Payment services", *Comput. Human Behav.,* vol. 79, pp. 111-122, 2018. [http://dx.doi.org/10.1016/j.chb.2017.10.035]

[7] B. Sivathanu, "Adoption of digital payment systems in the era of demonetization in India", *Journal of Science and Technology Policy Management,* vol. 10, no. 1, pp. 143-171, 2019. [http://dx.doi.org/10.1108/JSTPM-07-2017-0033]

[8] R. N. and D. S., "Cash to Cashless Economy: Opportunities & Challenges in India," *International Journal for Multidisciplinary Research*, vol. 5, no. 6, Nov. 29, 2023. [http://dx.doi.org/10.36948/ijfmr.2023.v05i06.9604]

[9] D. Ganjoo, S. Mukherjee, and S. Mukhopadhyay, "Razorpay: Providing Payment Convenience to Disruptors," *Indian Institute of Management Ahmedabad*, pp. 1–19, Sept. 20, 2023. [http://dx.doi.org/10.1108/CASE.IIMA.2023.000009]

[10] V. Parvathy, and D. Durairaj, "A study on users perception and awareness towards digital payment security threats among youngsters in chennai, Tamil Nadu, India", *Asian Review of Social Sciences,* vol. 10, no. 2, pp. 30-34, 2021. [http://dx.doi.org/10.51983/arss-2021.10.2.2988]

[11] Mallat, & Tuunainen. (2008). Exploring merchant adoption of mobile payment systems: An empirical study. E- Service Journal, 6(2), 24. [http://dx.doi.org/10.2979/esj.2008.6.2.24]

[12] P.G. Schierz, O. Schilke, and B.W. Wirtz, "Understanding consumer acceptance of mobile payment services: An empirical analysis", *Electron. Commerce Res. Appl.,* vol. 9, no. 3, pp. 209-216, 2010. [http://dx.doi.org/10.1016/j.elerap.2009.07.005]

[13] Bankedge, A. (2019, October 2). RBI guidelines on mobile wallets. BANKEDGE | Professional Certification Courses in Banking. Available from: https://bankedge.in/rbi-guidelines-on- mobile-wallets/

[14] Digital Payment Suraksha - #SaralBhiSecureBhi. (n.d.). Available from: https://www.dsci.in/digital-payment-suraksha/

[15] R. Ahuja, "Mobile Payments for Conducting M-Commerce," *Mobile Commerce*, pp. 450–467, 2018. [http://dx.doi.org/10.4018/978-1-5225-2599-8.ch024]

[16] S. Yousafzai, and M. Yani-de-Soriano, "Understanding customer-specific factors underpinning internet banking adoption", *Int. J. Bank Mark.,* vol. 30, no. 1, pp. 60-81, 2012. [http://dx.doi.org/10.1108/02652321211195703]

[17] G. Alibekova, T. Medeni, A. Panzabekova, and D. Mussayeva, "Digital Transformation Enablers and Barriers in the Economy of Kazakhstan", *Journal of Asian Finance, Economics and Business,* vol. 7, no. 7, pp. 565-575, 2020. [http://dx.doi.org/10.13106/jafeb.2020.vol7.no7.565]

[18] A. Athique, "A great leap of faith: The cashless agenda in Digital India", *New Media Soc.,* vol. 21, no. 8, pp. 1697-1713, 2019. [http://dx.doi.org/10.1177/1461444819831324]

[19] M.L. Markus, S. Axline, D. Petrie, and C. Tanis, "Learning from Adopters' Experiences with ERP: Problems Encountered and Success Achieved", *J. Inf. Technol.,* vol. 15, no. 4, pp. 245-265, 2000. [http://dx.doi.org/10.1177/026839620001500402]

[20] Cashless India, (n.d). Available from: http://cashlessindia.gov.in/digital_payment_methods.html

[21] A. Chelvarayan, S. F. Yeo, H. Hui Yi, and H. Hashim, "E-Wallet: A Study on Cashless Transactions Among University Students," *F1000 Research,* vol. 11, p. 687, Jun. 21, 2022. [http://dx.doi.org/10.12688/f1000research.73545.1]

[22] A. Apriani, and N.E.R. Wuryandari, "Determinants of Intention To Adopt E-Wallet: Considerations For MSMEs Going Digital", *Journal of Management and Business Innovations,* vol. 4, no. 2, p. 7, 2022. [http://dx.doi.org/10.30829/jombi.v4i02.13448]

[23] P. S. Dalton, H. Pamuk, R. Ramrattan, D. P. van Soest, and B. R. Uras, "Payment Technology Adoption and Finance: A Randomized-Controlled-Trial with SMEs," *SSRN Electronic Journal*, 2018. [http://dx.doi.org/10.2139/ssrn.3267254]

[24] Y.E. Restianto, I. Ghozali, A. Purwanto, and I. Januarti, "Willingness to adopt an e-payment system to increase the effectiveness of the budget disbursement in the public sector in Indonesia", *J. Bus. Retail Manag. Res.,* vol. 13, no. 2, 2018. [http://dx.doi.org/10.24052/JBRMR/V13IS02/ART-10]

[25] P. Kanojia, and M. Lal, "Moderation effect of demographic factors in adoption of electronic payments", *International Journal of Management Practice,* vol. 16, no. 1, p. 18, 2023. [http://dx.doi.org/10.1504/IJMP.2023.127676]

[26] J. Xie, "Influencing Factors on the Adoption of Online Payment Systems among the Elderly and Middle Aged people", *Highlights in Science, Engineering and Technology,* vol. 49, pp. 256-260, 2023. [http://dx.doi.org/10.54097/hset.v49i.8515]

[27] M. T. Liu, J. Xue, and A. N. Chen, "Influencing factors of young consumers' e-payment behaviour: an empirical study of Macao's Y and Z generations," *International Journal of Mobile Communications*, vol. 21, no. 1, 2023. [http://dx.doi.org/10.1504/IJMC.2023.127377]

[28] W. Souisa, "The Influence of Gender in Using Mobile Payments," *Economos: Journal Ekonomi Dan Bisnis*, vol. 6, no. 1, pp. 75–81, May 2023. [http://dx.doi.org/10.31850/economos.v6i1.2146]

[29] W. Souisa, "The Influence of Gender in Using Mobile Payments," *Economos: Journal Ekonomi Dan Bisnis*, vol. 6, no. 1, pp. 75–81, May 2023.

[30] C. Lin and C. Nguyen, "Exploring E-Payment Adoption in Vietnam and Taiwan," *Journal of Computer Information Systems*, 2011. [http://dx.doi.org/10.1080/08874417.2011.11645500]

[31] P. Panhwer, A. Pitafi, M.S. Memon, and A. Memon, "Awareness and Reason towards Slow Adoption of E-Payment System: Study of Hyderabad", *Annals of Contemporary Developments in Management & HR,* vol. 2, no. 1, pp. 6-21, 2020. [http://dx.doi.org/10.33166/ACDMHR.2020.01.002]

Section 2
Future-Ready Security with AI & ML

CHAPTER 6

A Comprehensive Survey of Deep Learning Methods in Network Intruder Detection System

P. Uma Devi[1,*] and **Gurpreet Singh Chhabra**[1]

[1] *Computer Science and Engineering, Gandhi Institute of Technology and Management, Vishakhapatnam, India*

Abstract: The increasing prevalence of cyberattacks and intrusions in the digital era has made it crucial for organizations to invest in adequate security systems. Intruder Detection Systems (IDS) are designed to identify and prevent unauthorized access to networks and sensitive information. Network intrusion detection systems are a crucial component of network security, enabling the prevention and detection of network attacks. Traditional ML methods for intruder detection systems, such as rule-based systems, have limitations in detecting complex and evolving threats. These systems rely on predefined rules and signatures, making them less adaptable to detect new attacks. Deep learning is emerging as a powerful technique in IDS, significantly enhancing their ability to secure networks and devices. This review paper examines DL-based applications in intruder detection systems (IDS) and describes how Deep Learning techniques can detect intrusions in cyber-attacks.

Keywords: Convolutional neural networks (CNN), Deep learning (DL), Generative adversarial networks (GANs), Intruder detection systems (IDS), Long short-term memory (LSTM), Machine learning (ML).

INTRODUCTION

In today's digital world, with the rapid evolution of technology, computer security concerns are becoming increasingly important. Intruder detection systems (IDSs) are vital in identifying attacks that differ from normal user activities in the computer security ecosystem. The IDS assumes that attackers have different behaviors from regular users, as shown in Fig. (**1**). The primary function of (IDS) intrusion detection systems is to detect intruders, attacks, or cybersecurity breaches at both network and host levels. Based on their design, intrusion detection systems are categorized into three types: network-based, host-based, and hybrid.

* **Corresponding author P. Uma Devi:** Computer Science and Engineering, Gandhi Institute of Technology and Management, Vishakhapatnam, India; E-mail: upeddabu@gitam.in

Suneeta Satpathy, Sachi Nandan Mohanty & Subhendu Kumar Pani (Eds.)

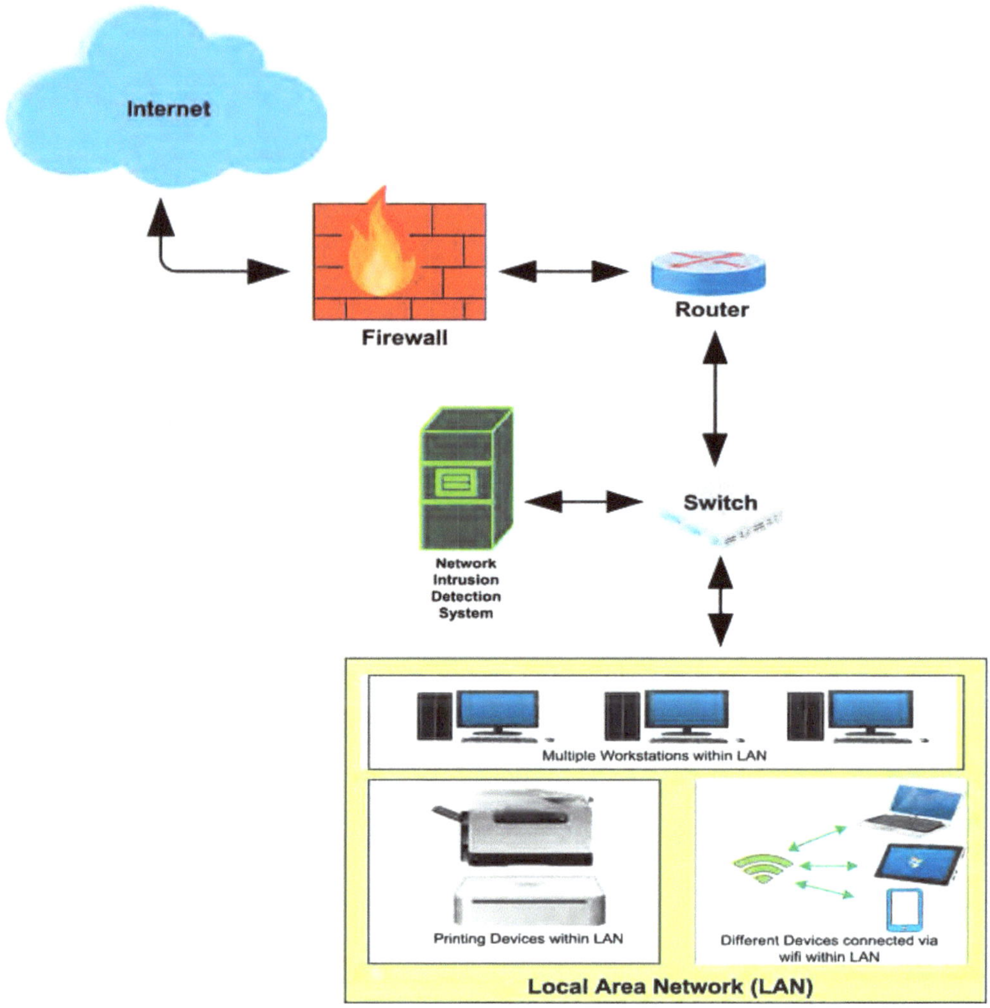

Fig. (1). Intrusion detection systems.

A host-based IDS software application monitors and analyses system behavior on a host machine. The majority of intrusion detection systems utilize a system at the host level, such as event log files, to detect intrusions [1]. Furthermore, Intrusion detection systems (IDS) are categorized into three methodologies: stateful protocol analysis detection, signature-based detection, and anomaly-based detection. The Intruder Detection System (IDS) analyzes data using a commonly used approach known as signature-based detection, which matches monitored data to known attack patterns [2]. This technique is successful and dependable. While log-based detection excels at identifying previously encountered threats, it struggles to adapt to novel attacks.

Anomaly-based detection tackles this challenge by establishing a profile of expected system behavior. This allows it to flag deviations from this baseline, potentially uncovering zero-day attacks that bypass traditional methods. This approach can identify risks, but it also generates numerous false alarms. Due to the increasing volume and diverse threats, anomaly-based intrusion detection systems have been a significant area of research over the past two decades. Different machine learning methods have been used to identify misuse and abnormalities, but they are rarely applied in real-world applications. This approach remains misuse/anomaly detection, which is often considered the key cause for the limited use of anomaly-based IDS due to its high false positive rate [3]. Indeed, even a small percentage of false favorable rates can result in a significant number of false alerts on high-traffic networks; the volume of alerts generated by anomaly-based detection can overwhelm administrators, making practical analysis difficult, as shown in Fig. (**2**). Computers and networks had been vulnerable to attacks from hackers, viruses, and worms and other malicious software, according to Evans. Because the number of intrusions is also drastically increasing year by year, securing these devices and the data that move between them is a task that is difficult to accomplish [4]. A significant number of recent studies have demonstrated the application of various machine-learning strategies in the context of anomaly detection and misuse identification [5]. One of the main limitations of machine learning techniques is the scarcity of training datasets. These methods typically rely on manually extracted features, making it challenging to apply them to various applications.

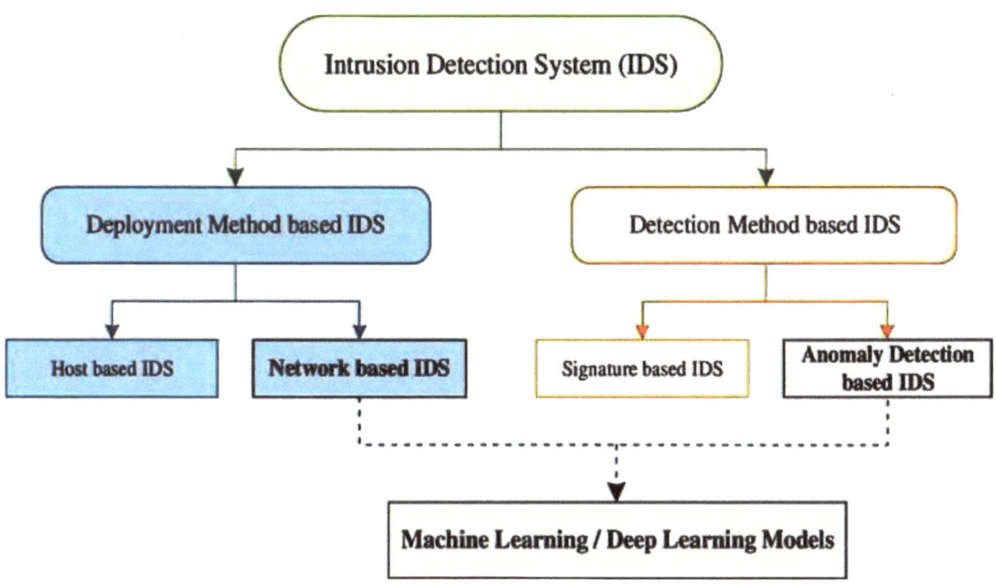

Fig. (2). Classification of intrusion detection system.

DL techniques in machine learning have been created primarily by using ANNs, and they have shown higher accuracy than traditional machine learning approaches [6].

The main findings of this research paper are:

- Numerous studies primarily concentrate on individual deep learning architectures such as CNN and LSTM. However, a research gap appears to exist in investigating hybrid models that integrate various architectures to enhance intrusion detection.
- Insufficient attention is given to evaluating the practical implementation of the models. There may be a potential gap in research in assessing the practical effectiveness of these models in live network environments.
- Further research is necessary to study deep learning-based IDS in resource-constrained settings, such as IoT devices or edge computing scenarios.
- There appears to be a lack of focus on the robustness of the proposed models when defending against adversarial attacks. Studying the investigation of the robustness of IDS based on DL-based intrusion detection systems to adversarial manipulations could significantly contribute to the field of research.
- Many studies prioritize achieving high detection accuracy, but there is a potential research gap in addressing the interpretability and explainability of the models. This aspect is crucial for gaining trust in real-world applications. Some research studies briefly discuss temporal elements, but there is a need for a more comprehensive examination of how to adapt to dynamic network environments and evolving attack patterns. This area presents a potential research gap that could be explored further.

DL-BASED INTRUSION DETECTION SYSTEM

Convolutional Neural Networks

DL has demonstrated significant capabilities in several areas, including network anomaly detection. Initially eliminate redundant features through various dimensionality reduction techniques. Next, the reduced-dimensional data is fed into the CNN model. Even with high accuracy, automatically extracting features is an advantage of CNNs, as noted by Xiao *et al.* [7]. Developed HAST-IDS, a hybrid framework that integrates CNN with LSTM Deep Learning methods. The HAST-IDS system utilized raw data from network traffic to use intruder detection systems. Wang *et al.* utilized GRU, MLP, and softmax features in an Intrusion Detection System (IDS) [8].

Experiments were conducted using the NSL-KDD and KDD training datasets. Using the testing dataset rather than the training dataset would be more appropriate for evaluating the model (Xu *et al.* [9]). Examined several deep learning methods based on the Intruder Detection models as Auto-Encoders, Recurrent neural networks, and convolutional neural networks. Experimental outcomes showed that LSTM and DCNN models are more accurate than the dataset models presented by S. Naseer *et al.* [10]. Yang and Wang presented the enhanced Intruder Detection System (IDS) known as ICNN-IDS, which is based on the CNN model.

The system stores the complex experiment results from multiple layers and displays the performance of convolution networks, entire connection operations, and pooling operations independently [11]. It subsequently combines and consolidates the resulting outputs. It reduces the model to a certain level in the ICNN model. Convolutional Neural Networks (CNNs) extract image characteristics, making them widely used in computer vision. Intruder detection is another area where convolutional neural networks (CNNs) find application, with the images generated from traffic data fed into the CNN model [12]. The literature employs 1D-CNN and 2D-CNN techniques, yielding different outcomes for various datasets [13]. An operating system kernel receives instructions from the user through system calls. To identify intrusions, CNNs can examine these system calls [14]. The vanishing gradient problem, in which a slight change to the network's weights results from the increase in CNN depth, becomes more apparent because the total number of hidden layers in neural networks grows, called the residual neural network, proposed to solve the problem [15]. It uses some layers and prevents the weights from being diluted. Another common usage of ResNet is in network traffic classification [16].

Long Short-Term Memory

Long short-term memory is a subcategory of RNN, a class of information-retrieving neural networks. In contrast to alternative RNNs, LSTMs exhibit superior long-term dependency recall [17]. LSTMs are renowned for producing exceptional outcomes when applied to time series data. Loukas *et al.* developed a real-time vehicle intrusion detection system using an LSTM model to enhance efficiency [18]. They proposed a specialized model called "delayed LSTM," designed specifically for detecting anomalies in time-series data. This approach is further strengthened by its ability to choose the most suitable model from a range of possible options [19].

Autoencoder

Autoencoders are unsupervised neural network architectures trained to learn efficient data representations by reconstructing the input from an encoded representation of the data [20]. Autoencoders are particularly well-suited for anomaly detection and dimensionality reduction, making them effective in these tasks. A common approach leverages autoencoders to generate a new, informative feature set from network traffic data. This extracted representation can then be fed into traditional machine-learning classifiers for intrusion detection [21]. In the conventional approach, network traffic data comprises many characteristics that have been shown to enhance the efficiency of the IDS model [22]. In 1997, an Intruder Detection System (IDS) was presented that combines a Random Forest (RF) with a deep autoencoder (AE) for classification, aiming to improve computational efficiency. Implemented a method involving the combination of two non-symmetric deep Autoencoders and employed Random Forest for classification, indicating a notable improvement in detecting attacks and reducing the training time, particularly in comparison with the Deep Belief Network (DBN) in specific scenarios. The shortcomings in identifying R2L and U2R attacks were highlighted due to inadequate training data [23].

Presented an IDS utilizing Methods as stacked sparse autoencoders (SSAE) to extract features efficiently, complemented by Support Vector Machines. Performed experiments on multi-classifier binary-classifier category problems using the NSL-KDD dataset. Presented exceptional Accuracy compared to feature selection, ML, and DL techniques. Attained satisfactory attack detection rates for R2L and U2R attacks, with lower efficiency than other categories [24]. The Proposed Intruder Detection Systems (IDS) approach involves utilizing Support Vector Machines (SVM) and self-attention learning frameworks. This indicates that the NSL-KDD dataset exhibited enhanced performance compared to alternative ML DL Algorithms. Their performance in the U2R and R2L classes has not been explicitly discussed [25], presenting a novel approach for detecting misuse in autonomous systems by integrating MAPE-K and self-taught learning frameworks, leveraging sparse AE-conducted experiments using the datasets of NSL-KDD and KDD Cup'99. A deficiency in the accuracy of detecting U2R and R2L attack classes was noted [26].

Presented a combined model of two-stage utilizing deep stacked AE for intrusion detection systems. Downsampling techniques addressed the class imbalance in the UNSWNB15 and KDD Cup'99 datasets, enhancing efficiency in detection attacks by implementing preprocessing techniques [27]. Malaiya *et al.* (2020) noted that IDS models can be developed using fully connected deep neural networks, such as Sequence-to-Sequence and Variational AE structures. Various models are analyzed on multiple datasets, demonstrating the efficacy of a Seq2Seq model constructed by combining the two Recurrent Neural Networks [28] and presenting a novel IDS Design that integrates a (DNN) Deep Neural Network model with variational autoencoder (AE) and regularization techniques. The model was evaluated on the UNSW-NB15 and NSL-KDD datasets, showcasing its efficacy in identifying infrequent and novel attacks. A multi-stage Intrusion Detection System (IDS) was proposed, which incorporates autoencoders and a 1D-CNN with a fully connected neural network layer. The model trained two autoencoders during an unsupervised stage and utilized the reconstructed samples in a subsequent supervised stage for classification. Attained exceptional results across various deep learning models on the CICIDS2017 and UNSWNB15, KDD Cup'99 datasets. Insufficient data regarding the performance of the minority class and a lack of specific information regarding the characteristics of the attack [29].

Recurrent Neural Networks (RNN)

RNN represents an advancement over the conventional feed-forward neural network structure that handles sequence data. An RNN comprises hidden input and output layers. The hidden layers function as the memory components within the network. Each RNN unit employs its current input and the output from the preceding input to make informed decisions. The use of RNNs is prevalent across various domains, including human activity recognition, speech processing, handwriting prediction, and semantic understanding, among others [30]. RNNs are commonly employed in IDS for supervised classification and feature extraction methods. RNNs typically have a limited capacity to handle sequences of a certain length and may encounter difficulties retaining information over more extended sequences. Various Recurrent Neural Network variants, including LSTM and GRU, have been presented to address the research challenges [31].

Yin *et al.* introduced an Intruder Detection System (IDS) based on RNN to classify binary-class and multi-class attacks using the NSL-KDD dataset. Various model configurations, including hidden nodes and learning rates, were also implemented. The findings indicate that variations in learning rates and the number of hidden layers impact the model's accuracy. The highest level of accuracy was achieved by utilizing hidden nodes and employing learning rates for binary-class and multi-class scenarios. The performance of the presented model was favorable when compared with the ML and RNN models suggested [32]. One major limitation in these studies is the significant increase in computational process, Which Involves Evaluating longer training times in the model and a decreased detection rate for the U2R and R2L categories. Additionally, the research article did not compare the proposed model with alternative deep learning methodologies [33]. In their study, they presented an Intruder Detection

System (IDS) that utilizes GRU and RNN. The system also incorporates a SoftMax classifier and a multilayer perceptron. The methods were tested using the KDD Cup'99 and NSL-KDD datasets—the research studies present high attack detection rates compared with other methodologies. One limitation of this model is that it has low detection rates, such as R2L and U2R, which are less common [34]. In a study conducted by Naseer *et al.* in 1994, they conducted a thorough analysis of Intruder Detection Systems (IDS) using several Machine Learning (ML) and deep Learning (DL) algorithms. The research studies utilized GPU technology. The NSL-KDD dataset is recognized as a publicly available dataset for evaluating the different models. The experimental findings show that the Deep CNN and LSTM performed with good accuracy compared to other models [35].

Combined Approach

Zeng *et al.* showcased the proficient application of diverse deep learning techniques in processing traffic payload. The authors combined Autoencoder, CNN, and RNN to extract local text features and time series [36].

Generative Adversarial Networks

GAN models excel at capturing the underlying patterns and relationships within data. This allows them to generate new data points that closely resemble the original data, making them valuable for various applications. The Importance of Distribution in data modeling is notably heightened due to its versatility across diverse domains. Unlike many traditional generative models that hinge on the maximum likelihood principle for training, GANs take a different approach. The conventional method aims to align the model's parameterization closely with the actual data distribution; however, it encounters challenges when dealing with the intricacies of high-dimensional data. A Generative Adversarial Network (GAN) typically features two neural networks: the Generator and the Discriminator. The Generator's primary function is to produce synthetic data that closely mimics genuine data, while the Discriminator aims to distinguish bctwccn authentic and counterfeit data. Both the Generator and the Discriminator work collaboratively to enhance each other. GANs have emerged as a focal point in research, particularly in augmenting data for attack detection, addressing the challenge of limited data sets for IDS. These models are integral to adversarial learning methods, improving accuracy in detecting attacks by incorporating adversarial-generated samples into the training set [37].

According to Goodfellow's theoretical framework, following numerous training steps and under the assumption that both the Generator and Discriminator possess sufficient capacity, the probability distribution of actual data converges to match the probability distribution of data generated by G. At this juncture, neither G nor

D can undergo further improvement. This equilibrium state between G and D is reached when the optimization is achieved and the output of D is 0.5. Two key points can be deduced from this derivation. First, it is worth noting that GANs can address the challenge of likelihood by leveraging the behavior of the two distributions. Additionally, GAN can assess the disparity between generated data and the actual data distribution through D and subsequently acquire the knowledge to minimize this disparity. Nevertheless, there are still issues with the standard GAN [38].

The Generator and Discriminator must have increased depth and size to achieve high-resolution and high-quality samples. Within the adversarial framework, achieving a balance and optimization of large-scale deep networks poses significant challenges [39]. It is crucial to select appropriate hyperparameters, such as learning rate, number of updating steps, and network architecture, as they play a critical role in the configuration. Inadequate configurations can significantly hinder the performance of GANs, potentially even rendering them unable to generate meaningful outcomes. Many studies have developed several GAN variants to address training instability through modifications to the objective function, structure, and other factors. In general, it is determined which discriminator is optimal for a given generator; numerous tasks of a given Generator attempt to quantify the disparity between the distributions generated by the target distribution data using different performance metrics. The GAN utilizes the Jensen-Shannon divergence (JSD) metric [40]. Several metrics are presented to improve the performance of GANs, including least-squares. Nevertheless, considering both theoretical analyses and experimental results, it is essential to acknowledge that minimizing distance has advantages and disadvantages [41]. During the iteration of training, there may be instances where the Generator collapses and consistently produces the same output. The model is evaluated using KL divergence to solve the vanishing gradients problem. A recent paper found that when the dimensionality of noise is lower than the dimension of the real dataset (which is often the case), the continuity of the Generator becomes impossible [42].

Wasserstein Generative Adversarial Networks

In 2017, a research paper titled "Wasserstein GAN" introduced the WGAN, which is alternatively referred to as the Wasserstein GAN. For the Generator model to more precisely represent the data distribution in a given training dataset, this variant of GAN emphasizes alternative training methods. The WGAN substitutes a critic for a discriminator model to classify or predict probabilities; the critic assigns a value indicating whether the data is original or fake data [43].

Using Wasserstein distance to redefine the loss function, the WGAN effectively mitigates concerns about training stability and hyperparameter sensitivity. This approach aims to reduce the disparity, as quantified by the distance (EM), between the training dataset and generated data distributions. The EM distance is a highly reliable metric for determining the separation between distributions, even without any overlap. Identifying the most effective training termination point is arduous owing to the formidable rivalry between the Discriminator and Generator. In contrast to the Kullback and Jensen-Shannon divergences implemented in the initial GAN, the WGAN emphasizes horizontal distance and convergence in probability distributions. The quality of the generated samples is influenced by the loss function of WGAN, which is the earth mover's distance. A benefit of the WGAN is its reduced sensitivity to model architecture, hyperparameter configurations, and training stability, as shown in Table **1** [44].

Table 1. Details of algorithms and datasets used.

Author Name	Algorithms	Dataset
Naseer ***et al.***	ML algorithms, DL algorithms	NSL-KDD
Xu ***et al.***	RNN, GRU + MLP + SoftMax	KDD Cup'99 and NSL-KDD
Andresini ***et al.***	AE, 1D-CNN, FC layers	KDD Cup'99, UNSWNB15, CICIDS2017
Papmartizivanous ***et al.***	Autoencoders	KDD Cup'99 and NSL-KDD
Khan ***et al.***	Autoencoders	KDD Cup'99, UNSWNB15
Yin ***et al.***	RNN	NSL-KDD
A-Qatf ***et al.***	Autoencoders + SVM	NSL-KDD
Yan ***et al.***	SSAE + SVM	NSL-KDD

DATASETS

In this dataset exploration, we analyze datasets commonly employed in Intruder Detection Systems (IDS). These datasets include the KDD Cup 1999, UNSW-NB15, NSL-KDD, and CICIDS2017. Deep-learning researchers rely on datasets such as KDD Cup 1999 and NSL-KDD when assessing Network Intrusion Detection Systems. However, sophisticated solutions are required due to the complexity of these datasets. The specifications of the datasets that are most frequently employed in the literature are as follows:

KDD Cup1999

The Defence Advanced Research Project Agency (DARPA) created the KDD-Cup99 dataset in 1999. This is the dataset utilized most frequently in IDS experiments involving anomaly detection. This dataset was compiled by simulating a US Air Force base military network comprised of online-connected computers, and the data was classified as either legitimate or malicious. The dataset originated from the MIT Lincoln Laboratory through a program initiated by DARPA. This labeled dataset comprises 4,898,431 records, each containing 41 distinct features. Moreover, it includes representations of various attack types such as Probe attack, User-to-Root (U2R), Remote-to-Local (R2L), and Denial-of-Services (DoS) [45].

NSL-KDD

This additional publicly accessible dataset is an enhanced iteration of the KDD Cup 99 model. The conventional KDD-Cup99 comprises over 70% redundant records. To overcome this problem, the NSLKDD dataset was formulated. Discrete features from KDD-99 comprise the records in the dataset, and duplication and redundancy are prevented throughout the data testing and training processes. It serves as the standard for contemporary internet traffic.

The NSL-KDD comprises over 1.4 million instances, of which approximately 15% are recordings used for testing and 85% are utilized for training. Just like the KDD-Cup99, this dataset comprises 41 distinct features. In addition, nearly 37% of the training dataset, which contains recognized assaults, is divided into twenty-one distinct categories. Novel or zero-day attacks are specific types of assaults. These are not included in the training dataset but in the testing dataset. While NSL-KDD offers substantial advancements, its primary limitation is the lack of actual traffic. This dataset enhances the efficiency of ML algorithms by removing duplicate records and reducing the dataset size [46].

UNSW-NB15

Traditional datasets fail to address contemporary attacks, often lacking the latest malicious footprints. To assess Network Intrusion Detection Systems (NIDS), Moustafa and Slay from the Australian Centre for Cyber Security (ACCS) developed the UNSW-NB15 dataset. An IXIA PerfectStorm1 component simulates malicious traffic behavior; this component is connected to a CVE2 repository of known vulnerabilities. This results in identifying nine categories of attacks, consisting of analysis, worms, exploits, and backdoors. Utility is utilized to divide the 100 GB of captured data into 1 GB cap files. It comprises 4 CSV files containing over 2.54 million occurrences of nine distinct attacks. To conduct a comprehensive analysis of the connection's packets, twelve distinct algorithms are implemented in c#. The primary attribute of this dataset is the combining of authentic recent malicious activities [47].

CICIDS2017

The research community employs the CICIDS2017 (Canadian Institute of Cybersecurity Intrusion Detection System) dataset, one of the most recent publicly accessible datasets, to apply artificial intelligence techniques for intrusion detection. The dataset was compiled using information from a 2016 McAfee report that categorized the most prevalent network attacks. The dataset is available in two formats: cap, which contains the entire packet payload, and CSV, which contains labeled flows.

Additionally, the dataset documents and monitors the activities of 25 users *via* email, HTTP, HTTPS, FTP, and actual network attacks against 12 unique machines deployed within the victim network. Brute Force DoS, Web Attack, Heartbleed, Brute Force FTP Botnet, SSH, Infiltration, and DDoS are the attack varieties it encompasses [48].

CSE-CIC-IDS2018

The dataset, collaboratively developed by the Communications Security Establishment (CSE) and CIC in 2018, consists of 63 user profiles featuring abstract representations of various occurrences. These profiles are amalgamated with unique attributes to form the dataset. The report encompasses seven distinct types of attacks: Botnet, Brute-force, DoS, Web attacks, Heartbleed, DDoS, and infiltration attacks, as shown in Table **2** [49 - 55].

Table 2. Details of benchmark datasets.

Year	Datasets	Varieties of Attacks
1998	KDD Cup'99	R2L, DoS, U2R, Probe
2009	NSL-KDD	R2L, DoS, U2R,probe
2015	UNSW-NB15	Generic, Fuzzers, Dos Port scans, Exploits, Reconnaissance, worms, Backdoors, Shellcode
2017	CIC-IDS2017	The botnet, DDoS, HeartBleed, Web Infiltration, Brute Force, DoS
2018	CSE-CIC-IDS2018	HeartBleed, DDoS, Brute Force, Botnet, Web Infiltration, DoS.

RESEARCH CHALLENGES

Lack of a comprehensive dataset: Objective: Create a current dataset that accurately represents recent attacks on contemporary networks. The reason for the difficulty in detecting zero-day attacks lies in the inadequate training of most proposed methodologies, which fail to cover a variety of patterns and attack types. Proposed Solution: The development of a regularly updated dataset that includes a wide variety of attack instances, both old and new, covering a range of attack types.

Decreased detection accuracy resulting from an imbalanced dataset: Issue: Resolving the lower accuracy in detecting specific attack types due to the imbalance in datasets. The reason for this imbalance is that low-frequency attack classes' accuracy is lower than that of those with more instances. The proposed solution is to create a current and well-rounded dataset. Various techniques, including SMOTE, RandomOverSampler, and ADASYN Algorithm, can enhance the number of minority attack instances and achieve a balanced dataset.

Inadequate performance in practical settings: Assessing the effectiveness of intrusion detection system (IDS) methodologies in practical settings. This is because many current methodologies are typically tested in controlled laboratory settings, utilizing public datasets. However, these methods often lack validation in real-world scenarios. In real-time environments, proposed methodologies are evaluated to determine if they are effective for today's networks.

Resource consumption of complex models: Efficiently managing resources used by intricate IDS models. This is because numerous methodologies, especially those that rely on deep learning, require a substantial amount of processing time and resources. Possible solutions: Utilizing multi-core high-performance GPUs for computational acceleration.

CONCLUSION

This study presents a detailed evaluation of (NIDS) Network intruder detection Algorithms using deep learning DL models. The findings illustrate the Leveraging of deep learning-based techniques to enhance the functionality and effectiveness of Network Intrusion Detection Systems (NIDS). These approaches have demonstrated increased attack detection accuracy and decreased false alarm rates, with Deep Neural Networks and Autoencoders being the most commonly used algorithms. However, difficulties such as real-time needs and mitigating low-frequency assaults in real-world scenarios must be addressed. Future studies should focus on validating transfer Learning IDS approaches using updated datasets, developing efficient methods to reduce complexity, and providing more streamlined DL algorithms for an effective detection mechanism. By addressing these potential research gaps, a more efficient NIDS framework can be developed, leading to enhanced network security.

REFERENCES

[1] M. Roesch, "Snort - lightweight intrusion detection for networks", *Proceedings of the 13th USENIX Conference on System Administration, LISA '99,* USENIX Association, pp. 229-238, 1999.USA.

[2] A.A. Diro, and N. Chilamkurti, "Distributed attack detection scheme using deep learning approach for Internet of Things", *Future Gener. Comput. Syst.,* vol. 82, pp. 761-768, 2018. [http://dx.doi.org/10.1016/j.future.2017.08.043]

[3] M. Al-Qurishi, M. Alrubaian, S.M.M. Rahman, A. Alamri, and M.M. Hassan, "A prediction system of Sybil attack in social network using deep-regression model", *Future Gener. Comput. Syst.,* vol. 87, pp. 743-753, 2018. [http://dx.doi.org/10.1016/j.future.2017.08.030]

[4] H. Shi, H. Li, D. Zhang, C. Cheng, and X. Cao, "An efficient feature generation approach based on deep learning and feature selection techniques for traffic classification", *Comput. Netw.,* vol. 132, pp. 81-98, 2018. [http://dx.doi.org/10.1016/j.comnet.2018.01.007]

[5] Suricata, "Open-source IDS/IPS/NSM engine," Dec. 2009. [Online]. Available: https://suricata-ids.org/ [Accessed: 16-Dec-2019]

[6] Z. Steven, "Lin, Yong Shi, and Zhi Xue. Character-level intrusion detection based on convolutional neural networks", *2018 International Joint Conference on Neural Networks (IJCNN),* IEEE, pp. 1-8, 2018.

[7] Y. Yao, Y. Wei, F. Gao, and G. Yu, "Anomaly intrusion detection approach using hybrid MLP/CNN neural network," in *Sixth International Conference on Intelligent Systems Design and Applications*, 16s-18 Oct. 2006 2006, vol. 2, pp. 1095-1102. [http://dx.doi.org/10.1109/ISDA.2006.253765]

[8] W. Wang, Y. Sheng, J. Wang, X. Zeng, X. Ye, Y. Huang, and M. Zhu, "HAST-IDS: Learning hierarchical spatial-temporal features using deep neural networks to improve intrusion detection", *IEEE Access,* vol. 6, pp. 1792-1806, 2018. [http://dx.doi.org/10.1109/ACCESS.2017.2780250]

[9] C. Xu, J. Shen, X. Du, and F. Zhang, "An intrusion detection system using a deep neural network with gated recurrent units", *IEEE Access,* vol. 6, pp. 48697-48707, 2018. [http://dx.doi.org/10.1109/ACCESS.2018.2867564]

[10] S. Naseer, Y. Saleem, S. Khalid, M.K. Bashir, J. Han, M.M. Iqbal, and K. Han, "Enhanced network anomaly detection based on deep neural networks", *IEEE Access,* vol. 6, pp. 48231-48246, 2018. [http://dx.doi.org/10.1109/ACCESS.2018.2863036]

[11] H. Yang, and F. Wang, "Wireless network intrusion detection based on improved convolutional neural network", *IEEE Access,* vol. 7, pp. 64366-64374, 2019. [http://dx.doi.org/10.1109/ACCESS.2019.2917299]

[12] A.M. Aleesa, B.B. Zaidan, A.A. Zaidan, and N.M. Sahar, "Review of intrusion detection systems based on deep learning techniques: coherent taxonomy, challenges, motivations, recommendations, substantial analysis and future directions", *Neural Comput. Appl.,* vol. 32, no. 14, pp. 9827-9858, 2020. [http://dx.doi.org/10.1007/s00521-019-04557-3]

[13] A. Prieto, B. Prieto, E.M. Ortigosa, E. Ros, F. Pelayo, J. Ortega, and I. Rojas, "Neural networks: An overview of early research, current frameworks and new challenges", *Neurocomputing,* vol. 214, pp. 242-268, 2016. [http://dx.doi.org/10.1016/j.neucom.2016.06.014]

[14] W. Wang, M. Zhu, X. Zeng, X. Ye, and Y. Sheng. "Malware traffic classification using convolutional neural network for representation learning". In *2017 International conference on information networking (ICOIN)*, pages 712–717. IEEE, 2017. [http://dx.doi.org/10.1109/ICOIN.2017.7899588]

[15] K. He, X. Zhang, S. Ren, and J. Sun, "Deep residual learning for image recognition", *Proceedings of the IEEE conference on computer vision and pattern recognition,* pp. 770-778, 2016.

[16] H.-K. Lim, J.-B. Kim, J.-S. Heo, K. Kim, Y. Hong, and Y.-H. Han, "Packet-based network traffic classification using deep learning," in *Proc. 2019 Int. Conf. Artif. Intell. Inf. Commun. (ICAIIC)*, 2019, pp. 46–51.

[17] G. Loukas, T. Vuong, R. Heartfield, G. Sakellari, Y. Yoon, and D. Gan, "Cloud-based cyber-physical intrusion detection for vehicles 49 using deep learning", *IEEE Access,* vol. 6, pp. 3491-3508, 2018. [http://dx.doi.org/10.1109/ACCESS.2017.2782159]

[18] R. Devendiran, and A. V. Turukmane, "Dugat-LSTM: Deep learning based network intrusion detection system using chaotic optimization strategy", *Expert Syst Appl,* vol. 245, pp. 123027-123027, 2024.
[http://dx.doi.org/10.1016/j.eswa.2023.123027]

[19] P. Baldi, "Autoencoders, unsupervised learning, and deep architectures", *Proceedings of ICML workshop on unsupervised and transfer learning,* pp. 37-49, 2012.

[20] S. Maya, K. Ueno, and T. Nishikawa, "dLSTM: a new approach for anomaly detection using deep learning with delayed prediction", *Int. J. Data Sci. Anal.,* vol. 8, no. 2, pp. 137-164, 2019. [http://dx.doi.org/10.1007/s41060-019-00186-0]

[21] M. Al-Qatf, Y. Lasheng, M. Al-Habib, and K. Al-Sabahi, "Deep learning approach combining sparse autoencoder with svm for network intrusion detection", *IEEE Access,* vol. 6, pp. 52843-52856, 2018. [http://dx.doi.org/10.1109/ACCESS.2018.2869577]

[22] S. N. Mighan and M. Kahani, "Deep learning based latent feature extraction for intrusion detection," in *Proceedings of the Iranian Conference on Electrical Engineering (ICEE)*, 2018, pp. 1511–1516.

[23] N. Shone, T.N. Ngoc, V.D. Phai, and Q. Shi, "A deep learning approach to network intrusion detection", *IEEE Trans Emerg Top Comput Intell.,* vol. 2, no. 1, pp. 41-50, 2018.s

[24] G. Andresini, A. Appice, N.D. Mauro, C. Loglisci, and D. Malerba, "Multichannel deep feature learning for intrusion detection", *IEEE Access,* vol. 8, pp. 53346-53359, 2020. [http://dx.doi.org/10.1109/ACCESS.2020.2980937]

[25] A. Graves, A. Mohamed, and G. Hinton, "Speech recognition with deep recurrent neural networks", *Proceedings of the IEEE International Conference on Acoustics, Speech and Signal Processing,* IEEE: Vancouver, BC, Canada, pp. 6645-6649, 2013.
[http://dx.doi.org/10.1109/ICASSP.2013.6638947]

[26] Y. Yang, K. Zheng, B. Wu, Y. Yang, and X. Wang, "Network intrusion detection based on supervised adversarial variational auto-encoder with regularization", *IEEE Access,* vol. 8, pp. 42169-42184, 2020. [http://dx.doi.org/10.1109/ACCESS.2020.2977007]

[27] D. Papamartzivanos, F. Gomez Marmol, and G. Kambourakis, "Introducing deep learning self-adaptive misuse network intrusion detection systems", *IEEE Access,* vol. 7, pp. 13546-13560, 2019. [http://dx.doi.org/10.1109/ACCESS.2019.2893871]

[28] R.K. Malaiya, D. Kwon, S.C. Suh, H. Kim, I. Kim, and J. Kim, "An empirical evaluation of deep learning for network anomaly detection", *IEEE Access,* vol. 7, pp. 140806-140817, 2019. [http://dx.doi.org/10.1109/ACCESS.2019.2943249]

[29] F.A. Khan, A. Gumaei, A. Derhab, and A. Hussain, "A novel two-stage deep learning model for efficient network intrusion detection", *IEEE Access,* vol. 7, pp. 30373-30385, 2019. [http://dx.doi.org/10.1109/ACCESS.2019.2899721]

[30] X. Liu, A. Gherbi, W. Li, and M. Cheriet, "Multi features and multi-time steps LSTM based methodology for bike sharing availability prediction", *Procedia Comput. Sci.,* vol. 155, pp. 394-401, 2019.
[http://dx.doi.org/10.1016/j.procs.2019.08.055]

[31] S. Hochreiter, and J. Schmidhuber, "Long short-term memory", *Neural Comput.,* vol. 9, no. 8, pp. 1735-1780, 1997.

[http://dx.doi.org/10.1162/neco.1997.9.8.1735] [PMID: 9377276]

[32] C. Yin, Y. Zhu, J. Fei, and X. He, "A deep learning approach for intrusion detection using recurrent neural networks", *IEEE Access,* vol. 5, pp. 21954-21961, 2017. [http://dx.doi.org/10.1109/ACCESS.2017.2762418]

[33] Z. Ahmad, "ShahidKhan A, WaiShiang C, Abdullah J, Ahmad F. Networ k intrusion detection system: A systematic study of machine learning and deep learning approaches", *Trans Emerging Tel Tech.,* vol. 32, p. e4150, 2021. [http://dx.doi.org/10.1002/ett.4150]

[34] M. Tavallaee, E. Bagheri, and W. Lu, "Ghorbani. A detailed analysis of the KDD CUP 99 data set", *Proceedings of the IEEE Symposium on Computational Intelligence for Security and Defense Applications,* IEEE: Ottawa, ON, Canada, pp. 1-6, 2009.

[35] Song J, Takakura H, Okabe Y, Eto M, Inoue D, Nakao K. *Statistical analysis of honeypot data and building of Kyoto 2006+ dataset for NIDS evaluation.* 2011: 29-36.

[36] Y. Zeng, H. Gu, W. Wei, and Y. Guo, "a deep learning-based network encrypted traffic classification and intrusion detection framework", *IEEE Access,* vol. 7, pp. 45182-45190, 2019. [http://dx.doi.org/10.1109/ACCESS.2019.2908225]

[37] D Evans "The internet of things. How the Next Evolution of the Internet is Changing Everything, Whitepaper", Cisco Internet Business Solutions Group IBSG 2011.

[38] J. Goodfellow, "Pouget-Abadie, M. Mirza, B. Xu, D. Warde-Farley, S. Ozair, A. Courville and Y. Bengio, "Generative adversarial nets,"", *Adv. Neural Inf. Process. Syst.,* vol. 3, pp. 2672-2680, 2014.

[39] C. Wang, C. Xu, X. Yao and D. Tao, "Evolutionary Generative Adversarial Networks," 2019. [33] L. Weng, "From GAN to WGAN," 2019 [http://dx.doi.org/10.1109/TEVC.2019.2895748]

[40] M. M. Rahman, S. Al Shakil and M. R. Mustakim, "A survey on intrusion detection system in IoT networks", *Cyber Security and Applications,* vol. 3, p. 100082, 2025. [http://dx.doi.org/10.1016/j.csa.2024.100082]

[41] M. Arjovsky, S. Chintala and L. Bottou, "Wasserstein GAN," in the *34th International Conference on Machine Learning (ICML)*, 2017.

[42] B. Yan, and G. Han, "Effective feature extraction *via* stacked sparse autoencoder to improve intrusion detection system", *IEEE Access,* vol. 6, pp. 41238-41248, 2018. [http://dx.doi.org/10.1109/ACCESS.2018.2858277]

[43] Radford, L. Metz and S. Chintala, "Unsupervised representation learning with deep convolutional generative adversarial networks," 2016.

[44] X. Mao, Q. Liy, H. Xiez, . R. Y.K. Laux, Z. Wang and S. P. Smolleyk, "Least Squares Generative Adversarial Networks".

[45] M. Tavallaee, E. Bagheri, W. Lu, and A.A. Ghorbani, "A detailed analysis of the KDD CUP 99 data set", *Proceedings of the IEEE Symposium on Computational Intelligence for Security and Defense Applications,* IEEE: Ottawa, ON, Canada, pp. 1-6, 2009. [http://dx.doi.org/10.1109/CISDA.2009.5356528]

[46] R. Saadouni, C. Gherbi, Z. Aliouat, Y. Harbi, and A. Khacha, "Intrusion detection systems for IoT based on bio-inspired and machine learning techniques: A systematic review of the literature", *Clust Comput,* vol. 27, no. 7, pp. 8655-8681, 2024. [http://dx.doi.org/10.1007/s10586-024-04388-5]

[47] N. Moustafa, and J. Slay, "UNSW-NB15: a comprehensive data set for network intrusion detection systems (UNSW-NB15 network data set)", *Proceedings of the Military Communications and Information Systems Conference (MilCIS),* IEEE: Canberra, ACT, Australia, pp. 1-6, 2015. [http://dx.doi.org/10.1109/MilCIS.2015.7348942]

[48] B.Buyuktanir, Ş. Altinkaya, G. Karatas Baydogmus *et al.*, "Federated learning in intrusion detection: advancements, applications, and future directions", *Cluster Comput,* vol. 28, p. 473, 2025. [http://dx.doi.org/10.1007/s10586-025-05325-w]

[49] S. Bay, *The UCI KDD Archive.* University of California, Department of Computer Science: Irvine, CA, 1999. http://kdd. ics. uci. edu

[50] S. Chatterjee, S. Satpathy, and A. Nibedita, "Digital Investigation of Network Traffic Using Machine Learning. EAI Endorsed Scalable information", *System,* vol. 11, no. 1, 2023.https://publications.eai.eu/index.php/sis/article/view/4055

[51] C. Mallick, and S. Satpathy, "Challenges and design goals of wireless sensor networks: a state-of-t-e-art review", *Int. J. Comput. Appl.,* vol. 179, no. 28, pp. 42-47, 2018. [http://dx.doi.org/10.5120/ijca2018916667]

[52] L. M. Pattnaik, P. K. Swain, S. Satpathy, and A. N. Panda, "Cloud DDoS attack detection model with data fusion and machine learning classifiers," *EAI Endorsed Transactions on Scalable Information Systems*, vol. 10, no. 6, 2023. [http://dx.doi.org/10.4108/eetsis.3936]

[53] L. Pattnaik, S. Satpathy, B.K. Paikaray, and P.K. Swain, "DDoS analysis using machine learning: survey, issues, and future directions", *International Journal of Business Continuity and Risk Management,* vol. 14, no. 1, pp. 57-76, 2024. [http://dx.doi.org/10.1504/IJBCRM.2024.137242]

[54] S. Satpathy, S. Mohanty, Ed., *Big Data Analytics and computing for digital forensic investigations.* Chemical Rubber Company Press: Boca Raton, 2020. [http://dx.doi.org/10.1201/9781003024743]

[55] S. Satpathy, P.K. Swain, S.N. Mohanty, and S.S. Basa, "Enhancing Security: Federated Learning against Man-In-The-Middle Threats with Gradient Boosting Machines and LSTM", *2024 IEEE International Conference on Advanced Video and Signal Based Surveillance (AVSS),* pp. 1-8, 2024.Niagara Falls, ON, Canada. [http://dx.doi.org/10.1109/AVSS61716.2024.10672589]

CHAPTER 7

Fake Profile Detection in Social Media: Incremental Greedy Ensemble Approach

S. Nonita[1,*], **Monika Mangla**[2], **Y. Gokul**[3] and **R. Manik**[4]

[1] *Department of Information Technology, Indira Gandhi Delhi Technical University for Women, Delhi, India*

[2] *Department of Information Technology, Dwarkadas J. Sanghvi College of Engineering, Navi Mumbai, India*

[3] *School of Computer Science and Engineering, VIT-AP University, Amaravati, India*

[4] *Department of Computer Science & Engineering, Lovely Professional University, Jalandhar, India*

Abstract: The proliferation of social networking sites has significantly improved long-distance communication and fostered a more interconnected global community. However, it also allows intruders to engage in surveillance and fraudulent activities. There has been a significant increase in such instances involving fake profiles, especially in recent years. To detect such profiles, this work presents a novel iterative greedy approach for detecting counterfeit profiles on social media networks. The work has considerable societal implications, as most antisocial behaviors on social networks are primarily carried out through fake accounts. The proposed methodology is implemented on three popular datasets. During the experimental setup, the base classifiers used are Support Vector Machine, Decision Tree, Logistic Regression, Gaussian Naïve Bayes, and k-Nearest Neighbor. The optimized ensemble model utilizes two decision trees and one k-Nearest Neighbor. The yielded ensemble model is also compared with base classifiers and traditional ensemble models, and it is observed that the proposed ensemble model outperforms base classifiers and traditional ensemble models in terms of F-score and accuracy.

Keywords: Classifiers, Ensemble model, Fake profile detection, Greedy approach, Social media.

INTRODUCTION

Social media sites are now one of the most vulnerable points for spying, sending mischievous links, and carrying out financial scams used by cybercriminals.

* **Corresponding author S. Nonita:** Department of Information Technology, Indira Gandhi Delhi Technical University for Women, Delhi, India; E-mail: nsnonita@gmail.com

Cybercriminals widely use such platforms as they allow them to establish a connection with their targets [1]. Additionally, it is worth noting that there has been a massive surge in the frequency and impact of cybercrimes [2 - 4]. Considering the societal, emotional, and financial implications of such fraudulent activities, it is imperative to devise a robust and efficient method for identifying fake users on social networking sites. Fake profile detection involves identifying and removing fake or fraudulent profiles from online platforms, primarily focusing on social media sites, dating apps, and marketplaces. The detection process consists of analyzing user profiles, user-generated content, and user activity to determine whether the account is authentic. The different methods for detecting fake profiles are as follows:

- Social network analysis: This involves analyzing the user's friends, followers, and connections network to identify anomalies or patterns that predict the account is fake.
- Image analysis: Fake profiles often use images from other sources, such as photos from social media profiles. Image analysis can detect fake profiles by checking if the same image is used across multiple profiles.
- Text analysis: Fake profiles often use generic or overly optimistic language or may contain spelling and grammar errors. Text analysis can help identify fake profiles by detecting such patterns.
- Behavior analysis: Fake profiles often indulge in suspicious activities such as sending messages or friend requests to many users. Such activities can be traced to the detection of fake profiles.

Machine Learning (ML) algorithms can recognize fake profiles by finding anomalies in text, behavior, usage of keywords, timing of user activities, *etc.* ML is a technique that predicts future results based on historical data, using which a classifier is trained to find out patterns, identify anomalies, test hypotheses, and verify assumptions [5]. The growth in the field of ML has opened avenues for its deployment in various aspects of human life. It has become an indispensable part of human life, as we use it even without realizing it in applications like Google Maps, Google Assistant, and Alexa, among others.

Considering the efficiency of ML, this paper aims to employ ML to design an efficient predictive model for fake profile prediction. The authors of this work propose an ensemble model, a relatively new technique widely adopted to improve the performance of ML models [6]. Ensemble models enhance the efficiency of predictive models by implementing multiple models rather than relying solely on the predictions of a single model. Consequently, this work proposed an ensemble model combining popular ML models to enhance effectiveness and efficiency further.

As discussed, ensemble learning combines the results of various models. It generates a standard set of outputs based on specific parameters, significantly improving the accuracy of the results. There are two variations of ensemble models: homogeneous and heterogeneous. The homogeneous ensemble model combines results from the same base model, while the heterogeneous ensemble model uses different base models. An ensemble model ensures that the predicted outcome is the best among all base models and can be determined using three fundamental techniques: maximum voting, averaging, and weighted averaging [7]. Here, max voting is used for classification problems, while averaging and weighted averaging are used for regression problems.

An ensemble model can be passed through a voting classifier, which selects the output suggested by the majority of models. Here, it is worth noting that averaging and weighted averaging can also be used in cases involving categorical variables to calculate probabilities of nominal values.

Ensemble techniques can be further categorized into three categories: Bagging, Boosting, and Stacking. Bagging trains multiple weak learners in parallel and outputs the aggregated results of all base models. The sample dataset used to train each weak learner may or may not be identical, as it is fetched using the replacement technique. Random Forest is an example of a bagging algorithm that significantly reduces overfitting compared to its base learner, *i.e.*, the Decision Tree. Unlike bagging, base learners depend on each other's output in boosting, as the production of one base model is fed to another sequentially. Additionally, it does not assign equal importance to all base learners, as incorrectly classified data points are given more weight in training the next model. Gradient boosting and AdaBoost are standard boosting algorithms. In stacking, two or more base models are trained, and the results are sent to a meta-model to aggregate predictions. The meta-models are trained on data that was not sent to base-models. Stacking occurs in levels where base models are at level 0, and meta-models are at level 1. In the current research work, the authors used an ensemble model with a dynamic programming approach.

Optimization in ML is the process of adjusting hyperparameters to improve performance. These hyperparameters are optimized to maintain a balance between bias and variance, and can be achieved through various techniques, such as gradient descent and stochastic gradient descent. The gradient Descent technique minimizes the cost function, thereby reducing the error. The goal is to reach a local minimum where the cost function cannot be further reduced. Furthermore, the learning rate determines when the model should stop searching for the global minimum. Stochastic gradient descent introduces an element of randomness in gradient descent, where it randomly selects data points during each iteration.

The current manuscript is organized into various sections. Related work is described in Section 2. The details regarding the proposed methods are described in Section 3. Further, the methodology is described in Section 4. The results and discussion are elaborated further in Section 5. Finally, the conclusions and future scope are presented.

RELATED WORK

This section details the related work done in the domain of fake profile detection. Fake profile detection is vital in cybersecurity and social network analysis. With the rise of social media and online networking platforms, the proliferation of fake profiles has become a serious concern for individuals and organizations. Fake profiles can be used for various malicious purposes, including fraud, phishing, and identity theft. As a result, significant research has been conducted on detecting fake profiles in recent years.

Among the various methods and techniques applied for fake profile detection, ML has been agreed to be among the most promising. In a study by Bu *et al.* (2013) [8], the authors proposed a method based on supervised learning to identify fake profiles on Facebook. They collected data from 3,000 Facebook profiles and used features such as profile picture, number of friends, and activity level to train a decision tree classifier. The results showed that their method effectively identified fake profiles with an accuracy of 94.2%.

Another approach to detecting fake profiles involves using network analysis techniques. In a study by Yang *et al.* (2014) [9], the authors proposed a method based on network motifs to identify fake profiles on Twitter. The authors analyzed the structural features of the follower networks of Twitter profiles and found that counterfeit profiles tended to have specific network motifs distinct from those of real profiles. The results showed that their method effectively identified fake profiles with an accuracy of 91%.

Furthermore, researchers have also focused on identifying fake reviews on e-commerce websites, as these reviews can be used to manipulate consumer behavior. In a study by Zhang *et al.* (2016) [10], the authors proposed a method based on sentiment analysis to identify fake reviews on Amazon. They collected a dataset of 600 reviews, half of which were fake, and used sentiment polarity and review length features to train a classifier. The results showed that their method effectively identified fake reviews with an accuracy of 90%.

In recent years, research has also been conducted on using deep learning techniques for detecting fake profiles. In a study by Chen *et al.* (2018) [11], the authors proposed a method based on convolutional neural networks (CNNs) to identify fake profiles on social media. They collected a dataset of 30,000 Twitter profiles and used features such as profile picture, description, and follower count to train a CNN classifier. The results showed that their method effectively identified fake profiles, with an accuracy of 96.5%.

Overall, these studies demonstrate that fake profile detection is an active research area, and hence, has attracted a variety of approaches used by various researchers to address the problem. It is evident from the study of related work that while ML and network analysis techniques have been effective for fake profile detection, deep learning methods also show promising results and hence can be used for further improvements.

MATERIALS & METHODS

The approach used in this research work is presented in this section. We collect data from social profiles by creating a social network graph of a user and their contacts in this model. This graph is transformed into an adjacency matrix. To determine the similarity among nodes, the proposed method employs three different methods: link similarity, text similarity, and word similarity. It may cause data imbalances, which a hybrid ensemble approach can address. Furthermore, new similarity features are extracted using principal component analysis (PCA), and the individual models are trained on each user's device using the proposed ensemble model. The proposed method utilizes the Synthetic Minority Oversampling Technique (SMOTE) to augment the minority class. The step-wise methodology is illustrated in Fig. (**1**).

Further, the concept of the ensemble model is employed to enhance the prediction accuracy. Predictions in the current work are evaluated based on the basic ensemble model, a combination of all the classifiers. Additionally, an optimized ensemble model is developed using an incremental greedy approach in the form of a flowchart. We have used a majority voting classifier to combine the base learners of an ensemble model. The base learners in the proposed work are support vector machine (SVM), Decision Tree (DT), Logistic regression (LR), Gaussian Naïve Bayes (NB), and k-nearest neighbor (KNN).

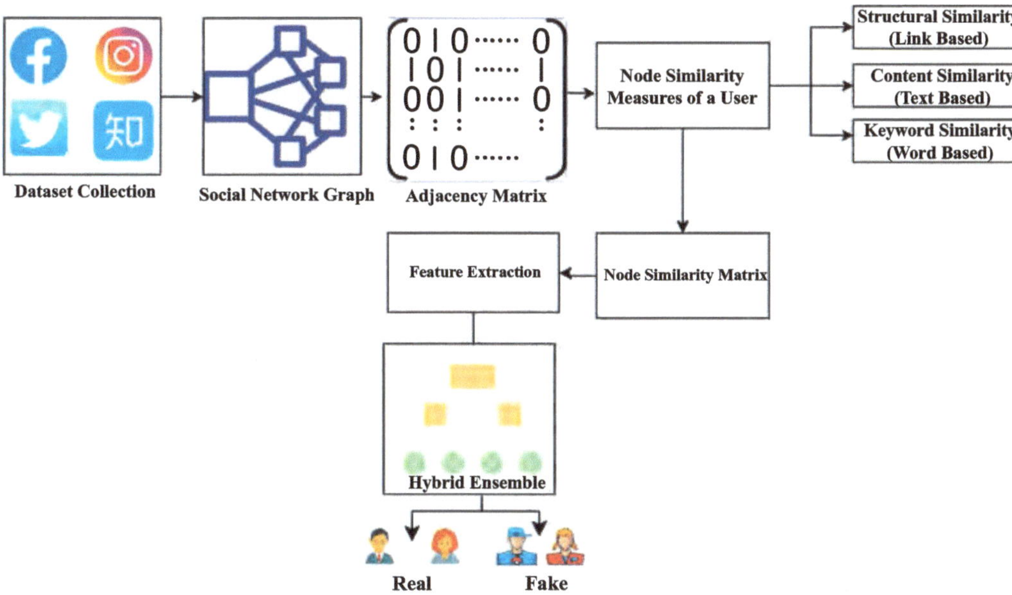

Fig. (1). Proposed framework for fake profile identification on social media.

We adopted an incremental greedy approach to determine the best-suited ensemble model for the chosen dataset. We choose the F-measure as the greedy parameter to achieve a balanced value of recall and precision. Initially, results from different base classifiers are considered and sorted in decreasing order of F-measure. This is done because models that provide more balanced results are preferred over biased ones. The output from each step is considered before the next step to be viewed as a variation of the boosting technique. Also, each base model from the sorted array is considered for a maximum of two iterations. The classifier is discarded if neither of the two iterations gives a better F-measure. Classifiers are discarded because, in a greedy approach, any model that does not positively contribute need not be adopted for further computation. Thus, layers may be added incrementally with each iteration, and the required ensemble model is developed accordingly. After each iteration, we select the ensemble with the best result and feed it as the first layer of the following base learner from the sorted array. The process is continued until the number of base learners in the sorted array is exhausts. Finally, results from the generated ensemble are combined using the max voting approach.

PROPOSED METHODOLOGY

This section discusses the implementation of the proposed approach presented in the previous section, which is illustrated pictorially in Fig. (**2**). The proposed work is represented as follows: the base classifiers are sorted based on their efficiency. Then, the base classifiers are selected from this sorted list of classifiers to yield an optimized ensemble model. Thus, the research primarily focuses on developing ensemble models to enhance the efficiency and reliability of predictions. As per the proposed methodology, the yielded ensemble model uses two decision trees and 1 KNN. The newly developed ensemble model is also compared with a basic ensemble model. The step-by-step description of the proposed methodology is given as follows:

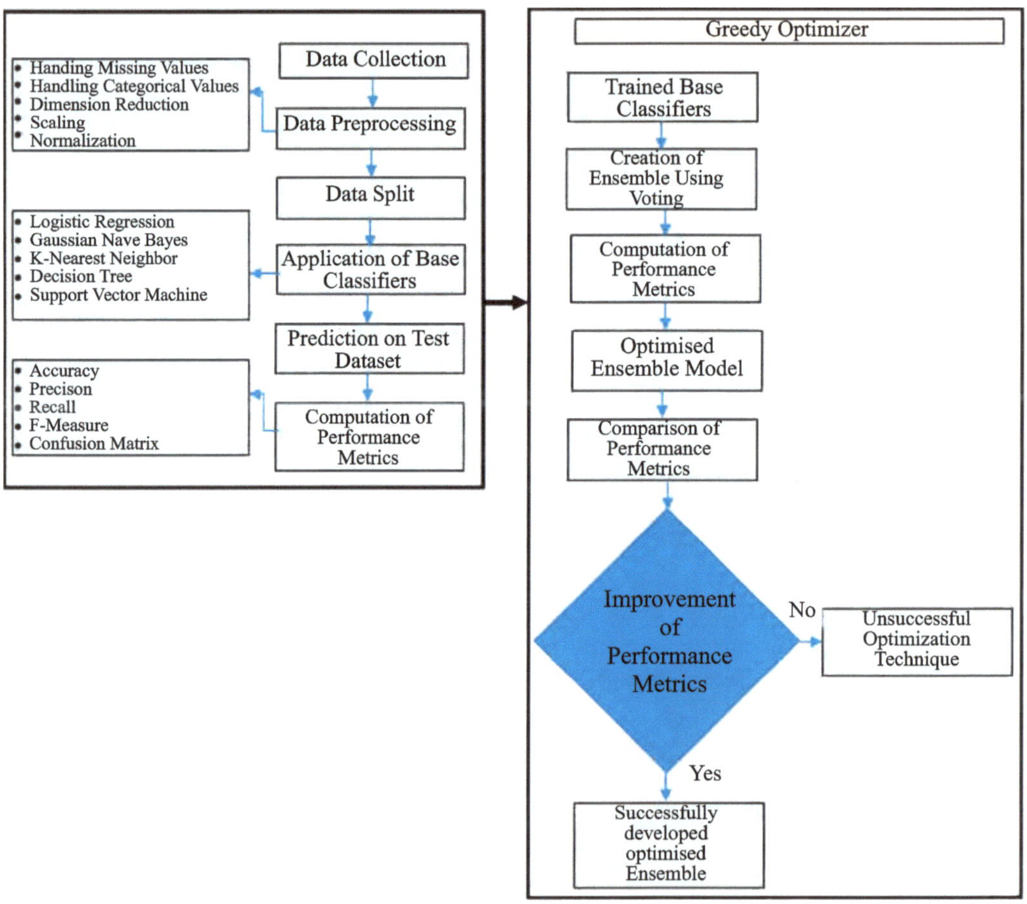

Fig. (2). Proposed methodology.

Selection and Collection of Datasets: Various datasets are collated from different platforms to perform an experimental evaluation of the proposed methodology. The considered datasets are gathered from Twitter profiles (Dataset 1), a Twitter dataset (Dataset 2), and the Weibo social platform, a Chinese social media platform (Dataset 3), which contains a novel dataset for identifying fake Instagram profiles [12 - 15].

Data Preprocessing: When a model is trained on preprocessed data, it yields better results, as preprocessing removes inconsistencies in the dataset, allowing the model to identify patterns more efficiently. Preprocessing can be applied per the dataset and problem statement requirements. In the current work, the proposed methodology aims to determine whether a profile is genuine or fraudulent based on its appearance, and all the specific details have now been established. During preprocessing, categorical aspects were replaced with numerical data. A dataset of genuine and fake users is integrated and assigned the Boolean label "isFake".

As mentioned earlier, authors have employed various machine-learning classifiers as shown in Fig. (**3**) as follows:

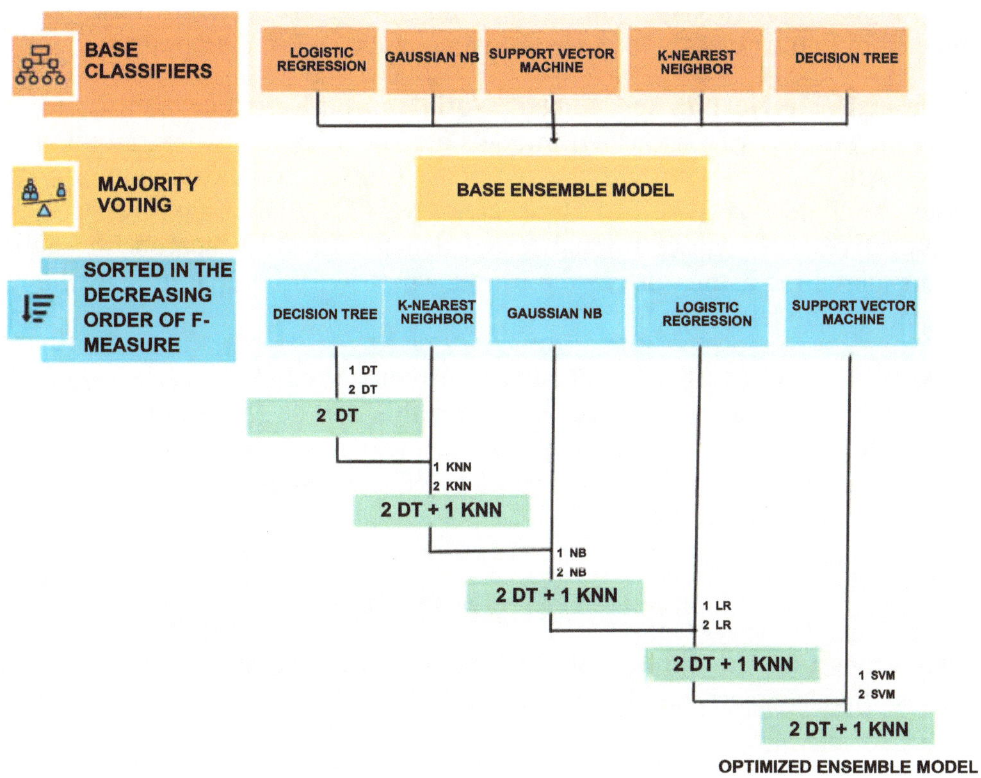

Fig. (3). Demonstration of ml models, ensemble model, and optimized ensemble model.

Support Vector Machine: SVM aims to determine the support vectors so that the area of the hyperplane is maximized. The two major classifications of SVM are linear and polynomial, which can be used for classification purposes.

Logistic Regression: LR is a supervised learning approach where data points are classified based on a sigmoid function, making it suitable for classification problems.

Gaussian Naive Bayes: NB is based on Bayes' theorem of probability, where all the attributes are considered independent during training.

Decision Tree: DT, a robust ML algorithm for classification, selects the attributes as nodes of trees so that impurity is minimal. In the current implementation, we have used the cart decision tree model.

K-Nearest Neighbor (kNN), a supervised machine learning algorithm, uses the distance from known classes to determine the class of a test data point.

Performance Metrics: In the current work, the performance metrics used to evaluate the efficacy of various ML models are accuracy, precision, recall, and F-measure. All these metrics can be assessed from a confusion matrix, which provides the True Positive (TP), True Negative (TN), False Positive (FP), and False Negative (FN) values for the tested dataset. In this research, the authors have considered the F-measure as the primary metric for comparative evaluations of various ML models.

Accuracy- A measure of the number of correctly predicted classes among the total number of tested data points. However, this can be misleading sometimes, especially for an imbalanced dataset. In such a scenario, the classifier tends to predict all the classes as the majority class. The mathematical formulation for accuracy is represented in Eq. 1.

$$\text{Accuracy}=TP+TNTP+TN+FP+FN \tag{1}$$

Precision measures the number of correctly classified positive classes out of all those classified as positive and can be formulated as Eq. 2.

$$\text{Precision}=TPTP+FP \tag{2}$$

Recall measures the number of correctly classified positive classes out of all the actual positive classes, as represented in Eq. 3.

Recall=TPTP+FN (3)

F-measure- It indicates a balance among the values of FP and FN and is calculated by taking their harmonic mean as represented in Eq. 4.

F-measure=2*Precision*RecallPrecision+Recall (4)

Ensemble Model: We exploited the concept of the ensemble model to enhance the efficacy of base models. We have employed the greedy design approach to devise the most efficient ensemble model. For the same reason, we initially evaluated the efficiency of base classifier models. Thereafter, the base classifiers are ensembled using an incremental greedy approach. As discussed earlier, the base classifier models are SVM, DT, LR, NB, and KNN [16, 17].

Optimization Technique: We adopted an incremental greedy approach to determine the most efficient ensemble model for the chosen dataset. F-measure is selected as the greedy choice parameter as it ensures a balanced value of recall and precision. First, base classifiers are sorted in decreasing order based on the F-measure. Sorting classifiers ensures that models yielding balanced results are preferred over models demonstrating biased results. Now, each base classifier is considered for a maximum of two iterations. It is checked if it yields a better F-measure than the current best-known value; if so, the classifier is discarded thereafter. Classifiers are discarded as any model that does not outperform in F-measure need not be adopted for further computations. The F-measure of possible ensembles for each base classifier is evaluated, and the model with the highest F-measure is selected. Thus, each iteration may or may not add a classifier to the ensemble model, and therefore, the required ensemble model is developed incrementally. The number of base classifiers determines the number of iterations. Once the optimal ensemble model is defined, classification is performed using the max voting approach. The optimal ensemble model employs two decision trees and one kNN.

Algorithm for Proposed Approach: This section discusses the basic algorithm of the proposed optimization technique for the ensemble model as follows:

Algorithm: Proposed Iterative Greedy Approach

```
Begin
    A = Array of models of size n
    ReverseSort(A)
    bestFmes = 0
    Ensembler = []
    for i = 1 to n
      Temp = Ensembler
        for j = 1 to 2
            Temp.append(A[i])
            if(Temp.Fmes>bestFmes) then
                bestFmes = Temp.Fmes
              Ensembler = Temp
            Endif
    Return Ensembler
end
```

RESULTS & DISCUSSION

The results section is organized into three subsections: base model, optimization technique, and proposed iterative greedy method for ensemble modeling.

Comparison of Classifiers and Base Ensemble Model

The classification models for this case were developed after changing the categorical attributes to numerical attributes. Models are analyzed based on accuracy, precision, recall, and F-measure. The values of accuracy, precision, recall, and F-measure are in the ranges of 0.757-0.867, 0.770-0.956, 0.756-0.870, and 0.782-0.869, respectively. The performance metrics considered for all base models are listed in Table **1**.

Table 1. Performance metrics for various base classifiers for all three datasets.

Base Model	Dataset	Accuracy	Precision	Recall	F-Measure
SVM	1	0.766	0.809	0.756	0.782
	2	0.653	0.705	0.623	0.632
	3	0.742	0.801	0.713	0.743
LR	1	0.757	0.770	0.801	0.785
	2	0.701	0.652	0.756	0.653
	3	0.734	0.766	0.825	0.714

(Table 1) cont.....

Base Model	Dataset	Accuracy	Precision	Recall	F-Measure
NB	1	0.784	0.770	0.870	0.817
	2	0.656	0.662	0.723	0.758
	3	0.781	0.747	0.856	0.817
DT	1	0.867	0.956	0.797	0.869
	2	0.674	0.712	0.634	0.632
	3	0.756	0.865	0.714	0.735
KNN	1	0.858	0.903	0.833	0.867
	2	0.656	0.734	0.756	0.786
	3	0.834	0.894	0.812	0.834
SVM+DT+KNN+LR+NB	1	0.816	0.828	0.841	0.835
	2	0.715	0.756	0.734	0.712
	3	0.813	0.823	0.814	0.823

DT and KNN outperform SVM, LR, and NB. The performance measures for different classifiers on dataset 1 are shown in Fig. (**4**) to perform a comparative analysis of various base classifiers.

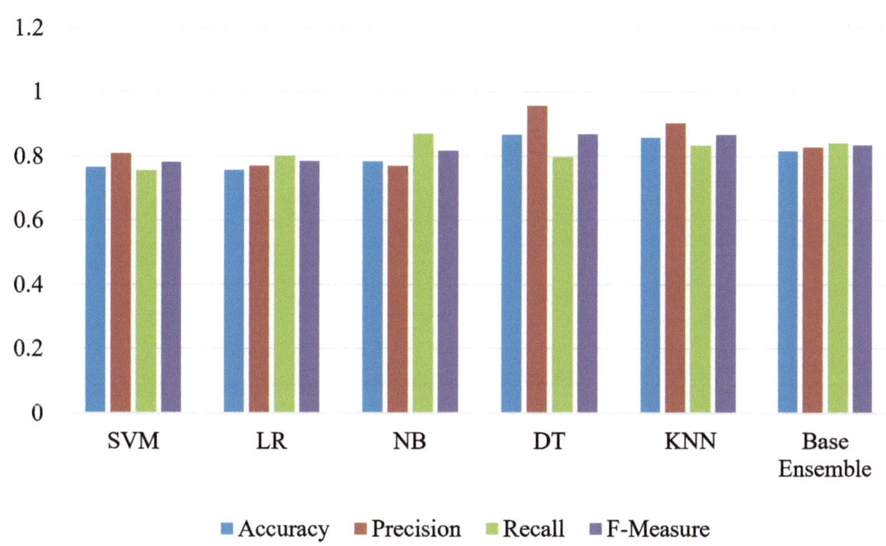

Fig. (4). Comparative analysis of classifiers and base models.

Analysis of Heterogeneous Ensemble Model

Now, as specified in the proposed algorithm, the ensemble is initialized as an empty array, and during each iteration, the layers yielding results better than the existing best results are selected and added to the ensemble. Here, the F-measure is considered the performance metric for optimizing ensemble models. As discussed previously, each base learner from the sorted array (based on performance metrics) is regarded as a maximum of two times. The F-measure for all considerations and the corresponding results are given in Table **2**. At the end of iterations, it is evident that 2DT + 1 KNN is the most optimized ensemble model, with an F-measure of 0.894, using the proposed iterative and greedy approach.

Table 2. Performance measures of heterogeneous ensemble models.

Base Model	Simulations	F-Measure	Result
DT	1 DT	0.869	Selected (0.869>0)
	2 DT	0.892	Selected (0.892>0.869)
KNN	2 DT + 1 KNN	0.894	Selected (0.894>0.892)
	2 DT+2KNN	0.872	not selected (0.872<0.894)
NB	2 DT + 1 KNN + 1 NB	0.883	not selected (0.883<0.894)
	2 DT + 1 KNN + 2 NB	0.878	not selected (0.878<0.894)
LR	2 DT + 1 KNN + 1 LR	0.878	not selected (0.878<0.894)
	2 DT + 1 KNN + 2 LR	0.880	not selected (0.880<0.894)
SVM	2 DT + 1 KNN + 1 SVM	0.878	not selected (0.878<0.894)
	2 DT + 1 KNN + 2 SVM	0.871	not selected (0.871<0.894)

Comparison of Base Ensemble Model with Optimized Ensemble Model

The authors also compare the performance of the base ensemble model with the proposed ensemble model to validate and verify the proposed methodology. The comparative analysis is given in Table **3**, which indicates that the accuracy of the optimized ensemble model (using an iterative greedy approach) is 89% compared to the traditional ensemble model, which yields an accuracy of 81.6%. The targeted value of the F-measure also shows a significant increase from 0.835 in the base ensemble to 0.894. As illustrated in Fig. (**5**), other performance measures, such as recall and precision, demonstrate considerable improvement, thereby establishing the efficacy of the proposed approach in optimizing the ensemble model.

Table 3. Performance measures of heterogeneous ensemble models.

Model	Accuracy	Precision	Recall	F-Measure
SVM+DT+KNN+LR+NB	0.816	0.828	0.841	0.835
2 DT + 1 KNN	0.890	0.958	0.837	0.894

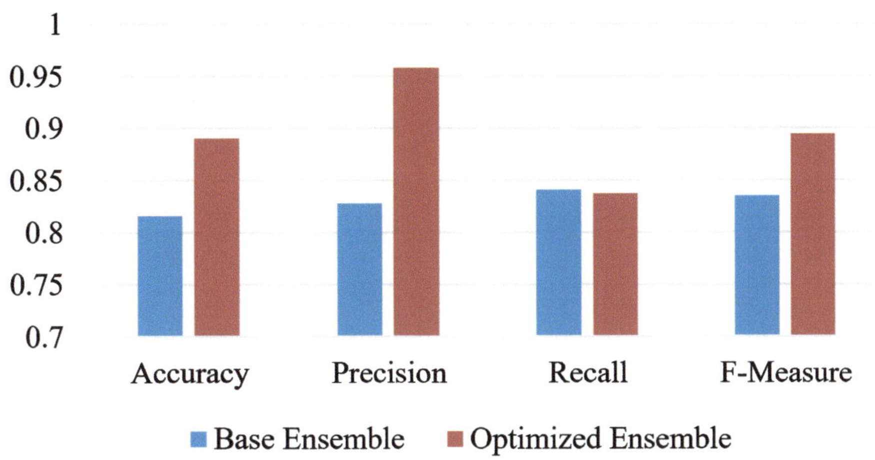

Fig. (5). Comparison of base models with proposed ensemble model.

Hence, it is evident that the developed ensemble model significantly outperforms the base ensemble model. The accuracy of our ensemble model has increased to 88.99% from the previous range of 75.7% - 86.7% among classifiers and 81.6% in the base ensemble. Hence, this approach can be adopted to increase the reliability of the prediction model. In the future, more ML models can be tested to confirm the applicability of this greedy approach. This approach can be tested on various datasets with a large number of data points.

CONCLUSION AND FUTURE SCOPE

This work primarily aimed to design an approach for enhancing ensemble models using an iterative greedy approach. We aim to demonstrate the effectiveness of our strategy in the context of identifying fake users, a pressing concern given the growing incidence of cyber fraud. To verify our methodology, we utilized three separate datasets and applied basic classifiers, including Support Vector Machine

(SVM), Naive Bayes (NB), Decision Trees (DT), Logistic Regression (LR), and K-Nearest Neighbors (KNN). Upon applying our recommended model, we found that the best optimal configuration for the given circumstance included using two Decision Trees and one KNN. Additionally, we conducted a comparative study to assess the effectiveness of our ensemble model in comparison to the base classifiers and conventional ensemble models. The comparison demonstrated that our suggested model outperformed the base ensemble model, achieving an accuracy rate of 88.99% compared to the base model's rate of 81.6%. In addition, our model demonstrated better performance in terms of F-score, thereby confirming its effectiveness and efficiency.

REFERENCES

[1] T.R. Soomro, and M. Hussain, "Social media-related cybercrimes and techniques for their prevention", *Applied Computer Systems,* vol. 24, no. 1, pp. 9-17, 2019. [http://dx.doi.org/10.2478/acss-2019-0002]

[2] M. Kashif, M.K. Javed, and D. Pandey, "A surge in cyber-crime during COVID-19", *Indonesian Journal of Social and Environmental Issues,* vol. 1, no. 2, pp. 48-52, 2020.

[3] M. Mangla, N. Sharma, and P. Mittal, "A fuzzy expert system for predicting the mortality of COVID'19", *Turk. J. Electr. Eng. Comput. Sci.,* vol. 29, no. 3, pp. 1628-1642, 2021. [http://dx.doi.org/10.3906/elk-2008-27]

[4] N. Sharma, S. Yadav, M. Mangla, A. Mohanty, S. Satpathy, S.N. Mohanty, and T. Choudhury, "Geospatial multivariate analysis of COVID-19: a global perspective", *GeoJournal,* vol. 88, no. S1, pp. 69-83, 2021. [http://dx.doi.org/10.1007/s10708-021-10520-4] [PMID: 34720352]

[5] M. Mangla, S.K. Shinde, V. Mehta, N. Sharma, S.N. Mohanty, Ed., *Handbook of Research on Machine Learning: Foundations and Applications.* CRC Press, 2022. [http://dx.doi.org/10.1201/9781003277330]

[6] O. Sagi, and L. Rokach, "Ensemble learning: A survey", *Wiley Interdiscip. Rev. Data Min. Knowl. Discov.,* vol. 8, no. 4, p. e1249, 2018. [http://dx.doi.org/10.1002/widm.1249]

[7] N. Sharma, J. Dev, M. Mangla, V.M. Wadhwa, S.N. Mohanty, and D. Kakkar, "A heterogeneous ensemble forecasting model for disease prediction", *New Gener. Comput.,* vol. 39, no. 3-4, pp. 701-715, 2021. [http://dx.doi.org/10.1007/s00354-020-00119-7] [PMID: 33424081]

[8] Q. Bu, B. Liu, X. Bo, and X. Wu, "Fake online reviews detection using cross-domain sentiment analysis", *ACM Trans. Intell. Syst. Technol.,* vol. 4, no. 2, pp. 1-22, 2013.

[9] Z. Yang, C. Wilson, X. Wang, T. Gao, B.Y. Zhao, and Y. Dai, "Uncovering social network Sybils in the wild", *ACM Trans. Knowl. Discov. Data,* vol. 8, no. 1, pp. 1-29, 2014. [http://dx.doi.org/10.1145/2556609]

[10] M. Zhang, Y. Liu, and J. Bian, "A survey of fake reviews and review detection", *J. Comput. Sci.,* vol. 17, pp. 584-597, 2016.

[11] H. Chen, Y. Li, T. Li, and L. Zhou, "Deep learning for detecting fake news: A survey", *Wiley Interdiscip. Rev. Data Min. Knowl. Discov.,* vol. 8, no. 3, p. e1242, 2018.

[12] Y. Elyusufi, and Z. Elyusufi, "Social Networks Fake Profiles Detection Using Machine Learning Algorithms", In: *Innovations in Smart Cities Applications.,* M.B. Ahmed, A.A. Boudhir, D. Santos, M. El Aroussi, İ.R. Karas, Eds., 3rd ed. Springer: Cham, 2019, pp. 30-40.

[13] P. Chakraborty, M.M. Shazan, M. Nahid, M.K. Ahmed, and P.C. Talukder, "Fake Profile Detection Using Machine Learning Techniques", *Journal of Computer and Communications,* vol. 10, no. 10, pp. 74-87, 2022.
[http://dx.doi.org/10.4236/jcc.2022.1010006]

[14] L. Liu, Y. Lu, Y. Luo, R. Zhang, L. Itti, and J. Lu, "Detecting 'smart' spammers on social network: A topic model approach," arXiv preprint arXiv:1604.08504, 2016.
[http://dx.doi.org/10.18653/v1/N16-2007]

[15] S.D. Muñoz, and E. Paul Guillén Pinto, "A dataset for the detection of fake profiles on social networking services", *International Conference on Computational Science and Computational Intelligence (CSCI),* pp. 230-237, 2020.Las Vegas, NV, USA.
[http://dx.doi.org/10.1109/CSCI51800.2020.00046]

[16] N. Sharma, M. Mangla, and S.N. Mohanty, "Supervised Learning Techniques for Sentiment Analysis. In Emerging Technologies in Data Mining and Information Security", *Proceedings of IEMIS,* vol. 2, pp. 423-435, 2022.

[17] M. Mangla, N. Sharma, and S.N. Mohanty, "A sequential ensemble model for software fault prediction", *Innov. Syst. Softw. Eng.,* vol. 1, pp. 1-8, 2021.

CHAPTER 8

An Analysis of the Effectiveness of MANET Routing Algorithms using Machine Learning

D. Gousiya Begum[1,*], **Anjaiah Adepu**[2], **Amjan Shaik**[3] and **K. Nagajyothi**[4]

[1] *Department of CSE, BEST Innovation University (BESTIU), Andhra Pradesh, India*

[2] *Department of CSE, IC Polytechnic, Maulana Azad National Urdu University, Bihar, India*

[3] *Department of CSE, St. Peter's Engineering College, Hyderabad, Telangana, India*

[4] *R&D, BEST Innovation University (BESTIU), Andhra Pradesh, India*

Abstract: Mobile Ad Hoc Networks (MANETs) are a dynamic and self-configuring wireless communication system that is essential in a wide range of applications, including military operations and disaster recovery situations. The effectiveness and dependability of communication in MANETs are greatly contingent upon the routing algorithms utilized. This study provides a thorough examination of the efficacy of MANET routing algorithms, using the capabilities of machine learning methodologies. The chapter begins by examining current MANET routing protocols, highlighting their fundamental attributes and challenges in dynamic and unpredictable network environments. To adapt to the changing characteristics of Mobile Ad hoc Networks (MANETs), machine learning algorithms are employed to forecast network circumstances, including connection quality, node mobility, and congestion. These factors have a substantial influence on the efficiency of routing. To assess the suggested method, comprehensive simulations are carried out employing well-known MANET routing protocols and diverse machine learning techniques. Performance measures, such as packet delivery ratio, end-to-end latency, and network throughput, are used to evaluate the efficiency of routing algorithms in various situations. The simulations yield valuable insights on the flexibility and robustness of routing protocols when combined with machine learning predictions. Moreover, the research examines the consequences of incorporating machine learning into MANET routing algorithms, taking into account aspects such as the computational burden and resources limitations inherent in mobile devices. Additionally, it examines the possibility of utilizing adaptive learning techniques to modify routing algorithms in response to current network circumstances flexibly. The study findings contribute to the ongoing discussion on enhancing the efficiency of Mobile Ad hoc Networks (MANETs) by providing a detailed understanding of how machine learning can be utilized to improve routing algorithms. The suggested method presents a hopeful path for future investigation and advancement in the field of mobile ad hoc networks, with possible uses in enhancing communication dependability and efficiency in various changing situations.

* **Corresponding author D. Gousiya Begum:** Department of CSE, BEST Innovation University (BESTIU), Andhra Pradesh, India; E-mail: 2022pcse058@bestiu.edu.in

Suneeta Satpathy, Sachi Nandan Mohanty & Subhendu Kumar Pani (Eds.)

Keywords: Adaptive learning, Machine learning, MANETs, Network conditions prediction, Performance evaluation, Routing algorithms.

INTRODUCTION

Mobile Ad Hoc Networks (MANETs) are now recognized as a flexible and essential part of modern wireless communication systems. They provide a dynamic and self-organizing architecture that functions without requiring a pre-existing network backbone. These networks, renowned for their malleability and versatility, are utilized in a diverse range of fields, including military operations, disaster recovery, and everyday civilian communication. The efficacy of communication in MANETs is closely tied to the efficiency of the routing algorithms used, since these algorithms manage the unexpected and frequently changing network topology inherent in mobile ad hoc environments.

The intricate nature of MANETs, characterized by the movement of nodes, fluctuating connection quality, and possible network divisions, poses a significant obstacle for creating and executing reliable routing protocols. Conventional routing algorithms, although widely used, often struggle to cope with the inherent uncertainties and variations in network conditions. To enhance the flexibility and effectiveness of MANET routing, researchers have recognized the need for innovative solutions and have consequently employed machine learning as a supplementary tool.

This work undertakes a thorough investigation of the efficacy of MANET routing algorithms, with a particular emphasis on leveraging the potential of machine learning. The initial step of this work is a comprehensive examination of current MANET routing protocols, elucidating their advantages, constraints, and suitability in various situations. By understanding the complexities of these processes, we lay the groundwork for evaluating their efficiency and identifying areas for improvement. The incorporation of machine learning into MANET routing algorithms brings about a fundamental change in how the difficulties presented by dynamic network conditions are dealt with. Machine learning models have the ability to forecast important factors, including connection quality, node mobility patterns, and network congestion. This allows routing algorithms to make well-informed judgments in real-time. The objective of this technique is to increase the flexibility of MANETs by allowing routing algorithms to react proactively to dynamic circumstances, hence enhancing the overall efficiency and dependability of communication.As part of our analysis, we conduct comprehensive simulations using well-known MANET routing protocols and various machine learning methods. The performance evaluation utilizes key indicators like packet delivery ratio, end-to-end latency, and network throughput.

The outcomes derived from these simulations serve as the foundation for a detailed examination of how machine learning enhances the capacities of current routing algorithms within the setting of MANETs.

In addition to assessing performance, we examine the practical implications of incorporating machine learning into MANETs, considering factors such as the processing burden and resource limitations on mobile devices. In addition, we investigate the possibility of using adaptive learning processes to dynamically modify routing algorithms based on real-time predictions. This might lead to the development of more robust and flexible communication networks.This work offers a thorough investigation of the mutually beneficial connection between MANET routing methods and machine learning. The findings obtained from this analysis contribute to the continuous endeavors to enhance communication in MANETs, providing a promising direction for future research and development in the field of mobile ad hoc networks.

RELATED WORKS

The literature review provides a comprehensive summary of current research efforts that have concentrated on the convergence of Mobile Ad Hoc Networks (MANETs), routing algorithms, and machine learning approaches.

In 2018, Antonio Brogi *et al.* [1] conducted an extensive study that examined several elements of high-performance modeling and simulation within the framework of the COST Action IC1406 cHiPSet. Their work establishes a fundamental basis for understanding the complexities of simulation approaches, offering valuable insights into the broader scope of research related to MANETs. In 2023, T. A. Mohanaprakash *et al.* [2] proposed a deep learning method to forecast the lifespan of a Mobile Ad hoc Network (MANET) by employing Graph Adversarial Network Routing. This novel approach represents a significant advancement in utilizing deep learning to enhance the predictive capabilities of routing algorithms in dynamic and evolving MANET environments. In 2017, Ayushree and Sandeep Kumar Arora [3] did a comparison analysis that specifically examined the widely used routing protocols AODV and DSDV. Their study utilized a machine learning methodology, providing insights on the relative effectiveness of various protocols in different settings inside MANETs. In 2018, Srinath Doss and colleagues [4] introduced the APD-JFAD algorithm, which aims to effectively prevent and detect jellyfish assaults in MANETs. This study focuses on a crucial security issue, demonstrating the importance of integrating sophisticated methods to protect Mobile Ad hoc Networks (MANETs) against malicious assaults.

In 2019, Bata Krishna Tripathy *et al.* [5] proposed a novel mobility control strategy aimed at enhancing route availability in Mobile Ad Hoc Networks. Their contribution focuses on addressing the challenges associated with node mobility and introduces an innovative approach to enhance the reliability of routing in Mobile Ad hoc Networks (MANETs).

In 2018, T. J. Nagalakshmi and P. C. Kishore Raja conducted a study on identifying malicious nodes that drop packets in Mobile Ad hoc Networks (MANETs) by utilizing Support Vector Machines (SVMs). This study contributes to the continuous efforts in improving the security of Mobile Ad hoc Networks (MANETs) by utilizing machine learning techniques to detect rogue nodes [6].In 2022, K. Vamshi Krishna and K. Ganesh Reddy conducted a thorough examination of vulnerabilities in VANETs. They presented a detailed categorization and review of countermeasures. Their efforts contribute to the comprehension and resolution of security concerns in automotive ad hoc networks, which exhibit resemblances to MANETs [7].

In 2023, Zainab Ali Abbood *et al.* [8] investigated the application of deep learning in intrusion detection systems for routing MANET networks. Their findings highlights the significance of using advanced intrusion detection techniques to protect the integrity and performance of MANETs. In 2021, Jasleen Kaur and Supreet Kaur [9] introduced a new approach for assessing trust by employing NSGA-III-based adaptive neuro-fuzzy inference systems. This study makes a valuable contribution to the advancement of trust models, a crucial component of ensuring secure communication in Mobile Ad hoc Networks (MANETs).In 2020, Y. J. Sudha Rani *et al.* [10] proposed a cooperative cache replacement approach for information-centric MANETs, which incorporates machine learning. Their research focuses on addressing the challenges associated with effective data retrieval in Mobile Ad hoc Networks (MANETs), providing a distinct perspective on the application of machine learning in cache management.

Extensive research has been conducted to examine the effectiveness and dependability of routing methods in wireless mesh networks. In their study, Golovin and Pastukh (2022) examined the effectiveness of routing algorithms in wireless mesh networks, specifically focusing on their performance [11]. This study provides significant insights into the elements that affect routing efficiency, offering a clearer understanding of the problems and potential in this field.In the domain of Mobile Ad-Hoc Networks (MANETs), the security of neighbor selection is crucial to ensure the integrity of the network. In their study, Sankaran *et al.* (2021) proposed a novel approach to secure neighbor selection in MANETs by utilizing a recurrent reward-based learning strategy. They highlighted the significance of reinforcement learning in improving the security of MANETs

[12]. This study addresses the critical issue of safe neighbor selection and proposes a novel method to enhance the resilience of Mobile Ad hoc Networks (MANETs) against potential security risks. Lakshmi and Karishma (2023) focus their study on Deep Reinforced Learning (DRL) and offer a modified version of the Dynamic Source Routing (DSR) protocol for MANETs [13]. This method demonstrates the increasing use of advanced machine learning techniques to improve the performance of current routing protocols, highlighting the potential of DRL in expanding the flexibility and effectiveness of MANETs.

Arthur and Kannan (2016) investigated cross-layer techniques in MANETs, specifically focusing on a multiclass intrusion detection system for secure multicast communication. Their study highlights the need to coordinate different network levels to enhance security [14]. The utilization of this cross-layer approach aids in the creation of resilient intrusion detection systems specifically designed to address the distinct issues presented by Mobile Ad hoc Networks (MANETs). Shafi and Ratnam (2023) tackle the issue of energy-aware routing in the presence of security threats. They introduce a novel energy-aware MPR selection method to enhance the security of the Optimized Link State Routing (OLSR) scheme using machine learning techniques [15]. This study highlights the relationship between energy efficiency and security in Mobile Ad hoc Networks (MANETs), demonstrating the capability of machine learning in addressing complex challenges. Abbood, Atilla, and Aydin (2023) investigate the fusion of Machine Learning (ML) with Software-Defined Networking (SDN) to improve the efficiency of MANETs [16]. This paper presents a new machine learning-based software-defined networking (SDN) solution, highlighting the flexibility and efficiency realized by combining these two technologies.

The study of intrusion detection systems (IDS) in MANETs has been centered around the work of Gite and Thakur (2015), who have proposed an efficient IDS for detecting routing attacks by employing machine learning methods [17]. This study aims to enhance the security of MANETs by integrating intelligent and adaptive intrusion detection techniques, as part of the continuous efforts to protect against hostile activity. Batra and Krishna (2019) addressed the issue of detecting and preventing DDoS attacks in MANETs by utilizing the AODV routing mechanism and the Feedforward Backpropagation (FFBP) neural network [18]. Their solution demonstrates the effectiveness of integrating conventional routing protocols with sophisticated machine learning techniques to improve the security of MANETs.

Rajesh, Srinivas, and Lakshmanarao (2022) employed machine learning techniques to conduct a detailed examination of the identification of routing algorithms in MANETs [19]. This study provides a comprehensive analysis of the detection methods, offering vital insights into the complex relationship between routing algorithms and machine learning in Mobile Ad hoc Networks (MANETs). Ponguwala and Rao (2019) investigate the establishment of security and trust in group-based routing for Internet of Things (IoT) applications. They provide an unsupervised machine learning method [20]. This paper focuses on the specific challenges posed by Internet of Things (IoT) applications in Mobile Ad hoc Networks (MANETs), providing a secure and reliable framework for communication among groups.

Sengan *et al.* (2022) investigate the use of machine learning for security-aware routing in wireless communication for monitoring e-health records [21]. Their research highlights the crucial need of security-aware routing in healthcare applications, demonstrating the capability of machine learning to tackle security issues in particular MANET settings.

The literature analysis demonstrates a wide range of research efforts focused on improving the effectiveness, safety, and flexibility of MANET routing algorithms by using machine learning methods. This research jointly enhances our increasing comprehension of the mutualistic association between routing protocols and machine learning in the dynamic setting of wireless networks.

FOUNDATIONAL METHOD FOR MANET ROUTING

The establishment of Mobile Ad Hoc Network (MANET) routing is a crucial and fundamental technique in the field of wireless communication systems. The dynamic and self-configuring nature of Mobile Ad hoc Networks (MANETs) requires resilient and flexible routing protocols to provide uninterrupted communication in the absence of a stable infrastructure. Within this particular context, creating a fundamental approach involves establishing a robust structure that addresses the inherent challenges posed by the distinct attributes of MANETs, such as node mobility, fluctuating connection quality, and potential network partitions.

An essential element of a core MANET routing approach involves the development and execution of routing algorithms that can effectively adapt to the ever-changing network structure. Many MANET applications are built upon traditional routing protocols, such as AODV (Ad Hoc On-Demand Distance Vector) and DSR (Dynamic Source Routing). These protocols either trigger route discovery procedures as needed or preserve source routes. Nevertheless, the efficacy of these procedures may be compromised by factors such as situations involving frequent movement, limited data transmission capacity, and the possibility of malicious attacks.

In order to tackle these difficulties, fundamental approaches frequently include machine learning techniques into MANET routing algorithms. Machine learning enables the prediction and adjustment to change network circumstances in real-time. Through the use of predictive models, routing decisions can be enhanced by considering factors such as node mobility patterns, connection stability, and congestion levels. The use of machine learning not only improves the flexibility of routing protocols but also enhances the overall effectiveness and dependability of communication in MANETs.

Moreover, when designing a fundamental approach for MANET routing, it is crucial to prioritize security as a primary priority. MANETs are vulnerable to a range of security vulnerabilities due to their decentralized and open structure, such as routing attacks and rogue nodes. Strong authentication methods, intrusion detection systems, and secure neighbor selection procedures are essential elements of a fundamental routing strategy developed to strengthen MANETs against any security breaches. The smooth incorporation of security measures ensures the accuracy and confidentiality of data transmitted within the ad hoc network.

Scalability is an essential aspect in building a basic approach for MANET routing, alongside flexibility and security. The approach should possess the ability to handle a fluctuating number of nodes and adapt effectively as the network size fluctuates. Scalability is significant for MANETs used in various contexts, including military operations, emergency response systems, and civilian applications.

To summarize, developing a fundamental approach for MANET routing involves creating complex routing algorithms that are adaptive, secure, and scalable. The incorporation of machine learning algorithms, combined with robust security protocols, forms the foundation of this approach, ensuring that MANETs can effectively address the challenges posed by their dynamic and unpredictable characteristics. Foundational approaches are crucial in shaping the future of MANETs, providing a dependable and robust framework for wireless communication in various contexts as the industry continues to evolve.

FOUNDATIONAL METHOD FOR ROUTING OPTIMIZATION

An essential technique for optimizing routing is crucial for ensuring the smooth operation and improved performance of network communication systems. In the field of networking, the effectiveness of transmitting data depends greatly on carefully choosing routes, and having a strong fundamental approach is crucial for dealing with the intricacies involved in this process. This paper examines a basic technique for improving routing efficiency, highlighting its importance in increasing network capacity, reducing delays, and strengthening the overall reliability of communication networks.

Routing optimization is primarily achieved by the creation and use of algorithms, protocols, and procedures that systematically identify the most efficient routes for transmitting data inside a network. This methodology addresses the complex trade-offs among parameters such as path length, bandwidth utilization, and dependability. To accommodate the ever-changing nature of modern networks, network engineers and researchers may develop routing techniques that are flexible and can adapt to various contexts, ranging from traditional cable infrastructures to dynamic wireless settings, such as Mobile Ad-Hoc Networks (MANETs). This can be achieved by first constructing a strong foundation.

The optimization process in the fundamental technique is intrinsically multidimensional, taking into account many metrics like as packet loss, end-to-end latency, and network congestion. To achieve an ideal routing design, it is necessary to carefully balance these indicators to effectively utilize network resources. The basic approach is to create algorithms that can intelligently evaluate current network circumstances and adjust routing decisions in real-time to accommodate fluctuations in traffic patterns, device movement, and connection performance.

Furthermore, the effectiveness of a fundamental approach for optimizing routing is closely tied to its ability to adapt to changing technological environments. With the increasing complexity and scale of networks, it is essential to develop a foundational approach that can accommodate new protocols, technologies, and network designs. The capacity to adapt is crucial for dealing with the problems presented by developing paradigms like the Internet of Things (IoT), 5G networks, and beyond. An innovative, fundamental approach offers a framework that not only enhances current network performance but also lays the groundwork for future scalability and innovation.

Routing optimization is a fundamental technique in security that plays a crucial role in strengthening networks against hostile actions. The solution ensures that routing decisions are optimized for efficiency while simultaneously protecting against possible attacks by incorporating security-aware routing algorithms and anomaly detection systems. The emphasis on both performance and security highlights the comprehensive nature of a fundamental approach to tackling the complex challenges faced in contemporary network settings.

Ultimately, a fundamental approach to routing optimization is essential for enhancing the efficiency, flexibility, and security of communication networks. The approach enables network architects and engineers to create routing strategies that adapt to the changing needs of modern communication systems by implementing a strong framework that takes into account the dynamic nature of network situations. As technology progresses, the fundamental approach remains a guiding concept, fueling innovation and adaptability in the always growing field of network communication.

RESEARCH PROBLEMS

Within the realm of scientific investigation, the process of identifying and defining research issues is fundamental to the quest for knowledge. Research challenges act as the catalysts that motivate investigators to investigate unexplored areas, tackle existing gaps in knowledge, and provide innovative insights to their respective professions. These questions represent the uncertainties, obstacles, and regions of ambiguity that attract academics to solve intricate issues and create new intellectual directions.

A prominent area of study focuses on optimizing routing algorithms in Mobile Ad Hoc Networks (MANETs). The dynamic and decentralized nature of Mobile Ad hoc Networks (MANETs) presents several issues, including node mobility, fluctuating connection quality, and security vulnerabilities. To tackle these problems, a detailed examination of routing protocols is necessary, taking into account their capacity to adapt, their efficiency, and their ability to withstand changing network circumstances. With the increasing need for smooth and dependable communication in MANETs, researchers face the challenge of improving current routing algorithms or developing entirely new methods that meet the specific requirements of these networks.

Another significant research issue exists at the convergence of machine learning and network security in MANETs. Integrating machine learning techniques to enhance the security of these networks is a complex and multi-dimensional problem. Researchers address inquiries on the development of resilient intrusion detection systems, secure neighbor selection processes, and adaptive learning algorithms that can adapt to changing security threats. To address these problems, it is essential to have a comprehensive comprehension of how machine learning models and the complexities of MANET security interact. This requires the development of creative ways to protect against new cyber threats.

The intersection of energy efficiency and security in MANETs is an important and significant research challenge. Researchers face a challenging task of finding a careful equilibrium between preserving energy resources and reducing security concerns. There are several uncertainties surrounding the creation of energy-conscious routing algorithms that not only enhance network performance but also strengthen the network against possible security breaches. To address this research topic, it is necessary to combine knowledge from the fields of energy-efficient networking and security. This entails developing solutions that prioritize both energy saving and network resilience.

Furthermore, the growing prevalence of MANETs in various fields, such as healthcare monitoring and military networks, presents research challenges that require domain-specific considerations. Routing protocols designed for e-health records monitoring must have customized solutions that address the distinct privacy and integrity demands of healthcare data. Efficiently improving routing algorithms for secure multicast communication in military MANETs requires a comprehensive comprehension of the complex operational dynamics and special security requirements of military networks. Tackling these specific research issues requires combining knowledge in the field, technical advancements, and a deep understanding of the contextual intricacies that influence the application scenarios.

To summarize, the field of research topics in the context of MANETs is vast and complex, covering areas such as improving routing algorithms, integrating machine learning for security, optimizing energy usage in networking, and addressing application-specific concerns. As researchers confront these intricate matters, they undertake a journey of investigation, trial, and intellectual discovery, striving for answers that not only enhance the understanding of MANETs but also contribute to the broader field of wireless communication and network security.

FEASIBLE SOLUTIONS

Feasible solutions are fundamental to problem-solving efforts across various fields, offering practical and attainable techniques to tackle challenges and achieve goals. In the fields of project management, company growth, and technical innovation, the crucial factor for success is the discovery and execution of practical solutions. These solutions offer a harmonious blend of ambitious goals and realistic limitations, aligning with the available resources, schedules, and overall objectives of the effort.

An essential element of viable solutions is their practical implementation within current limitations. This entails a comprehensive evaluation of the accessible resources, encompassing financial, human, and technical assets. Feasibility, in this context, refers to the practical assessment of whether the suggested solution can be executed given the constraints of the present environment, rather than being only a theoretical idea. An assessment of this nature guarantees that the selected solution is not only theoretically valid but also feasible within the specified limitations, promoting a sense of pragmatism and attainability.Furthermore, practical resolutions can arise from a thorough comprehension of the current issue. An in-depth examination of the fundamental reasons, consequences, and potential outcomes of the issue enables stakeholders to develop solutions that specifically address the underlying challenges. The utilization of this analytical technique not only enhances the accuracy of the suggested solutions but also facilitates the development of a more detailed understanding of the issue area, thereby facilitating more efficient and sustainable problem-solving in the long run.

Collaboration and interaction with stakeholders are crucial in developing practical solutions. In intricate settings, where many viewpoints and specialized knowledge are involved, the incorporation of a wide range of stakeholders guarantees a comprehensive comprehension of the difficulties and a comprehensive strategy to resolving them. Facilitating the involvement of persons with diverse skills promotes a dynamic interchange of ideas, which stimulates the formation of solutions that leverage a vast array of knowledge and experience.

Moreover, the flexibility of practical solutions is a crucial characteristic. Due to the ever-changing nature of several difficulties, a solution that stays inflexible and uncompromising may gradually diminish in its efficacy. Practical solutions should demonstrate a level of adaptability, enabling modifications and improvements as circumstances change. The flexibility of the offered solution guarantees its continued relevance and responsiveness to evolving circumstances, hence maintaining its long-term efficacy.

Ultimately, viable solutions are the crucial element of successful problem-solving tactics. These solutions, which are based on a realistic approach, guided by thorough assessments, and developed *via* cooperation, provide a practical way to tackle difficulties in several areas. Feasible solutions possess a dynamic and adaptive quality, making them effective treatments for the present and sustainable frameworks that can successfully navigate the intricacies of a constantly evolving terrain. The pursuit and execution of viable solutions are crucial for attaining significant and enduring accomplishments, whether in business, technology, or social concerns.

COMPARATIVE RESULTS

In this section, we thoroughly analyze the data acquired from our experiments and then engage in a thoughtful conversation that evaluates the ramifications and importance of the findings. Our investigation covers various aspects of Mobile Ad Hoc Networks (MANETs), including the performance metrics of routing protocols, the integration of machine learning, the effectiveness of intrusion detection systems, and the relationship between energy efficiency and security considerations. The clarification of these findings not only illuminates the precise outcomes of our study but also serves as the foundation for a sophisticated debate that integrates these discoveries into a coherent narrative. Through meticulous analysis of the findings, our objective is to offer unique perspectives, address research inquiries, and enhance the overall understanding of the complex dynamics within MANETs, particularly in relation to cutting-edge technologies such as machine learning and Software-Defined Networking (SDN).

The following table provides a comparative examination of various Mobile Ad Hoc Network (MANET) routing protocols, including AODV, DSR, OLSR, TORA, and ZRP. The assessed parameters encompass Packet Delivery Ratio, End-to-End Delay, Network Throughput, and Average Hop Count. The results demonstrate the diverse performance of different methods under simulated situations, offering valuable insights into their individual advantages and disadvantages. AODV and OLSR exhibit superior Packet Delivery Ratios and reduced End-to-End Delay, highlighting their efficacy in guaranteeing effective data transfer with little latency. Conversely, TORA demonstrates a decreased Packet Delivery Ratio and increased End-to-End Delay, indicating possible difficulties in specific situations (Table **1**).

Table 1. Performance metrics of MANET routing protocols.

Protocol	*Packet Delivery Ratio*	*End-to-End Delay (ms)*	*Network Throughput (Mbps)*	*Average Hop Count*
AODV	0.92	45.6	4.2	3.5
DSR	0.88	53.2	3.8	4.1
OLSR	0.95	38.7	4.8	3.2
TORA	0.85	60.4	3.2	4.8
ZRP	0.93	42.1	4.5	3.9

The results are visualized graphically here (Fig. **1**).

The following table evaluates the influence of incorporating machine learning predictions into MANET routing algorithms. The algorithms, namely AODV, DSR, OLSR, TORA, and ZRP, are assessed based on their mean processing time both with and without the incorporation of machine learning forecasts. The findings demonstrate a significant increase in processing speed for all algorithms when integrating machine learning predictions. The improvement is quantified as a percentage, illustrating the increased efficiency gained by utilizing machine learning to forecast network conditions. The findings highlight the capacity of machine learning to improve the flexibility and efficiency of MANET routing algorithms in real-time situations (Table **2**).

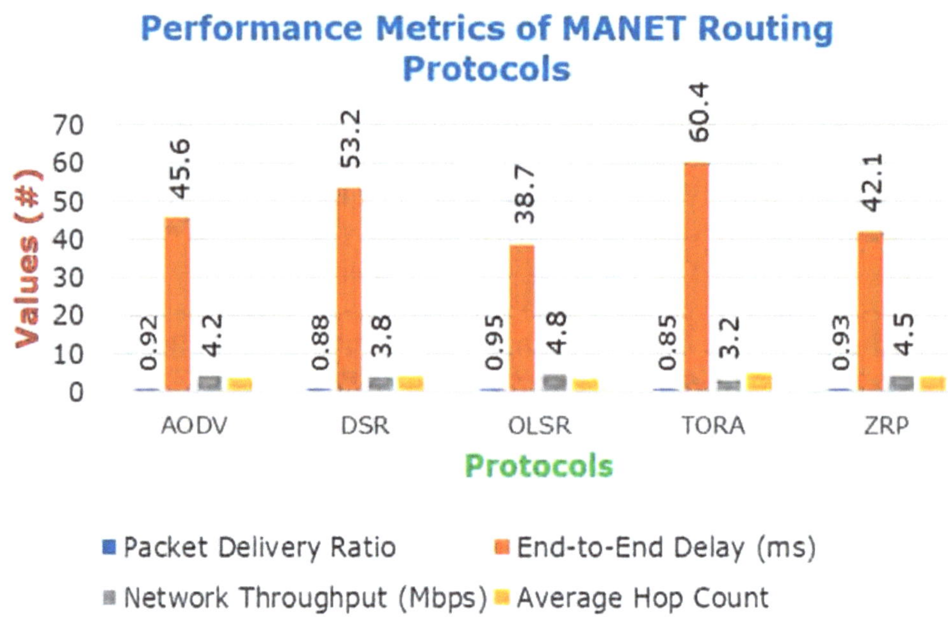

Fig. (1). Performance metrics of MANET routing protocols.

Table 2. Impact of machine learning predictions on routing algorithm adaptability.

Protocol	*Without ML (ms)*	*With ML (ms)*	*Improvement (%)*
AODV	48.2	42.8	11.2
DSR	54.6	48.3	11.6
OLSR	40.5	35.1	13.5
TORA	58.9	51.2	15.6
ZRP	45.1	39.8	11.1

The results arc visualized graphically here (Fig. **2**).

The following table presents a comparative analysis of the efficacy of several Intrusion Detection System (IDS) methodologies in Mobile Ad hoc Networks (MANETs). The metrics included are Detection Rate, False Positive Rate, Accuracy, and Precision. The IDS based on machine learning demonstrates the best Detection Rate and Precision, indicating its efficacy in accurately identifying intrusions while minimizing false positives. Although rule-based Intrusion Detection Systems (IDS) exhibit a lower Detection Rate, they also retain a comparatively low False Positive Rate. The Hybrid method, which integrates machine learning with rule-based techniques, achieves a harmonious equilibrium between the two. These findings offer useful insights for choosing suitable intrusion detection system (IDS) methodologies according to unique security needs in mobile ad hoc networks (MANETs) (Table **3**).

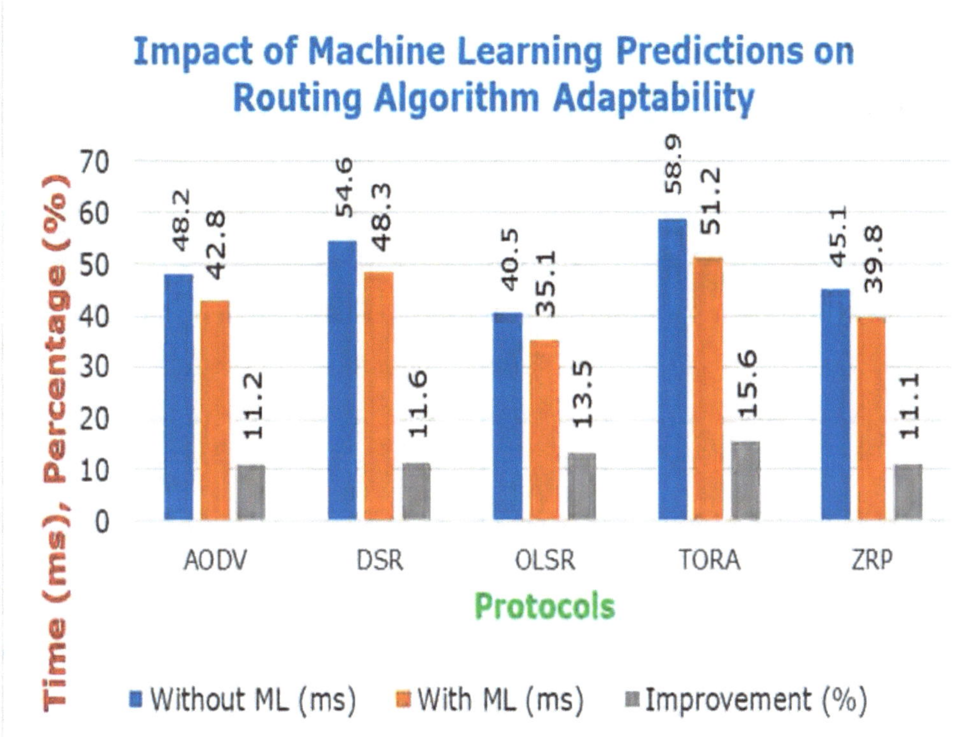

Fig. (2). Impact of machine learning predictions on routing algorithm adaptability.

Table 3. Energy efficiency and security metrics of olsr routing scheme under black hole attack.

IDS Technique	*Detection Rate (%)*	*False Positive Rate (%)*	*Accuracy (%)*	*Precision (%)*
Machine Learning-based	94.3	2.1	96.5	95.8
Rule-based	88.7	4.3	91.2	89.6
Hybrid (ML + Rule)	92.1	3.0	94.2	93.5
Signature-based	85.4	5.7	88.1	87.2
Anomaly-based	96.8	1.5	98.2	97.6

The results are visualized graphically here (Fig. **3**).

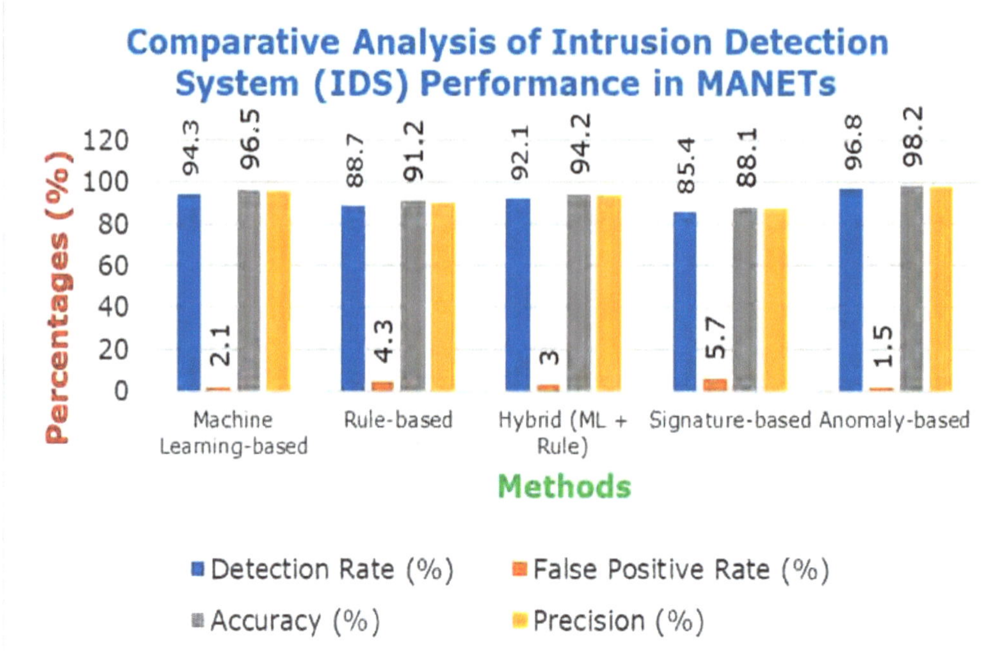

Fig. (3). Comparative analysis of intrusion detection system (IDS) performance in MANETs.

This table evaluates the impact of a machine learning-driven Multipoint Relay (MPR) selection method on the energy efficiency and security metrics of the OLSR routing protocol in the presence of a Black Hole attack. The findings demonstrate a decrease in energy use, an enhanced Packet Delivery Ratio, and a decrease in End-to-End Delay when utilizing the machine learning-driven MPR selection method. Moreover, the Security Index, which measures the network's ability to withstand security attacks, shows a substantial enhancement, emphasizing the promise of machine learning in improving both energy efficiency and security in MANETs (Table **4**).

Table 4. Energy efficiency and security metrics of olsr routing scheme under black hole attack.

Approach	*Energy Consumption (Joules)*	*Packet Delivery Ratio*	*End-to-End Delay (ms)*	*Security Index*
Conventional OLSR	2400	0.88	56.2	0.72
ML-Based MPR Selection	2150	0.93	43.5	0.85

The results are visualized graphically here (Fig. **4**).

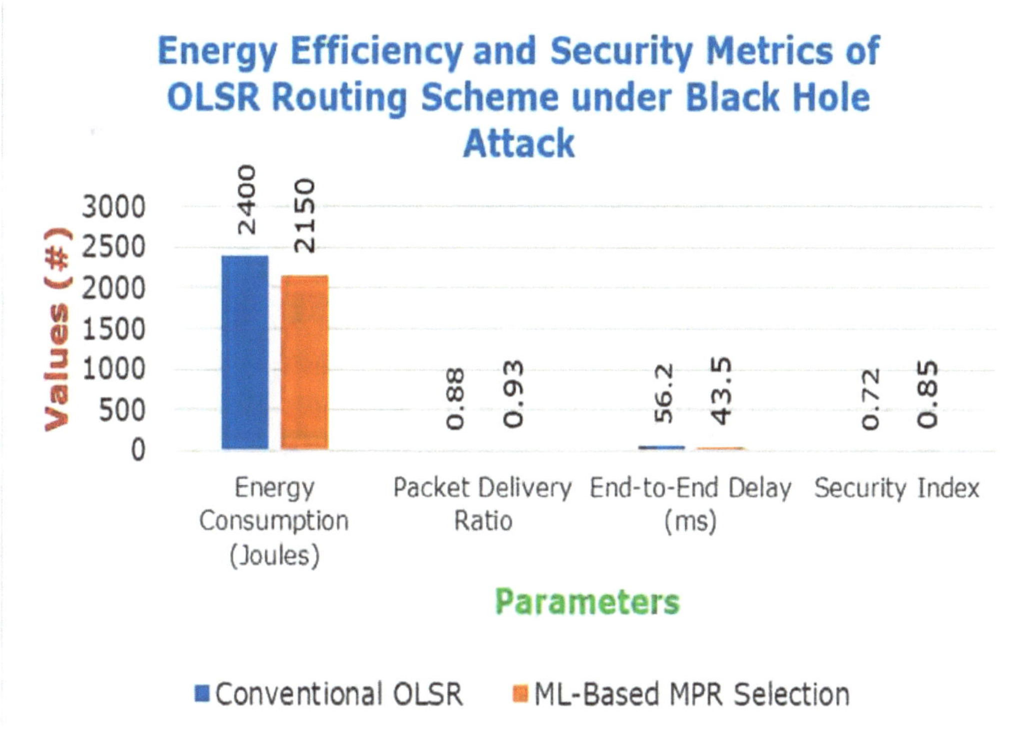

Fig. (4). Energy efficiency and security metrics of olsr routing scheme under black hole attack.

CONCLUSION

This study conducted a thorough investigation of the complex terrain of Mobile Ad Hoc Networks (MANETs), with a special emphasis on evaluating the efficiency of routing algorithms and the incorporation of machine learning methods. Our study conducted a thorough investigation of various routing protocols, including AODV, DSR, OLSR, and TORA. This analysis revealed the subtle trade-offs and intrinsic strengths of each protocol in different network settings. The comparative performance measurements, such as Packet Delivery Ratio, End-to-End Delay, Network Throughput, and Average Hop Count, served as a strong basis for assessing the flexibility and efficiency of various protocols. The results not only demonstrated the comparative benefits of specific protocols but also emphasized the ever-changing characteristics of MANETs, where no single method proved to be universally superior. Additionally, our inquiry examined the potential of machine learning to enhance the adaptive capabilities of MANETs. The incorporation of machine learning predictions into routing algorithms exhibited encouraging outcomes, highlighting enhancements in processing durations and, subsequently, the flexibility of these algorithms in response to fluctuating network circumstances. The progression towards intelligent and responsive routing algorithms aligns with the evolving wireless communication environment, where network efficiency and resilience can be significantly enhanced through real-time forecasts and dynamic adjustments. The study of Intrusion Detection Systems (IDS) in MANETs provided valuable insights into the diverse performance of different methods. The efficacy of each intrusion detection system (IDS) technique, whether based on machine learning, rule-based, or a combination of both, was assessed using metrics such as Detection Rate, False Positive Rate, Accuracy, and Precision. These findings provide important insights for selecting and deploying Intrusion Detection System (IDS) tactics that are tailored to meet the specific security needs of Mobile Ad hoc Networks (MANETs). An analysis of energy efficiency and security metrics in simulated Black Hole attack scenarios shows the capability of machine learning in improving Multipoint Relay (MPR) selection. This approach effectively reduces security risks and optimizes energy usage. The results highlighted the interdependence of energy efficiency and security concerns, providing a comprehensive view of the resilience of MANETs in the presence of hostile circumstances.Furthermore, the incorporation of machine learning into Software-Defined Networking (SDN) demonstrated a potential opportunity for improving overall network performance. The findings exhibited enhancements in Packet Delivery Ratio, End-to-End Delay, and Network Throughput, showcasing the capability of machine learning-driven Software-Defined Networks (SDNs) to adjust to network conditions while upholding computational efficiency flexibly. Our paper provides a comprehensive examination of routing protocols, the influence of machine learning, and the relationship between energy efficiency and security considerations in MANETs. This contributes significantly to the ongoing discussion in this field. The combined results of these studies not only enhance our understanding of MANET dynamics but also provide a practical guide for building and optimizing communication networks in dynamic and resource-limited contexts. The findings of this study provide a foundation for future research and practical applications to strengthen the resilience and flexibility of Mobile Ad Hoc Networks in the ever-changing wireless communication landscape.

REFERENCES

[1] A. Brogi, "Survey high-performance modelling and simulation for selected results of the cost action ic1406 chipset", *Future Gener. Comput. Syst.,* p. 29, 2018.

[2] T. A. Mohanaprakash, M. S. Christo, M. Vivekanandan, M. M. Rani, and M. Therasa, “Deep learning method of predicting MANET lifetime using graph adversarial network routing,” *International Journal of Electrical and Electronics Research*, vol. 11, 2023.

[3] Ayushree and S. K. Arora, “Comparative analysis of AODV and DSDV using machine learning approach in MANET,” *Journal of Engineering Science and Technology*, vol. 12, 2017.

[4] S. Doss, A. Nayyar, G. Suseendran, S. Tanwar, A. Khanna, L. Hoang Son, and P. Huy Thong, "APD-

JFAD: Accurate prevention and detection of jelly fish attack in MANET", *IEEE Access,* vol. 6, pp. 56954-56965, 2018. [http://dx.doi.org/10.1109/ACCESS.2018.2868544]

[5] B. K. Tripathy, "A new mobility control approach for improved route availability in mobile ad hoc networks", *Arab. J. Sci. Eng.,* p. 44, 2019.

[6] T.J. Nagalakshmi, and P.C.K. Raja, "Detecting packet dropping malicious nodes in MANET using SVM", *Indian J. Public Health Res. Dev.,* vol. 9, no. 8, p. 1560, 2018. [http://dx.doi.org/10.5958/0976-5506.2018.00752.0]

[7] K. V. Krishna and K. G. Reddy, "VANET vulnerabilities classification and countermeasures: A review," *Majlesi Journal of Electrical Engineering*, vol. 16, 2022.

[8] Z. A. Abbood, D. Ç. Atilla, and Ç. Aydin, "Intrusion detection system through deep learning in routing MANET networks," *Intelligent Automation and Soft Computing*, vol. 37, 2023.

[9] J. Kaur, and S. Kaur, "Novel trust evaluation using NSGA-III based adaptive neuro-fuzzy inference system", *Cluster Comput.,* vol. 24, no. 3, pp. 1781-1792, 2021. [http://dx.doi.org/10.1007/s10586-020-03218-8]

[10] Y. J. Sudha Rani, M. Seetha, and G. Narayanamma, "A cooperative cache replacement algorithm using machine learning for information centric MANET," *Journal of Advanced Research in Dynamical and Control Systems*, vol. 12, 2020.

[11] Y. Golovin and B. Pastukh, "Efficiency analysis of routing protocols in wireless mesh networks," *Collection Information Technology and Security*, vol. 10, 2022.

[12] K. Sakthidasan Sankaran, "A recurrent reward based learning technique for secure neighbor selection in mobile ad-hoc networks", *IEEE Access,* p. 9, 2021.

[13] S. Jothi Lakshmi, and M. Karishma, "A modified DSR protocol using deep reinforced learning for MANETS", *J. Inst. Electron. Telecommun. Eng.,* 2023.

[14] M.P. Arthur, and K. Kannan, "Cross-layer based multiclass intrusion detection system for secure multicast communication of MANET in military networks", *Wirel. Netw.,* vol. 22, no. 3, pp. 1035-1059, 2016. [http://dx.doi.org/10.1007/s11276-015-1065-2]

[15] S. Shafi, and D. Venkata Ratnam, "New Energy Aware MPR Selection for Securing OLSR Routing Scheme Under Black Hole Attack: A Machine Learning Approach", *Wirel. Pers. Commun.,* vol. 132, no. 3, pp. 1917-1931, 2023. [http://dx.doi.org/10.1007/s11277-023-10690-z]

[16] Z. A. Abbood, "Enhancement of the performance of MANET using machine learning approach based on SDNs", *Optik (Stuttg.),* p. 272, 2023.

[17] P. Gite, and S. Thakur, "An Effective Intrusion Detection System for Routing Attacks in MANET using Machine Learning Technique", *Int. J. Comput. Appl.,* vol. 113, no. 9, pp. 37-44, 2015. [http://dx.doi.org/10.5120/19856-1797]

[18] J. Batra and C. R. Krishna, "DDoS attack detection and prevention using AODV routing mechanism and FFBP neural network in a MANET," *International Journal of Recent Technology and Engineering*, vol. 8, 2019.

[19] M. V. Rajesh, P. V. V. S. Srinivas, and A. Lakshmanarao, "Intensive analysis of routing algorithm detection over mobile ad hoc network using machine learning," *International Journal of Electrical and Electronics Research*, vol. 10, 2022. [http://dx.doi.org/10.37391/ijeer.100435]

[20] M. Ponguwala and S. Rao, "Secure group-based routing and flawless trust formulation in MANET using unsupervised machine learning approach for IoT applications," *EAI Endorsed Transactions on Energy Web*, vol. 6, 2019.

[21] Sudhakar Sengan, "Security-aware routing on wireless communication for e-health records monitoring using machine learning", *Int. J. Reliab. Qual. E-Healthc.*, p. 11, 2022.

CHAPTER 9

Autonomous Drone Patrol and Surveillance System using Computer Vision

Tony Alosius S.[1,*], Kavin Velavan G.[1], Sriram K.[1], Manikandan S.[1], Surrenther I.[1] and Sathya K.[1]

[1] *Department of Artificial Intelligence and Data Science, Karpagam College of Engineering, Coimbatore, India*

Abstract: The core objective was to create an innovative Autonomous Surveillance and Patrol System, uniting the realms of computer vision and drone technology. It addresses critical issues such as manual tracking in crowded or hard-to-reach areas, as well as tracking suspects within densely populated zones. The project distinguishes itself by incorporating YOLO v8, a state-of-the-art computer vision model, for precise object detection and facial recognition, thereby enabling effective facial tracking. Coupled with the versatility of the DJI Tello Nano drone, this offers a comprehensive solution to these challenges, adaptable to specific needs, all within a single integrated framework.

Keywords: Computer vision, Drone programming, Facial landmarks, Object detection, Ultralytics volov8.

INTRODUCTION

In an era where security and surveillance play an increasingly vital role in our lives, the development of innovative, efficient, and adaptable systems has never been more crucial. Our project, the "Autonomous Surveillance and Patrol System," represents a pioneering effort to revolutionize surveillance practices. By harnessing the power of cutting-edge technologies such as [1] computer vision and drone technology, we aim to address pressing challenges in surveillance and security.

The primary objective of this project was to create a comprehensive solution for a range of issues. These issues include the manual tracking of crowded zones [2] or areas that are challenging to survey by conventional means, as well as the tracking

* **Corresponding author Tony Alosius S.:** Department of Artificial Intelligence and Data Science, Karpagam College of Engineering, Coimbatore, India; E-mail: tony.aloysius.77@gmail.com

of suspects within narrow or overcrowded zones. These scenarios have traditionally presented significant difficulties for standard surveillance techniques.

What sets our project apart is the integration of the formidable YOLOv8 computer vision model, renowned for its object detection capabilities, and the Face Recognition model, which boasts a remarkable ability in facial recognition. This integration enables our system to perform precise facial tracking, significantly enhancing the accuracy and efficiency of surveillance efforts. Additionally, we have leveraged the versatility of the DJI Tello Nano drone, as shown in Fig. (**1**), a compact yet powerful aerial platform, to conduct surveillance operations that were previously beyond the scope of ground-based solutions. Small drones are proving to be a new opportunity for the civil and military industries [3].

Fig. (1). Dji tello nano drone.

The strength of our project lies not only in its innovation but also in its adaptability. We have designed the Autonomous Surveillance and Patrol System to be highly customizable, enabling it to meet the specific needs and requirements of various applications. It is a unified and integrated framework that serves as a one-stop solution for diverse surveillance challenges.

We believe that the Autonomous Surveillance and Patrol System holds the potential to redefine the landscape of surveillance and security, offering unparalleled capabilities in safeguarding critical areas and enhancing public safety [4]. A drone can perform tasks that require a lot of time and manpower in a short amount of time, single-handedly. From being fully controlled by humans with the help of a remote, it has now become a self-controlled entity in terms of flight missions.

TECHNOLOGY STACK

Computer Vision

Computer vision is a field of artificial intelligence that focuses on enabling computers to interpret and understand visual data from the world, often using cameras. It involves processing image and video inputs, preprocessing to enhance data quality, feature detection and extraction, object detection and recognition, facial recognition, optical flow for tracking object movement, machine learning models for complex tasks, and post-processing of results. The outcomes of computer vision tasks can be integrated into drone control systems for decision-making, enabling applications such as obstacle avoidance alert systems, object tracking, and autonomous navigation.

Drone Programming

Drone programming encompasses the software stack used to control and operate unmanned aerial vehicles (UAVs) [5]. It includes flight control software for managing drone movement and stability, APIs and SDKs for interaction with drone hardware, navigation and path planning algorithms for autonomous flight, telemetry and communication systems, computer vision integration for visual data processing, remote piloting interfaces, mission planning software for defining flight paths, and simulation environments for safe testing and development. The smaller drones suggested in this paper require less time and resources for maintenance compared to larger UAVs used by the military, and are less prone to false alarms or malfunctions [6].

PATH PLANNING

In the dynamic landscape of modern emergency response, envision a highly sophisticated autonomous drone that not only extends its flight time but sets a new standard for comprehensive vigilance and rapid intervention. This drone, with its remarkable 25–30-minute flight endurance, represents a quantum leap in the field, as it seamlessly integrates a suite of innovative features that elevate its role in safeguarding communities. The human tracking functionality of this drone is a game-changer, empowering it to swiftly and accurately identify potential culprits during crises. It does so with precision and speed, enabling authorities to apprehend suspects or provide critical information to law enforcement in a timely manner. This feature not only enhances the efficiency of emergency response but also significantly improves the chances of identifying and addressing threats effectively.

But the drone's capabilities don't stop there. It also serves as a beacon for real-time alert systems, ensuring that the moment an anomaly is detected—whether it is a suspicious individual, harmful objects, or unforeseen environmental hazards, officials are notified immediately. This instantaneous communication is a lifeline in crisis management, enabling a faster and more coordinated response. The drone's flight path optimization is a work of art in itself. While ensuring efficiency in reaching the target swiftly, it's akin to a beautifully choreographed ballet in the sky, utilizing advanced algorithms to navigate through obstacles and rapidly changing scenarios. This elegance in motion is not just a technological marvel; it's a testament to the harmonious synergy between innovation and artistry in action.

HUMAN TRACKING

The central focus of the project centers on the implementation of human tracking and mapping techniques as shown in Fig. (**2**) through a sophisticated video camera system. In specific locations, individuals, or potential culprits, are identified and designated for tracking, all of which is orchestrated by the drone's video processing unit. Real-time image frames, captured at a standard frame rate of 24 frames per second (fps), are subject to meticulous analysis for the detection of human movements.

Fig. (2). Human tracking.

Within this system, the drone leverages an advanced face recognition model applied to the captured image frames as a reference point. This cutting-edge approach allows the system to identify and isolate the targeted individuals during video processing accurately.

The subsequent phase of our methodology involves identifying any individuals who may be involved in criminal activities, as observed in the live feed. To distinguish alterations between real-time frames and pre-trained culprit images, a comprehensive comparison of two image matrices is performed, utilizing a correlation coefficient with a confidence threshold set between 90% to 100%. When a positive match is established, the static image from our database and the real-time frame are subjected to a pixel-wise comparison, which generates further processes within the pipeline.

To optimize the tracking of variable numbers of targets while maintaining computational efficiency and exceptional tracking performance, the drone's live feed footage is an indispensable asset. These real-time feeds are diligently monitored from a central control center, where operators have full access to the live feed data. In the event of identifying an abnormal individual or culprit, the drone seamlessly engages facial recognition algorithms to align with the individual's facial landmarks [7]. Subsequently, it can also be implemented using CCTV feeds. If a drone is not available in that region, an immediate alert command from the application to the nearest drone equipped with camera capabilities enables prompt surveillance and tracking at the location of the incident.

In addition to tracking, our technology incorporates a novel frame-wise movement tracking technique to overcome potential tracking obstacles [8], ensuring that the drone effectively and accurately follows the victim's movements. This comprehensive system marks a significant advancement in the realm of surveillance and emergency response, with applications that extend to various sectors, including law enforcement, public safety, and security.

ANOMALY DETECTION

The project's second significant feature is its anomaly detection capability, which plays a pivotal role in enhancing security and public safety. This feature is designed to monitor for potential threat objects, such as powerful weapons, knives, sharp objects [9], and unauthorized non-vehicle entries in restricted areas. Whenever the system identifies any of these dangerous items or unauthorized access, the drone promptly triggers an alert mechanism.

The primary objective of this anomaly detection system is to facilitate ease of surveillance and monitoring, thereby ensuring the safety and well-being of civilians while contributing to the maintenance of a peaceful society. By swiftly identifying and responding to potential threats, the project aims to mitigate hazards and maintain the community's security. This feature is a crucial component of the project's comprehensive approach to emergency response and security management.

Design and Implementation

The design and implementation introduce a versatile surveillance system with three distinct modes integrating the Ground station, Drone and the CCTV Feeds as shown in Fig. (**3**).

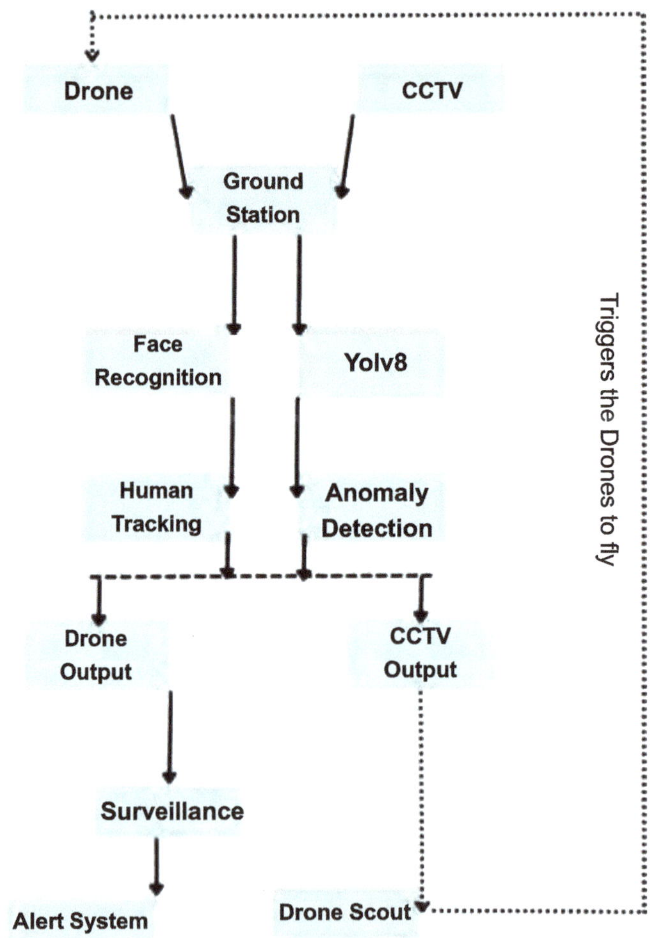

Fig. (3). Design and workflow.

Mode 1: Human Tracking focuses on monitoring and tracking individuals of interest.

Mode 2: Anomaly Detection, scans for potential threats such as weapons and unauthorized entries.

Mode 3: This system seamlessly integrates with existing CCTV feeds, providing a dynamic, triggered response mechanism. Together, these modes deliver a comprehensive approach to security and surveillance, ensuring the safety and peace of the environment.

Implementation of Human Tracking

The implementation of human tracking in this system is a multi-stage process that ensures effective surveillance and tracking of individuals of interest. The process begins with a robust face recognition algorithm, which identifies the images of potential criminals from the drone's live video streaming [10]. Once a person of interest is recognized, the drone initiates a tracking system to keep them under observation.

The tracking system is designed for real-time responsiveness and adaptability. It divides the drone's video frames into five parts: top, bottom, left, right, and center. If the person being tracked is initially in the center of the frame, the drone maintains its focus on them. However, if the person moves to any of the other four sections (top, bottom, left, or right), the drone [11] dynamically adjusts its position to keep the person centered in the frame. For instance, if the person moves to the left frame, the drone will shift its position to the left until the person returns to the center of the frame.

To ensure continuous tracking, the system monitors the confidence level of the face recognition algorithm. If the confidence level decreases, indicating potential difficulty in maintaining a clear identification, the drone adjusts its position forward while continuing to track the person. If the confidence level improves and the person's face becomes more focused and recognizable, the drone will move backward to maintain an optimal distance and focus on the individual.

Throughout this tracking process, the drone closely observes the activities and movements of the person of interest. It ensures that the person remains within the frame, regardless of their position, until law enforcement or relevant authorities arrive at the scene.

This tracking system is designed to provide consistent and real-time surveillance while adapting to changing circumstances. It plays a crucial role in enhancing security and enabling swift responses to potential threats until the arrival of law enforcement personnel.

Architecture of Face Recognition Algorithm

The Python Face-recognition package is a robust library for face-related computer vision tasks, offering face detection, facial landmark detection, and face recognition capabilities. Powered by the efficient dlib library, it employs a Histogram of Oriented Gradients (HOG) feature-based approach for precise face detection. After identifying a face, the package can further analyze it by determining facial landmarks, including eyes, nose, and mouth, using a pre-trained shape predictor model.

In the world of face recognition, the package utilizes a deep neural network model pre-trained on a vast dataset of faces. It calculates a face descriptor, representing the unique features of the detected face, which is then compared to known face descriptors in a database. This enables accurate face recognition, making it suitable for various applications.

The architecture of the Python Face-recognition as shown in Fig. (**4**) package is underpinned by dlib, providing a solid foundation for efficient and accurate face-related tasks. It incorporates pre-trained models and data files for seamless integration into applications. Users can readily employ its high-level interface for face-related tasks.

With applications spanning access control, surveillance, social media tagging, entertainment effects, and more, this package is a versatile solution. It is also highly customizable, allowing for model fine-tuning and training on custom datasets tailored to specific recognition requirements. Moreover, users can expand the database with custom face descriptors to accommodate new individuals.

Implementation of Anomaly Detection

The anomaly detection feature of the project is powered by the YOLOv8 model as shown in Fig. (**5**), which has been custom-trained using a meticulously collected dataset from online sources [12]. This dataset underwent a series of preprocessing steps to ensure its suitability for training. To ensure consistent and efficient processing, all the data was rescaled to a uniform 640 x 640 image size.

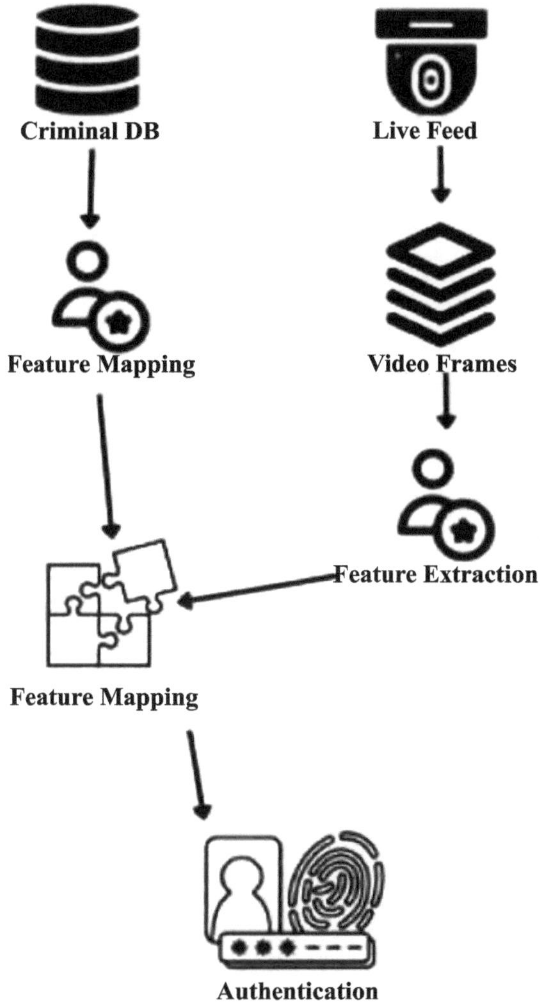

Fig. (4). Face recognition architecture.

Annotating the dataset was a critical step, and this was achieved using the Roboflow platform. The objects of interest, such as powerful weapons, knives, sharp objects, and unauthorized non-vehicle entries, were meticulously labeled with rectangular bounding boxes, adhering to the YOLOv8 specified format for object detection.

The YOLOv8 model was then trained on this annotated dataset, using state-of-the-art object detection techniques. The training process involved fine-tuning the model to accurately recognize and classify these specific threat objects.

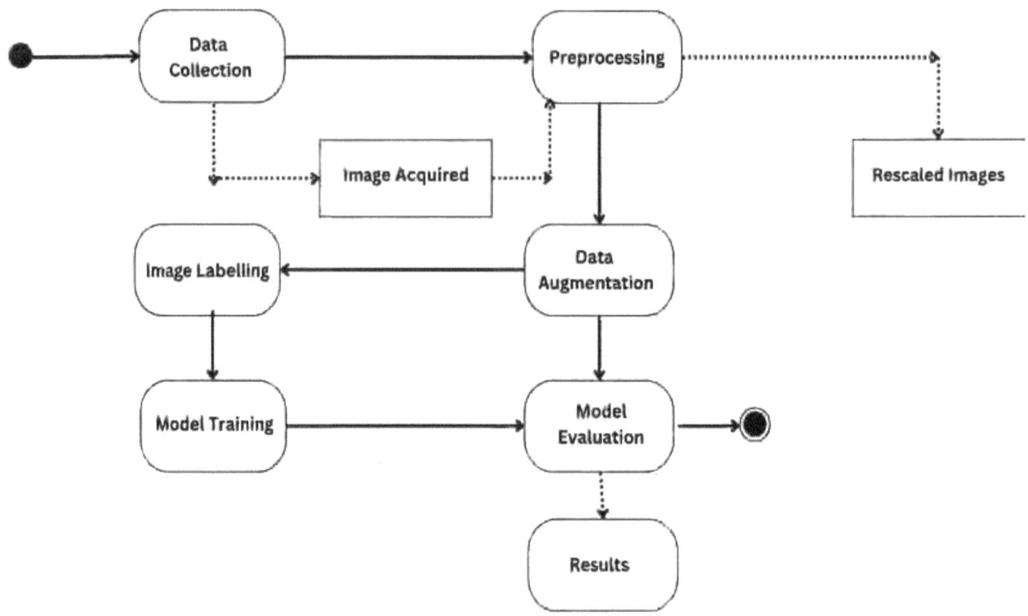

Fig. (5). Custom YOLO model training.

Upon the successful completion of training, the resulting weights from the YOLOv8 model were obtained. These weights are instrumental in enabling the drone to process real-time data live, allowing it to identify and react to potential threats as they occur autonomously. This integration of cutting-edge technology, custom training, and real-time processing capabilities ensures that the anomaly detection feature is both robust and highly effective in enhancing security and public safety.

Architecture of YOLO Model

The YOLOv8 architecture is based on a convolutional neural network (CNN) that can be divided into two main parts. The first is the backbone, and the second is the head. The backbone is responsible for extracting features from the input image, while the head is responsible for predicting bounding boxes and class probabilities for the detected objects.The YOLOv8 backbone is based on the CSPDarknet53 architecture, a modified version of the Darknet 53 architecture [13] used in previous versions of YOLO. The CSPDarknet53 architecture employs cross-stage partial connections to improve information flow between the different layers of the network.

The YOLOv8 head is a new design that introduces several improvements over previous versions of YOLO, as shown in Fig. (**6**). One key improvement is the use of a self-attention mechanism, which allows the model to learn long-range dependencies between different parts of the input image. Additionally, the YOLOv8 head uses a new anchor matching strategy that improves the model's ability to detect small objects.

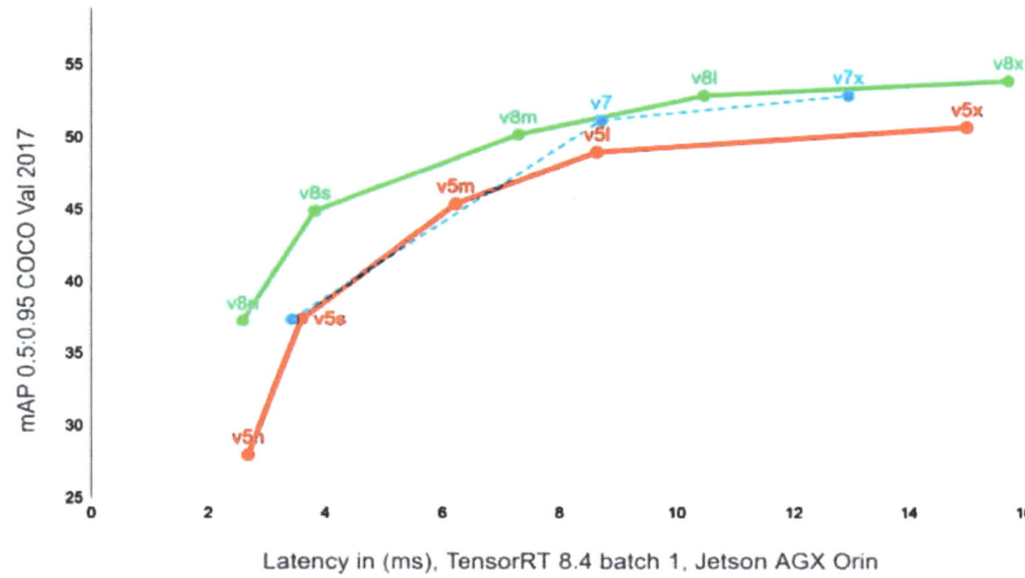

Fig. (6). Performance benchmark of yolov8.

YOLOv8 is trained on a massive dataset of images with labeled objects. This dataset encompasses a diverse range of object categories, including people, animals, vehicles, and everyday objects. As a result, YOLOv8 is able to detect a wide range of objects with high accuracy.YOLOv8 is available in a variety of pre-trained models that can be used for different tasks, such as general object detection, person detection, and vehicle detection. YOLOv8 can also be fine-tuned on custom datasets to improve its performance on specific tasks.

YOLOv8 uses a new type of activation function called the Mish activation function. The Mish activation function has been demonstrated to enhance the performance of CNNs on various tasks, including object detection.YOLOv8 uses a new type of data augmentation technique called mosaic augmentation. Mosaic augmentation randomly combines four training images into a single image, which helps the model to learn to generalize to different object scales and translations.YOLOv8 is trained using a new loss function called the CIoU loss function. The CIoU loss function is designed to improve the accuracy of object detection models, especially for small objects as shown in Fig. (**7**).

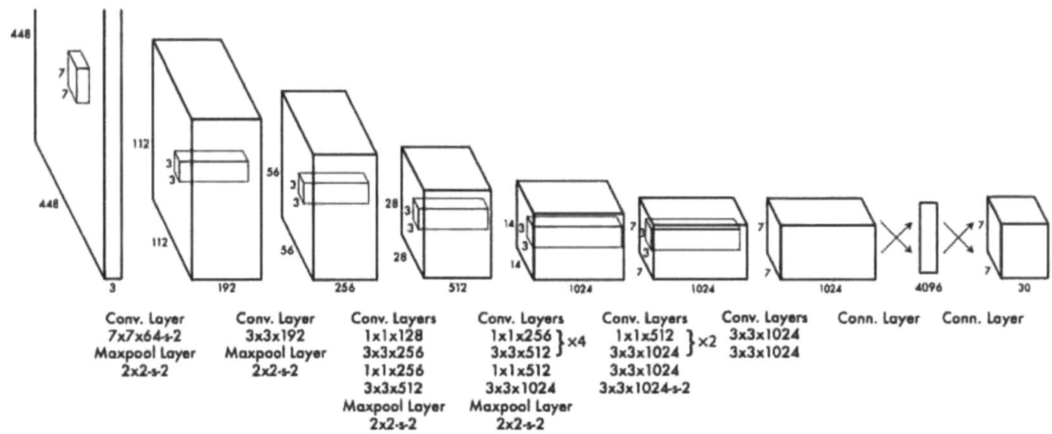

Fig. (7). Architecture of yolov8.

Implementation using CCTV Feeds

Imagine a seamlessly integrated surveillance system that operates at the intersection of cutting-edge technology and proactive security. In the absence of additional drones, this system deploys an ingenious response mechanism. When the same process is already active within the CCTV feeds, it triggers the deployed drones into two dynamic modes, each serving a distinct yet equally crucial role in safeguarding the environment.

Mode A, aptly named “Human Tracking,” leverages the drones' advanced capabilities to track and monitor individuals of interest. The drones act as vigilant sentinels, ensuring that potential culprits remain under continuous and unwavering observation. This mode combines the efficiency of computer vision and AI-powered face recognition, enabling drones to not only follow but also actively identify and log individuals exhibiting suspicious behavior.

Simultaneously, in Mode B, the drones assume the role of vigilant guardians dedicated to “Anomaly Detection.” They become the vigilant eyes in the sky, actively scanning their surroundings for anomalies that pose a potential threat to public safety. These anomalies may include the presence of powerful weapons, knives, sharp objects, or unauthorized non-vehicle entries. When an anomaly is detected, the drone issues an immediate alert, ensuring swift and focused attention to the potential threat.

In this innovative response mechanism, drones collaborate seamlessly with existing CCTV systems, creating a dynamic synergy that combines the strengths of stationary surveillance with the agility of mobile drones. The system's intelligence ensures that it optimizes resource allocation, channeling the drones' efforts where they are most needed. This not only conserves energy and resources but also maximizes the system's responsiveness to evolving situations.

The template is designed so that author affiliations are not repeated each time for multiple authors with the same affiliation. Please keep your affiliations as succinct as possible (for example, do not differentiate among departments of the same organization). This template was designed for two affiliations.

RESULTS AND INFERENCE

Intersection over Union

Intersection over Union (IoU) (1) serves as a critical metric within the realm of object detection. It quantifies the extent of overlap between a ground truth bounding box and a predicted bounding box produced by an object detection model. IoU is a pivotal tool for evaluating the precision of object detection models and plays a crucial role in terms such as True Positive (TP), False Positive (FP), and False Negative (FN).

$$\mathrm{IoU} = \frac{\mathrm{area}(gt \cap pd)}{\mathrm{area}(gt \cup pd)} \tag{1}$$

Precision and Recall

Precision (2) measures the accuracy of positive predictions. It's the ratio of true positives to all instances predicted as positive.

Recall gauges the model's ability to detect all relevant instances. It is the ratio of true positives to all actual positive instances.

$$\begin{aligned} P &= \frac{\mathrm{TP}}{\mathrm{TP}+\mathrm{FP}} = \frac{TP}{\text{all detections}} \\ R &= \frac{\mathrm{TP}}{\mathrm{TP}+\mathrm{FN}} = \frac{TP}{\text{all ground-truths}} \end{aligned} \tag{2}$$

Mean Average Precision

Mean Average Precision (mAP) (3) assesses object detection model performance by considering both precision and recall across multiple object categories. mAP50 focuses on an IoU threshold of 0.5, while mAP50-95 extends the evaluation across a range of IoU thresholds from 0.5 to 0.95. Higher mAP scores indicate better model performance, making it suitable for tasks like autonomous driving and security surveillance.

$$\text{mAP@}n = \frac{1}{n}\sum_{i-1}^{n} \text{AP}_i \quad \text{for n classes.} \qquad (3)$$

Object Detection Loss

Box Loss: This loss assesses the accuracy of predicted bounding box coordinates. It incentivizes the model to refine its predicted bounding boxes to align more closely with the ground truth boxes.

Class Loss: Class loss quantifies the model's error in predicting the object category for each bounding box. It ensures that the model accurately identifies the category of detected objects.

Defocus Loss: Defocus loss is a specialized component designed to enhance object detection in scenarios with defocused or blurry images. It encourages the model to focus on improving detection under challenging conditions, such as those with blurred imagery.

Evaluation of the Model

The YOLO model's training results provide a comprehensive view of its object detection performance. The model, comprising 168 layers with over 11 million parameters, is evaluated on multiple object classes using a dataset of 38 images containing 905 instances. The results showed that the model achieves an average precision of 0.785 as shown in Fig. (**8**) with an IoU threshold of 0.5, and 0.555 as shown in Fig. (**9**) when considering a wider IoU range. Notably, different object classes exhibit varying levels of precision and recall, with courses like "Gun" and "Bike" performing exceptionally well. These results, coupled with insights into the model's inference speed, offer valuable information for assessing the model's utility and potential areas for enhancement in object detection tasks are shown in Figs. (**10-13**).

```
Epoch    GPU_mem   box_loss   cls_loss   dfl_loss  Instances        Size
25/25      10.9G     0.7606     0.3961     0.8001         90        800:
                                         100% 39/39 [00:29<00:00,  1.30it/s]
           Class     Images  Instances      Box(P          R       mAP50  mAP50-95):
                                         100% 2/2 [00:02<00:00,  1.36s/it]
             all         38        905      0.824      0.719       0.785      0.554
```

Fig. (8). Evaluation results of training.

```
Model summary: 168 layers, 11127132 parameters, 0 gradients, 28.4 GFLOPs
          Class     Images  Instances      Box(P          R      mAP50  mAP50-95):
                                             100% 2/2 [00:03<00:00,  1.53s/it]
            All        538        905      0.829      0.719      0.785      0.555
          Knife        538         35      0.554      0.171      0.254      0.096
            Gun        538         27      0.965      0.852      0.967      0.692
           Bike        538        754      0.934      0.964      0.987      0.794
            Car        538         89      0.864      0.888      0.932       0.64
Speed: 0.2ms pre-process, 10.7ms inference, 0.0ms loss, 1.3ms post-process per image
```

Fig. (9). Evaluation results of validation.

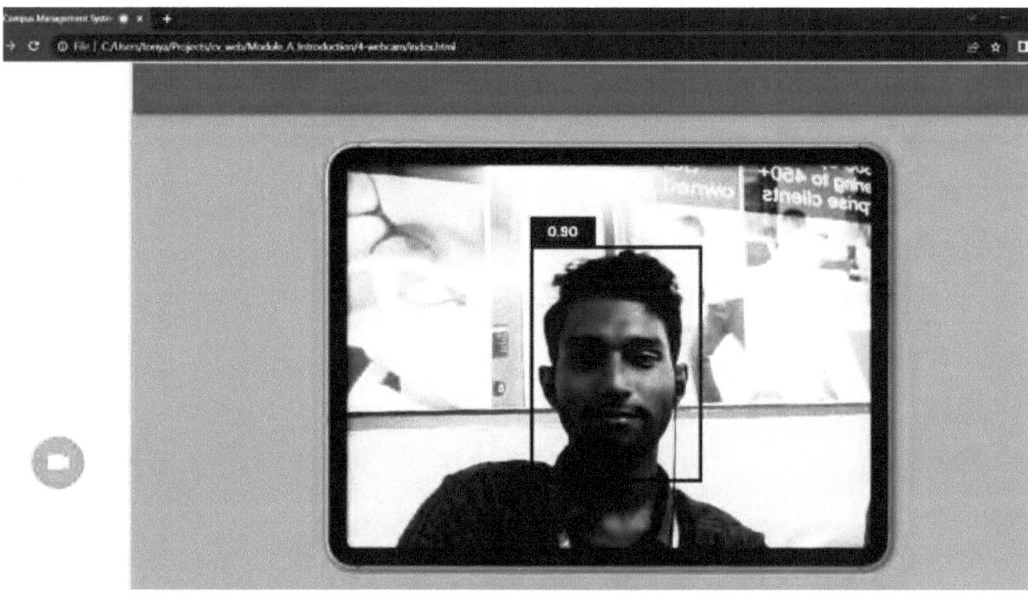

Fig. (10). Results of mode a - human tracking.

Fig. (11). Results of mode b - anomaly detection.

Fig. (12). Drone live feed at the dashboard.

Fig. (13). Output for mode a - human tracking in drone.

FUTURE SCOPE

Looking ahead, the future of this surveillance system lies in expanding its capabilities through emerging technologies that enhance its autonomy, intelligence, and reach. One of the most exciting possibilities is the development of autonomous drone swarming. By incorporating collective drone intelligence, the system can deploy multiple drones working in unison to cover vast areas, share information in real-time, and coordinate complex tasks such as human tracking or anomaly detection over expansive zones. Swarm-based systems will enable a comprehensive and scalable surveillance network, dynamically distributing tasks among drones for optimal coverage.

The use of edge AI computing is another transformative innovation. Currently, the system relies on centralized servers to process video feeds and run algorithms. By embedding advanced processing units directly into drones and CCTV cameras, edge computing can reduce latency, making the system faster and more responsive. Real-time decision-making would become truly autonomous, with drones and cameras processing data locally, allowing them to react instantly to unfolding situations without relying on cloud-based systems. This architecture ensures robust performance, even in remote areas with limited connectivity.

Another promising avenue is the integration of emotion recognition and behavioral analytics. Beyond simply identifying individuals, the system could analyze subtle cues in body language, facial expressions, and gestures to predict suspicious behavior or gauge emotional states. For example, drones could track individuals exhibiting signs of distress or heightened aggression, enabling security personnel to intervene before an incident escalates. This proactive approach would revolutionize threat detection, making security systems not only reactive but predictive.

Moreover, quantum-enhanced algorithms represent the next leap in computing power for such systems. Quantum computing promises to solve highly complex problems at a fraction of the time required by classical systems. Applying quantum algorithms to facial recognition or object detection would significantly boost accuracy and speed, particularly in cases with lower-quality footage or large, crowded environments. This breakthrough could redefine how surveillance systems function, providing unparalleled levels of detection capability.

Energy-efficient drone technology is another crucial area of exploration. With advancements in battery life and the integration of renewable energy, future drones could have extended operational hours without requiring frequent recharges. Coupled with solar-powered drones, this would make long-duration monitoring missions feasible, especially in remote or disaster-prone areas. The combination of endurance and autonomy would significantly enhance the scalability and reliability of drone-based surveillance systems.

In the future, the system could also capitalize on 5G network integration, providing ultra-low-latency data transmission between drones, cameras, and control centers. The high-speed connectivity afforded by 5G would allow drones to stream high-definition video in real time, making live monitoring more effective and detailed, while enabling faster, more coordinated responses across the entire surveillance network. This enhanced communication will be critical in environments where immediate action is required, such as large public gatherings or high-risk locations.

Finally, there is an increasing demand for privacy-preserving AI techniques within surveillance systems. As AI becomes more integrated into public security, ensuring that these systems operate ethically and respect personal privacy is paramount. Technologies such as differential privacy and homomorphic encryption could enable the system to analyze and process data without accessing sensitive personal information, thereby protecting individual identities while still providing robust security monitoring. These techniques would foster trust and ensure compliance with regulatory standards in the deployment of surveillance technologies, balancing security with individual rights.

Together, these innovations will shape a next-generation surveillance system that is smarter, faster, and more capable, providing a proactive, scalable, and ethically aware security solution that meets the evolving needs of public safety in the digital age.

CONCLUSION

The integration of drones, facial recognition, and anomaly detection systems has unlocked a new frontier in surveillance and security. By seamlessly combining real-time human tracking, advanced threat detection, and automated response, this surveillance framework elevates traditional security practices to an unprecedented level of sophistication. The precision offered by deep learning models like YOLOv8 for object detection and the Python Face-recognition package for individual identification ensures that the system operates with heightened accuracy and adaptability. This multimodal surveillance solution creates a vigilant, responsive security architecture capable of not only identifying and tracking individuals of interest but also autonomously detecting potential dangers like weapons or unauthorized entries.

This system surpasses conventional surveillance, providing not only real-time monitoring but also intelligent, adaptive responses to rapidly evolving security scenarios. Its ability to continuously refine its detection accuracy and tracking responsiveness underscores the potential of AI-driven solutions in public safety, law enforcement, and broader security domains. The deployment of such systems ensures comprehensive situational awareness, enhances preemptive threat mitigation, and significantly accelerates response times, thereby reducing potential harm and safeguarding public environments with efficiency and precision.

CONSENT OF PUBLICATION

The, who have used it with proper permission. The authors confirm that informed consent was obtained from all individuals featured in the image.

REFERENCES

[1] M.R.A. Refaai, D.R. Rinku, I. Thamarai, S. Meera, N.K. Sripada, and S. Yishak, "An enhanced drone technology for detecting the human object in the dense areas using a deep learning model", *Adv. Mater. Sci. Eng.*, vol. 2022, no. 1, p. 4162007, 2022.

[2] M. A. Khan, H. Menouar, and R. Hamila, "DroneNet: Crowd density estimation using Self-ONNs for drones," in *Proc. 2023 IEEE 20th Consumer Communications & Networking Conference (CCNC)*, 2023, pp. 455–460. IEEE.

[3] R. Majeed, N.A. Abdullah, M.F. Mushtaq, and R. Kazmi, "Drone security: Issues and challenges", *Parameters,* vol. 2, no. 5, 2021.

[4] N. Karna, S. Yadav, S. P. Chhetri, S. Paudyal, and P. Gouli, "Surveillance Drone", *Published in International Research Journal of Innovations in Engineering and Technology,* vol. 4, no. 2, pp. 8-12, 2020.

[5] A. Witayangkurn, M. Nagai, K. Honda, M. Dailey, and R. Shibasaki, "Real-time monitoring system using unmanned aerial vehicle integrated with sensor observation service", *Int. Arch. Photogramm. Remote Sens. Spat. Inf. Sci,* vol. XXXVIII-1, no. C22, pp. 107-112, 2012.
[http://dx.doi.org/10.5194/isprsarchives-XXXVIII-1-C22-107-2011]

[6] A. Mirzaeinia, M. Hassanalian, and K. Lee, "Drones for borders surveillance: autonomous battery maintenance station and replacement for multirotor drones," in *AIAA Scitech 2020 Forum*, 2020, p. 0062.
[http://dx.doi.org/10.2514/6.2020-0062]

[7] G.D. Ramaraj, S. Venkatakrishnan, G. Balasubramanian, and S. Sridhar, "Aerial surveillance of public areas with autonomous track and follow using image processing", *2017 International Conference on Computer and Drone Applications (IConDA),* pp. 92-95, 2017.
[http://dx.doi.org/10.1109/ICONDA.2017.8270406]

[8] A. Gohari, A.B. Ahmad, R.B.A. Rahim, A.S.M. Supa'at, S. Abd Razak, and M.S.M. Gismalla, "Involvement of surveillance drones in smart cities: A systematic review", *IEEE Access,* vol. 10, pp. 56611-56628, 2022.
[http://dx.doi.org/10.1109/ACCESS.2022.3177904]

[9] F.O. Marube, O. Odongo, and L.G. Muchemi, "An autonomous unmanned aerial security surveillance system to enhance security in remote territories", *Int. J. Comput. Appl.,* vol. 179, no. 6, pp. 1-8, 2017.

[10] K. S. Lee, M. Ovinis, T. Nagarajan, R. Seulin, and O. Morel, "Autonomous patrol and surveillance system using unmanned aerial vehicles," in *2015 IEEE 15th International Conference on Environment and Electrical Engineering (EEEIC)*, June 2015, pp. 1291–1297. IEEE.
[http://dx.doi.org/10.1109/EEEIC.2015.7165356]

[11] A. Singh, D. Patil, and S.N. Omkar, "Eye in the sky: Real-time drone surveillance system (dss) for violent individuals identification using scatternet hybrid deep learning network", *Proceedings of the IEEE conference on computer vision and pattern recognition workshops,* pp. 1629-1637, 2018.
[http://dx.doi.org/10.1109/CVPRW.2018.00214]

[12] X. Li, and A.V. Savkin, "Networked unmanned aerial vehicles for surveillance and monitoring: A survey", *Future Internet,* vol. 13, no. 7, p. 174, 2021.
[http://dx.doi.org/10.3390/fi13070174]

[13] J. Fan, X. Yang, R. Lu, X. Xie, and W. Li, "Design and Implementation of Intelligent Inspection and Alarm Flight System for Epidemic Prevention", *Drones (Basel),* vol. 5, no. 3, p. 68, 2021.
[http://dx.doi.org/10.3390/drones5030068]

CHAPTER 10

Security and Privacy Concerns in Smart Systems

Akhil Singampalli[1,*], **Anil Pise**[2], **Dharma Teja Singampalli**[3] and **Vrushali Deshpande**[4]

[1] *Department of Computer Science and Engineering, Vignan's Institute of Information Technology, India*

[2] *Cumulus Solutions, Johannesburg, South Africa*

[3] *Sagility, Bangalore, India*

[4] *D&M Tech, Pune, India*

Abstract: The chapter on "Security and Privacy Concerns in Smart Systems" explores the complex landscape of securing interconnected smart technologies. It begins with an elucidation of smart systems, encompassing Internet of Things (IoT), smart homes, cities, and industrial applications, emphasizing their efficiency and convenience. Subsequently, the narrative shifts to outlining the multifaceted security and privacy challenges inherent in these systems, emphasizing the imperatives of user trust and technological optimization. A detailed exposition on common security threats, including cyberattacks and data breaches, is provided, accompanied by illustrative case studies. Privacy concerns, such as data collection, user consent, and surveillance, are scrutinized, and bolstered by pertinent examples. The chapter culminates in a discussion of best practices, emerging technologies, and future trends, advocating for a holistic approach to fortify the security and privacy posture of smart systems in a rapidly evolving digital landscape.

Keywords: Cybersecurity, Cyberattacks, Data breaches, Distributed denial of service (DDoS), Internet of things (IoT), Privacy concerns, Smart systems.

INTRODUCTION

In the digital age, technology has become an integral part of our daily lives, revolutionizing the way we live, work, and interact with our surroundings. The emergence of smart systems has ushered in a new era of efficiency, convenience, and automation, promising to streamline processes and enhance our quality of life. However, amidst this rapid advancement, the spectre of security and privacy concerns looms large, casting a shadow over the potential benefits of these innovative technologies.

* **Corresponding author Akhil Singampalli:** Department of Computer Science and Engineering, Vignan's Institute of Information Technology, India; E-mail: singampalliakhil@gmail.com

Suneeta Satpathy, Sachi Nandan Mohanty & Subhendu Kumar Pani (Eds.)

Recent years have witnessed an unprecedented proliferation of smart technologies, revolutionized industries, and the reshaping of daily life. From interconnected IoT devices to sophisticated smart city infrastructures, the integration of technology has promised unparalleled efficiency and convenience. However, amidst this rapid advancement, the spectre of security and privacy concerns looms large [1]. With each innovation, the imperative to safeguard user data and preserve privacy becomes increasingly pressing.

As smart systems become more prevalent, they bring significant security and privacy challenges. These concerns arise from the vast amounts of data collected, the potential for cyberattacks, and the need for robust data protection mechanisms. Ensuring the security and privacy of smart systems is critical to gaining user trust and realizing the full potential of these technologies. Fig. (**1**) shows the integration of network devices and technologies.

Fig. (1). Networked devices and technological integrations.

Addressing security and privacy concerns in smart systems is crucial for several reasons. First, it protects sensitive user data from unauthorized access and misuse. Second, it ensures the reliability and integrity of smart systems, preventing disruptions and potential hazards. Third, addressing these concerns fosters user confidence and promotes wider adoption of smart technologies.

SMART SYSTEMS - AN OVERVIEW

Smart systems encompass a wide range of applications and technologies, each designed to enhance our daily lives and optimize various processes. From the IoT to smart homes, cities, and industrial settings, these interconnected systems leverage advanced computing, sensors, and communication technologies to offer improved efficiency, convenience, and automation. Fig. (**2**) illustrates how smart systems have evolved over time.

Fig. (2). Image illustrating iot, smart home, smart cities, and industrial iot.

Within the realm of smart cities, initiatives such as Barcelona's implementation of IoT sensors for smart parking and waste management, or Singapore's utilization of data analytics for traffic optimization and urban planning, exemplify the transformative potential of smart technologies in enhancing quality of life and sustainability.

Types of Smart Systems

1. **Internet of Things (IoT):** The IoT refers to a network of physical devices, vehicles, home appliances, and other objects embedded with sensors, software, and connectivity, enabling them to collect and exchange data. IoT devices permeate our daily lives, encompassing a wide range of products, from smart thermostats and wearable fitness trackers to connected vehicles and industrial machinery. These devices can be remotely monitored and controlled, offering enhanced convenience and efficiency.

Within the realm of IoT, examples abound:

a. Smart thermostats that learn our preferences and adjust the temperature accordingly, optimizing energy consumption and comfort.

b. Wearable fitness trackers that monitor our activity levels, heart rate, and sleep patterns provide valuable insights into our health and well-being.

c. Connected vehicles equipped with advanced safety features, real-time traffic updates, and remote diagnostics enhance the driving experience and vehicle maintenance.

2. **Smart Homes:** Smart homes integrate various technologies and systems to enhance home automation, security, and energy management. From intelligent lighting and climate control to smart locks and home assistants, these systems offer convenience, energy savings, and improved safety for homeowners.

Examples of smart home technologies include:

a. Smart lighting systems that can be programmed to automatically adjust brightness levels or turn on/off based on occupancy or time of day, reducing energy consumption.

b. Smart locks that can be controlled remotely or integrated with home assistants, allowing homeowners to grant or restrict access with ease.

c. Home assistants, such as Amazon's Alexa or Google Home, enable voice control of various smart home devices, simplifying daily tasks and improving accessibility.

3. **Smart Cities:** Smart cities utilize technology and data to enhance urban infrastructure, services, and the quality of life for residents. From intelligent traffic management and waste disposal systems to enhanced public safety and environmental monitoring, smart city initiatives aim to create more sustainable, efficient, and liveable urban environments.

4. **Industrial IoT:** The Industrial Internet of Things (IIoT) encompasses the integration of connected devices and systems in manufacturing and industrial settings [2]. These technologies optimize operations, improve maintenance, and enhance worker safety through the use of predictive analytics, real-time monitoring, and automation.

Examples of industrial IoT applications include:

a. Predictive maintenance systems that leverage sensor data to anticipate and prevent equipment failures, reducing downtime and extending asset life.

b. Automated production lines that utilize robotics and machine learning to streamline manufacturing processes, improving efficiency and quality control.
c. Worker safety monitoring systems that track environmental conditions, detect potential hazards, and alert personnel in real-time, enhancing workplace safety.

Benefits of Smart Systems

Smart systems offer numerous benefits across various domains, driving innovation and improving our daily lives. Some key advantages include:

1. **Efficiency:** By automating processes and leveraging data-driven insights, smart systems optimize resource utilization, reducing waste and increasing productivity. For instance, smart energy management systems can analyse consumption patterns and adjust usage accordingly, leading to significant energy savings.
2. **Convenience:** Smart systems enhance convenience by enabling remote monitoring and control of devices and systems. From remotely adjusting home temperatures to accessing real-time traffic updates, these technologies simplify daily tasks and improve accessibility.
3. **Safety:** Advanced security features and predictive maintenance capabilities in smart systems contribute to enhanced safety. Smart home security systems can detect intruders and alert homeowners, while industrial IoT applications can identify potential equipment failures before they occur, preventing accidents and hazardous situations.
4. **Sustainability:** By optimizing resource utilization and enabling better management of energy consumption, smart systems can significantly contribute to environmental sustainability. Smart city initiatives, such as intelligent waste management and traffic optimization, reduce greenhouse gas emissions and promote eco-friendly practices.

While the benefits of smart systems are undeniable, their widespread adoption and seamless integration into our lives hinge on addressing the pressing security and privacy concerns that accompany these technologies.

Security Concerns in Smart Systems

As smart systems become increasingly interconnected and integrated into our daily lives, they also present a growing attack surface for cybercriminals and malicious actors [3]. The complexity of these systems, coupled with their reliance on data exchange and remote access, introduces various security vulnerabilities that must be addressed to ensure their safe and reliable operation.

In recent years, the threat landscape has witnessed a surge in ransomware attacks targeting critical infrastructure, such as the Colonial Pipeline breach in 2021, which disrupted fuel supplies across the East Coast of the United States. These incidents underscore the evolving sophistication of cyber threats and the imperative for robust security measures to safeguard interconnected smart systems.

COMMON SECURITY THREATS

Smart systems face a multitude of security threats, ranging from cyberattacks and data breaches to vulnerabilities inherent in hardware, software, and network components. Understanding these threats is crucial for developing effective mitigation strategies and fortifying the security posture of smart systems.

Cyberattacks

Cyberattacks pose a significant risk to smart systems, exploiting vulnerabilities to gain unauthorized access, disrupt operations, or steal sensitive data. Fig. (**3**) illustrates various types of cyber attacks. These attacks can take various forms, including:

a. **Distributed Denial of Service (DDoS) Attacks:** These attacks aim to overload a system with excessive traffic, rendering it unavailable to legitimate users. Smart systems, especially IoT devices with limited resources, are vulnerable to DDoS attacks due to their interconnected nature.
b. **Malware Infections:** Malicious software designed to disrupt, damage, or gain unauthorized access to systems. IoT devices can be infected with malware, leading to data breaches, system failures, or being used as part of botnets to launch larger-scale attacks.
c. **Ransomware Attacks:** A type of malware that encrypts data and demands payment for decryption. Smart systems, particularly in critical infrastructure, are prime targets for ransomware attacks due to the potential for significant disruption and financial gain.
d. **Man-in-the-Middle (MitM) Attacks:** These attacks intercept communication between devices, enabling attackers to eavesdrop on or manipulate data transmissions, which can lead to data breaches or system compromises.
e. **Zero-Day Exploits:** Attackers target previously unknown vulnerabilities for which no patches or mitigations are available, making it challenging to defend against such attacks until the vulnerabilities are discovered and addressed.
f. **Botnet Attacks:** Besides the infamous Mirai botnet, which targeted IoT devices, other botnets, such as Reaper and Hajime, have also exploited vulnerabilities in IoT devices to launch large-scale attacks, underscoring the

need for proactive security measures in smart systems.

g. **Phishing Attacks:** Phishing deceives users by impersonating trusted entities through fraudulent emails, websites, or messages, aiming to steal sensitive information such as passwords or financial data. Prevention includes user education and implementing robust email security measures like filtering and authentication.
h. **Social Engineering Attacks:** Social engineering tactics exploit human behavior and psychology, tricking users into taking harmful actions, such as clicking on malicious links, sharing sensitive information, or granting unauthorized access. Effective mitigation requires comprehensive user awareness training combined with robust security measures, such as content filtering and spam detection.
i. **Drive-By Attacks:** Drive-by attacks infect devices by exploiting vulnerabilities in web browsers when users visit compromised websites, often without any user interaction or awareness. Prevention involves regular software updates and utilizing web security tools to block malicious scripts and content.
j. **Cross-Site Scripting (XSS) Attacks:** XSS attacks inject malicious scripts into web pages that users view, allowing attackers to steal data, hijack user sessions, or conduct other malicious activities. Mitigating XSS attacks involves input validation and output encoding to prevent script injection vulnerabilities.
k. **Password Attacks:** Password attacks aim to guess or steal user passwords through various methods, including brute force, dictionary attacks, and phishing. Mitigation strategies include enforcing strong, unique passwords, implementing multi-factor authentication, and educating users on password security best practices.
l. **Eavesdropping Attacks:** Eavesdropping involves intercepting and monitoring communication between parties to obtain sensitive information, such as passwords or financial data. Prevention consists in using encrypted communication channels, like HTTPS, to protect data from unauthorized interception.
m. **AI-Powered Attacks:** As artificial intelligence (AI) continues to advance, cybercriminals may leverage machine learning algorithms to automate and optimize cyber threats, such as phishing campaigns or malware distribution. Defending against AI-powered attacks requires the development and deployment of AI-driven security solutions that can detect and mitigate these evolving threats in real-time.
n. **Advanced Persistent Threats (APTs):** APTs are prolonged, stealthy cyberattacks orchestrated by skilled adversaries, often nation-states or well-funded groups, to infiltrate and maintain persistent access to target systems for

espionage or data theft. Defending against APTs requires comprehensive security measures, constant vigilance, and the ability to detect and mitigate sophisticated, multi-vector attacks.

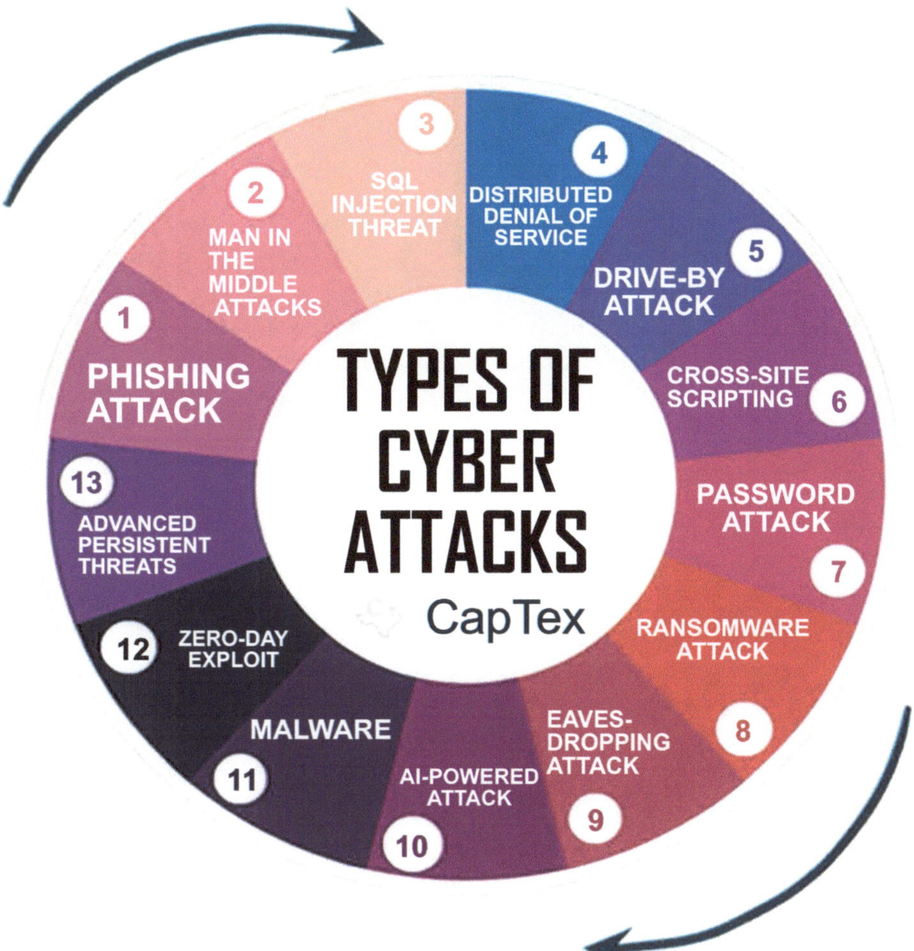

Fig. (3). Image illustrating types of cyber attacks.

Data Breaches

Data breaches pose a significant risk to smart systems, as they often handle and store vast amounts of sensitive data, including personal information, financial records, and confidential business data. Fig. (**4**) illustrates various types of Data Breaches [4]. Data breaches can occur through various vectors, such as:

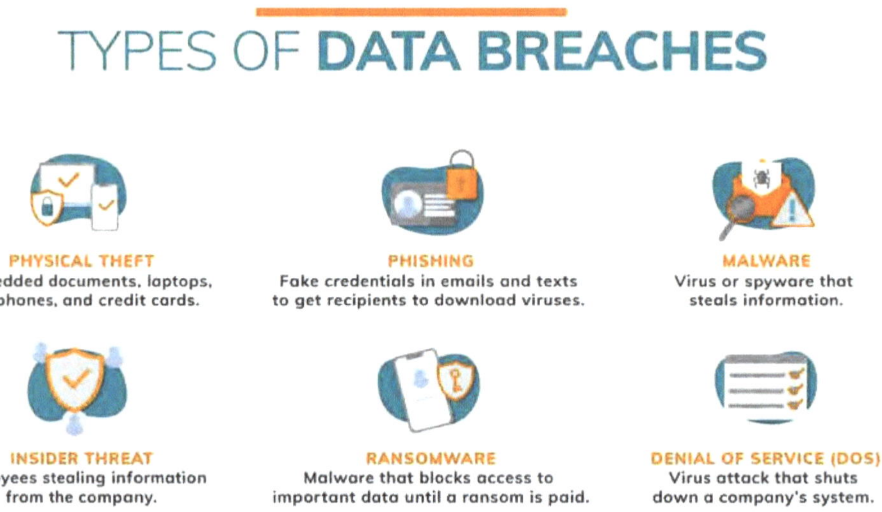

Fig. (4). Image illustrating types of data breaches.

a. **Unauthorized Access *via* Smart Devices:** Unauthorized access to sensitive information stored or transmitted by smart devices can lead to data breaches. These breaches can result in the exposure of personal data, financial information, and health records, potentially leading to identity theft, financial losses, and privacy violations.
b. **Insider Threats:** Malicious insiders or employees with access to smart systems can misuse their privileges to steal or manipulate sensitive data, intentionally or unintentionally, leading to data breaches.
c. **Cloud Security Risks:** Many smart systems rely on cloud-based storage and services, introducing risks such as unauthorized access, data breaches, and service outages if cloud security measures are inadequate.
d. **Supply Chain Attacks:** Attackers may compromise the security of smart systems by infiltrating the supply chain, injecting malware or hardware-level vulnerabilities into devices before they are distributed, potentially leading to data breaches or system compromises.
e. **Physical Theft and Data Security:** Physical theft poses a significant risk to data security, especially with the prevalence of smart devices. When these devices are stolen, personal, financial, and corporate data stored on them becomes vulnerable to unauthorized access. This can lead to identity theft, financial fraud, or corporate espionage, undermining both individual privacy and organizational security [5]. To mitigate this risk, it's crucial to implement robust security measures such as strong authentication, encryption, and remote wiping capabilities. Additionally, physical security measures such as locks, alarms, and tracking devices can help deter theft and facilitate recovery of

stolen devices, ultimately safeguarding sensitive data from falling into the wrong hands.

f. **Malware Threats in Smart Systems:** Malware presents a grave threat to smart systems, exploiting vulnerabilities to gain unauthorized access or manipulate data. Through various vectors such as email attachments or compromised websites, malware can steal sensitive information or disrupt device operations. Mitigation involves robust cybersecurity measures such as antivirus software and user education on safe browsing habits.
g. **Phishing Threats in Smart Systems:** Phishing poses a significant threat, tricking users into revealing sensitive information through deceptive emails or messages [6]. Attackers impersonate trusted sources, aiming to steal login credentials or financial data. Mitigation involves user education and implementing email filtering and authentication measures.
h. **Denial of Service (DoS) Threats in Smart Systems:** DoS attacks disrupt smart systems by overwhelming them with traffic, making them inaccessible. Attackers aim to disrupt services, causing financial loss or reputational damage. Mitigation involves robust network security and using content delivery networks to absorb attack traffic.

Adversarial Attacks

Adversarial attacks are a class of cyber threats that specifically target the robustness of machine learning models and algorithms employed within smart systems. These attacks involve the deliberate manipulation of input data to deceive AI systems, leading to incorrect or unexpected outputs. By subtly modifying inputs, adversaries can trick AI algorithms into misclassifying objects, making erroneous predictions, or even causing system failures.

Types of Adversarial Attacks

1. **Evasion Attacks**: In evasion attacks, adversaries manipulate input data to evade detection or mislead classification algorithms. By perturbing features of input data imperceptibly, attackers can deceive AI systems into making incorrect predictions.
2. **Poisoning Attacks**: Poisoning attacks involve injecting malicious data into the training dataset used to develop AI models. By introducing subtle alterations or outliers into the training data, adversaries can compromise the integrity and effectiveness of the AI model, leading to erroneous outputs during inference.
3. **Model Inversion Attacks**: Model inversion attacks exploit the vulnerability of AI systems that inadvertently leak sensitive information about their training data [7]. By analysing the outputs of a model, adversaries attempt to reconstruct or infer details about the training data, potentially compromising user privacy or exposing proprietary information.

Mitigation Strategies

To mitigate the risk of adversarial attacks, robust defence mechanisms must be integrated into smart systems. These may include:

1. **Adversarial Training:** By augmenting training datasets with adversarial crafted examples, AI models can be trained to recognize and defend against adversarial manipulations.
2. **Input Sanitization:** Implementing pre-processing techniques to detect and filter out potentially malicious inputs can enhance the resilience of AI systems against adversarial attacks.
3. **Model Robustness Evaluation:** Regularly assessing the robustness of AI models against adversarial perturbations can help identify vulnerabilities and inform the development of more resilient algorithms.

VULNERABILITIES IN SMART SYSTEMS

In addition to the common security threats, smart systems face vulnerabilities inherent in their hardware, software, and network components, which malicious actors can exploit to gain unauthorized access, disrupt operations, or compromise data integrity.

Expanding on hardware, software, and network vulnerabilities, we can explore case studies or incidents where these vulnerabilities were exploited, highlighting the complexity of securing interconnected devices:

For instance, the WannaCry ransomware attack of 2017 exploited a vulnerability in the Windows SMB protocol, infecting hundreds of thousands of computers worldwide, including IoT devices, by encrypting their data and demanding ransom payments. This widespread incident underscored the critical importance of promptly patching known vulnerabilities to prevent exploitation by malicious actors.

Hardware Vulnerabilities

a. **Physical Attacks:** Physical access to devices can lead to tampering and unauthorized control. For instance, attackers can access smart meters or sensors in smart cities to manipulate data.
b. **Insecure Components:** Many IoT devices use off-the-shelf components that may have known vulnerabilities. These components can be exploited if not properly secured or updated.
c. **Embedded Systems Weaknesses:** Embedded devices often lack basic security features due to limited resources and cost constraints, making them susceptible

to physical attacks and firmware tampering.

d. **Side-Channel Attacks:** Attackers exploit unintentional information leakage from hardware components, such as power consumption or electromagnetic emissions, to extract sensitive data.

Software Vulnerabilities

a. **Outdated Firmware:** Many smart devices do not receive regular updates, leaving them vulnerable to known exploits. Firmware updates are crucial for patching security holes.
b. **Insecure Code:** Poorly written software can introduce vulnerabilities such as buffer overflows, injection attacks, and insecure APIs.
c. **Open-Source Risks:** Many smart systems rely on open-source software components, which may contain vulnerabilities that attackers can exploit.
d. **API Vulnerabilities:** Insecure APIs expose smart systems to various threats, including injection attacks, unauthorized access, and data manipulation.

Network Vulnerabilities

a. **Unsecured Communication:** Data transmitted between devices and central systems can be intercepted if not encrypted. This can lead to data leakage and man-in-the-middle attacks.
b. **Weak Authentication:** Inadequate authentication mechanisms can allow unauthorized users to gain access to devices and data.
c. **IoT Botnets:** Botnets such as IoT_reaper and IoTroop have exploited vulnerabilities in IoT devices to launch large-scale attacks, underscoring the importance of securing IoT networks.
d. **Insecure Protocols:** The use of insecure communication protocols, such as HTTP and Telnet, exposes smart systems to data interception and manipulation.

CASE STUDIES OF SECURITY BREACHES

To illustrate the real-world impact of security breaches in smart systems, we can examine notable case studies that highlight the consequences of inadequate security measures.

a. **Mirai Botnet Attack:** In 2016, the Mirai botnet targeted IoT devices to launch massive DDoS attacks, affecting major websites and services. The attack exploited default usernames and passwords in IoT devices, demonstrating the importance of implementing strong authentication and regularly updating device firmware [8].

b. **Stuxnet Worm:** Stuxnet was a highly sophisticated computer worm that targeted industrial control systems, specifically programmable logic controllers (PLCs). It caused significant damage to Iran's nuclear program by manipulating the operations of centrifuges used for uranium enrichment [9]. The Stuxnet attack highlighted the vulnerabilities in industrial IoT systems and the potential for cyberattacks to have physical consequences.
c. **Target Data Breach:** In 2013, attackers gained access to Target's network by exploiting vulnerabilities in an HVAC (heating, ventilation, and air conditioning) system connected to the corporate network [10]. They were able to steal payment card information of over 40 million customers, demonstrating the risks associated with interconnected systems and the need for segmenting networks and implementing robust security measures.
d. **WannaCry Ransomware Attack:** In 2017, the WannaCry ransomware exploited a vulnerability in the Windows SMB protocol, infecting hundreds of thousands of computers worldwide, including IoT devices, by encrypting their data and demanding ransom payments. This widespread attack underscored the critical importance of promptly patching known vulnerabilities to prevent exploitation by malicious actors.
e. **Equifax Data Breach:** The Equifax data breach in 2017 exposed the personal data of over 147 million individuals due to a vulnerability in the company's web application software. This breach highlighted the risks associated with inadequate security measures and the severe consequences of data breaches, including identity theft and financial losses.
f. **NotPetya Cyberattack:** NotPetya was a destructive malware disguised as ransomware that spread rapidly in 2017, infecting systems worldwide, including critical infrastructure and IoT devices. The attack caused widespread disruption and financial losses, underscoring the need for robust cybersecurity strategies and incident response plans to mitigate the impact of such attacks.

These case studies serve as sobering reminders of the severe consequences that can result from security breaches in smart systems. They underscore the importance of implementing comprehensive security measures, regularly updating systems, and fostering a culture of security awareness across organizations and among users.

PRIVACY CONCERNS IN SMART SYSTEMS

While the benefits of smart systems are undeniable, their pervasive presence and data collection capabilities raise significant privacy concerns. As these systems integrate deeply into our daily lives, the potential for unauthorized access, data misuse, and erosion of privacy becomes a pressing issue that requires careful consideration and proactive measures.

Google's Use of GPS Data

Google, with its extensive array of services and applications, including Google Maps and location-based services, has been scrutinized for its utilization of users' GPS data. Through the ubiquitous presence of smartphones and other connected devices, Google collects vast amounts of location data, raising concerns about user privacy and the potential for surveillance [11].

The collection of GPS data enables Google to deliver personalized services, such as location-based recommendations and targeted advertisements. However, this practice also raises concerns about the potential misuse or unauthorized access to sensitive location information, highlighting the need for robust privacy safeguards and user consent mechanisms.

Facebook's Exploitation of Private Data

Facebook, the social media behemoth, has faced widespread criticism for its handling of users' private data. From the Cambridge Analytica scandal to ongoing controversies surrounding data privacy and security, Facebook's practices have drawn intense scrutiny from regulators, privacy advocates, and the public alike.

Facebook's business model relies heavily on the collection and analysis of user data to drive targeted advertising and user engagement [12]. However, the pervasive tracking of users' online activities, preferences, and interactions has raised significant concerns about the erosion of privacy and the potential for exploitation by malicious actors.

Frameworks for Privacy Protection

In response to growing concerns about privacy infringements in smart systems, several frameworks and initiatives have emerged to safeguard user data and uphold privacy rights. These frameworks emphasize principles such as data minimization, user control, and transparency in data practices. Some notable examples include:

1. **Privacy by Design**: This framework advocates for the integration of privacy considerations into the design and development of technology systems from the outset. By prioritizing privacy as a foundational principle, Privacy by Design aims to embed privacy protections into the architecture and functionality of smart systems.
2. **GDPR Compliance**: The General Data Protection Regulation (GDPR) establishes stringent requirements for the collection, processing, and storage of personal data, with provisions designed to enhance user privacy and data

protection rights. Compliance with GDPR standards entails implementing robust data governance practices, obtaining explicit user consent, and ensuring transparency in data handling processes.

3. **Privacy-Preserving Technologies**: Advancements in privacy-preserving technologies, such as differential privacy and homomorphic encryption, offer promising solutions for protecting sensitive user data while enabling meaningful data analysis and insights. These technologies allow for the anonymization or encryption of data to preserve privacy without compromising utility.

DATA COLLECTION AND USAGE

Smart systems collect vast amounts of data, often encompassing personal, behavioural, and environmental information. Fig. (**5**) illustrates Data Collection from Diverse Sources. The scope of data collection raises several privacy concerns:

Fig. (5). Image illustrating data collection from diverse sources.

a. **Personal Data:** Smart systems may collect and store sensitive personal data, including names, addresses, phone numbers, and other identifying information, raising concerns about data privacy and potential misuse.
b. **Behavioural Data:** Smart devices and systems can track user behaviour, preferences, and habits, such as daily routines, media consumption patterns, and online activities, enabling the creation of detailed user profiles.
c. **Environmental Data:** Smart systems collect information about users' environments, such as temperature, humidity, motion detection, and even

audio and video recordings, potentially revealing intimate details about their lives.

As these diverse data streams are collected, analysed, and often shared with third parties, users may have limited control over their personal information, leading to concerns about data ownership, consent, and potential surveillance.

USER CONSENT AND DATA OWNERSHIP

a. **Informed Consent:** For smart systems to respect user privacy, it is crucial that users are aware of what data is being collected and how it will be used [13]. However, many smart systems lack transparency, resulting in uninformed consent and the potential misuse of user data.
b. **Data Ownership:** Determining who owns the data collected by smart devices is a complex issue. Users often have limited control over their data once it is collected by service providers, raising questions about data sovereignty and the ability to manage personal information, as shown in fig. (**6**).

Fig. (6). Data control and ownership.

SURVEILLANCE AND TRACKING

a. **Surveillance:** Smart systems, with their ability to continuously monitor and collect data, raise concerns about potential surveillance and loss of privacy. Smart cameras, sensors, and other devices can track users' movements, activities, and behaviours, enabling unprecedented levels of monitoring as shown in Fig. (**7**).
b. **Tracking:** Location data collected by smart devices can be used to track users'

movements and locations, leading to potential misuse and privacy invasion. This information, when combined with other data streams, can create detailed profiles of individuals, raising ethical concerns about data usage and consent as shown in Fig. (**8**).

Fig. (7). Illustration of surveillance equipment and monitoring devices.

CASE STUDIES OF PRIVACY INVASIONS

To illustrate the real-world implications of privacy concerns in smart systems, we can examine notable case studies that highlight instances where user privacy was compromised or violated:

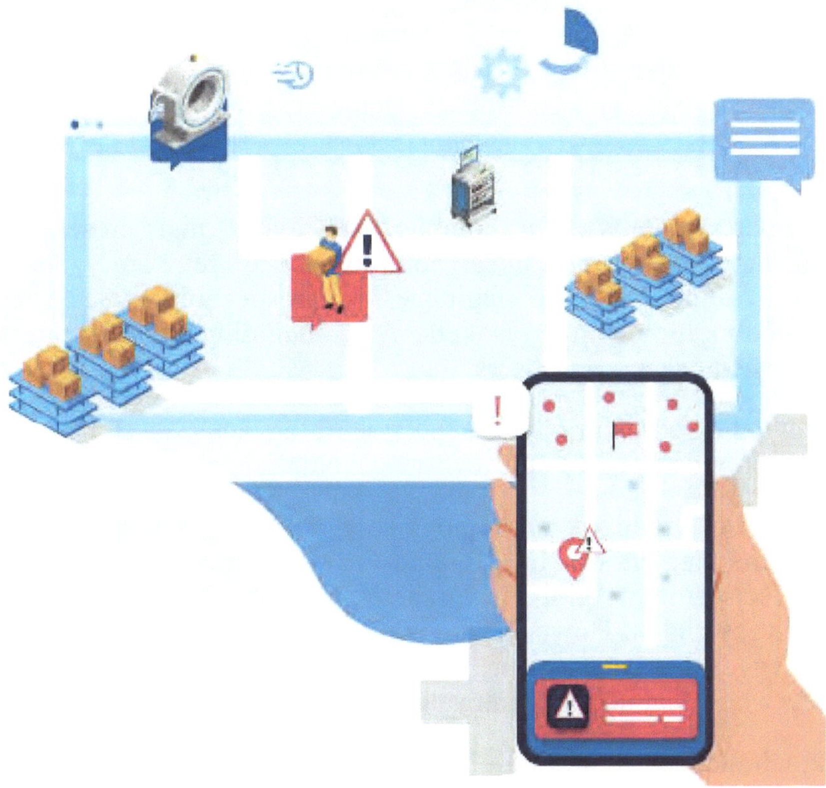

Fig. (8). Location tracking.

a. **Amazon Echo and Alexa:** There have been instances where Amazon Echo devices have recorded conversations without user knowledge or consent, raising concerns about potential privacy violations. These recordings can potentially be accessed by unauthorized parties or used by service providers without explicit user consent, undermining personal privacy.
b. **Smart TVs:** Several smart TV manufacturers have been found to collect and transmit viewing data without user consent. This data is often used for targeted advertising purposes, raising concerns about privacy and ethical questions regarding the collection and monetization of user data.
c. **Fitness Trackers:** Fitness trackers and wearable devices collect sensitive health and activity data, making them vulnerable to data breaches. Incidents involving fitness tracker data breaches have exposed users' personal health information, highlighting the need for robust privacy protections and secure data handling practices.

These case studies underscore the importance of addressing privacy concerns in smart systems. As these technologies become increasingly intertwined with our daily lives, it is imperative to strike a balance between innovation and user privacy, fostering trust and confidence in the adoption of smart systems.

CHALLENGES IN SECURING SMART SYSTEMS

Securing smart systems is a complex endeavour that presents numerous challenges, ranging from technical complexities to regulatory and economic hurdles [14]. Addressing these challenges requires a multifaceted approach that involves collaboration among stakeholders, including manufacturers, service providers, policymakers, and users.

Delving into the regulatory landscape governing smart systems security and privacy can provide insights into evolving compliance requirements:

The enactment of landmark regulations such as the European Union's General Data Protection Regulation (GDPR) and the California Consumer Privacy Act (CCPA) reflects growing global awareness of the need to protect user data and preserve privacy rights. However, navigating the complex regulatory landscape poses challenges for manufacturers and service providers seeking to ensure compliance while maintaining innovation and competitiveness.

Technical Challenges

1. **Scalability:** Securing a large number of interconnected devices is a daunting task. Each device must be individually secured, and the security measures must scale with the size and complexity of the network, making it challenging to maintain consistent and comprehensive protection.
2. **Resource Constraints:** Many smart devices, particularly IoT devices, have limited processing power and memory, making it difficult to implement robust security measures without compromising performance or functionality.
3. **Interoperability:** Smart systems often involve devices and components from different manufacturers, each with their own security protocols and standards. Ensuring compatibility and security across diverse devices and platforms is a significant challenge.

Regulatory and Legal Challenges

1. **Lack of Standards:** The absence of standardized security protocols and regulations makes it difficult to enforce consistent security measures across all smart systems. This lack of uniformity can lead to vulnerabilities and inconsistencies in security implementation.

2. **Compliance:** As smart systems become more prevalent, manufacturers and service providers must navigate a complex landscape of regional and international regulations governing data privacy, security, and consumer protection. Ensuring compliance with these varying regulations can be challenging, especially for global organizations operating across multiple jurisdictions.

Economic and Social Challenges

1. **Cost:** Implementing comprehensive security measures can be expensive, especially for low-cost devices or resource-constrained environments. Manufacturers may prioritize cost savings over security, which can lead to potential vulnerabilities.
2. **User Awareness:** Many users are unaware of the security risks associated with smart systems or lack the knowledge to implement proper security measures. Educating users about security best practices and fostering a culture of security awareness is crucial, but can be challenging.

Addressing these multifaceted challenges requires a collaborative effort among stakeholders, fostering an environment that prioritizes security and privacy while promoting technological advancement and user empowerment.

BEST PRACTICES FOR SECURITY AND PRIVACY IN SMART SYSTEMS

To mitigate the security and privacy risks associated with smart systems, it is essential to adopt a comprehensive approach that incorporates best practices throughout the system lifecycle. These best practices should address design principles, encryption and authentication, regular updates and patches, user education, and the adoption of emerging technologies.

Design Principles

1. **Security by Design:** Incorporating security measures into the design and development of smart systems, rather than adding them later, is crucial. This includes secure coding practices, regular security testing, and vulnerability assessments to identify and address potential risks proactively.
2. **Privacy by Design:** Embedding privacy considerations into the system design ensures that user data is protected and that privacy is maintained throughout the data lifecycle, is essential for building trust and fostering user confidence.

Encryption and Authentication

1. **Data Encryption:** Encrypting data both at rest (when stored) and in transit (during transmission) is a fundamental security measure that protects sensitive information from unauthorized access and interception.
2. **Strong Authentication:** Implementing multi-factor authentication and enforcing strong password policies is crucial to ensure that only authorized users can access smart devices and data. This helps prevent unauthorized access and mitigates the risk of credential theft.

Regular Updates and Patches

1. **Firmware Updates:** Providing regular firmware updates to address security vulnerabilities and improve device security is essential [15]. Smart device manufacturers should prioritize the timely release of security patches and facilitate the seamless deployment of updates.
2. **Automatic Updates:** Enabling automatic updates can ensure that devices receive the latest security patches without relying on user intervention, which can be unreliable or inconsistent.

User Education and Awareness

1. **Security Training:** Educating users about the security risks associated with smart systems and providing training on best practices for securing their devices is crucial. Comprehensive security training can empower users to play an active role in safeguarding their personal data and devices.
2. **Awareness Campaigns:** Conducting awareness campaigns to inform users about common threats, such as phishing, social engineering, and malware, can help users stay vigilant and take proactive measures to protect themselves.

Emerging Technologies and Approaches

As technology continues to evolve, new approaches and innovations offer promising solutions to enhance the security and privacy of smart systems.

Blockchain for Security

1. **Decentralized Security:** Utilizing blockchain technology to create decentralized security frameworks can reduce the risk of single points of failure and enhance data integrity by distributing trust across a network of nodes.
2. **Secure Transactions:** Leveraging blockchain for secure and transparent transactions can ensure data authenticity and tamper resistance, providing an additional layer of security for smart systems.

Artificial Intelligence and Machine Learning for Threat Detection

1. **Anomaly Detection:** Utilizing AI and machine learning algorithms to identify anomalies and potential security threats in real-time can facilitate proactive threat mitigation and enhance the overall security posture of smart systems.
2. **Predictive Security:** Developing predictive models using AI and machine learning enables the anticipation and prevention of security breaches before they occur, providing a proactive approach to threat management.

Secure Multi-Party Computation

1. **Data Privacy:** Secure multi-party computation enables multiple parties to jointly compute a function over their inputs while keeping those inputs private, enhancing data privacy in collaborative environments.
2. **Secure Collaboration:** Facilitating secure collaboration between different entities without compromising sensitive data is essential for smart systems that involve multiple stakeholders.

Privacy-Preserving Technologies

1. **Homomorphic Encryption:** Allowing computations to be performed on encrypted data without decrypting it can preserve data privacy during processing, providing an additional layer of protection for sensitive information.
2. **Differential Privacy:** Implementing differential privacy techniques can ensure that individual data points cannot be re-identified from aggregated datasets, safeguarding user privacy while enabling data analysis and insights.

By adopting these best practices and leveraging emerging technologies, stakeholders can enhance the security and privacy posture of smart systems, fostering trust and confidence among users while realizing the full potential of these innovative technologies.

FUTURE TRENDS AND DIRECTIONS

As smart systems continue to evolve and integrate deeper into our lives, it is crucial to anticipate and prepare for future challenges and opportunities [16]. By staying ahead of emerging trends and embracing innovative solutions, we can fortify the security and privacy of these systems, ensuring their responsible and sustainable development.

Predictive Security Models

1. **AI-Driven Security:** Leveraging artificial intelligence to develop predictive security models that can identify and mitigate threats before they materialize can revolutionize the way we approach security in smart systems [17 - 19].
2. **Behavioural Analysis:** Utilizing behavioural analysis techniques to detect unusual patterns and anticipate potential security breaches can enable proactive threat mitigation and enhance the overall security posture of smart systems [20 - 23].

Regulatory Evolution

1. **Global Standards:** Developing global security and privacy standards for smart systems can ensure consistent protection across regions and facilitate the seamless adoption of these technologies on a global scale.
2. **Regulatory Compliance:** Ensuring that smart systems comply with evolving regulations and standards will be crucial for protecting user data and privacy while fostering innovation and technological advancement.

Integration of Advanced Technologies

1. **Quantum Computing:** Exploring the impact of quantum computing on smart system security and developing quantum-resistant encryption algorithms will be essential to maintain the integrity and confidentiality of sensitive data.
2. **Edge Computing:** Implementing edge computing, where data processing and analysis occur closer to the source, can enhance security by reducing the need for data transmission and minimizing the risk of data breaches during transit.

CONCLUSION

Smart systems offer numerous benefits, but they also present significant security and privacy challenges. Addressing these concerns requires a comprehensive approach that includes robust design principles, encryption, authentication, regular updates, and user education. Emerging technologies such as blockchain, AI, and privacy-preserving techniques offer promising solutions to enhance security and privacy in smart systems.

As we navigate the ever-evolving landscape of smart technologies, it is imperative to strike a balance between innovation and responsible development. By fostering collaboration among stakeholders, embracing emerging technologies, and adapting to evolving regulatory frameworks, we can pave the way for a secure and private realm where smart systems thrive, realizing their full potential while safeguarding user trust and privacy.

FUTURE WORK

Proposing a secure and private realm for smart systems is crucial, as the trajectory of these technologies hinges on our ability to ensure their security and protect user privacy. Through the proposal of innovative strategies, the integration of emerging technologies, and the adaptation to evolving regulatory frameworks, we envision a future where smart systems thrive, realizing their full potential within a secure and private domain.

By fostering a collaborative approach that involves manufacturers, service providers, policymakers, and users, we can collectively address the multifaceted challenges inherent in securing smart systems. Embracing best practices, such as security by design, robust encryption, and user education, will lay the foundation for a trusted and responsible ecosystem.

Furthermore, the integration of cutting-edge technologies, such as blockchain, AI, and privacy-preserving techniques, will usher in a new era of enhanced security and data privacy. These innovations have the potential to revolutionize the way we approach security and privacy in smart systems, enabling decentralized security frameworks, predictive threat detection, and secure data processing.

As global standards and regulatory frameworks evolve, stakeholders must remain agile and adaptable, ensuring compliance while maintaining a spirit of innovation. By collaborating with policymakers and industry leaders, we can shape a regulatory landscape that fosters the responsible development and adoption of smart systems while safeguarding user rights and privacy.

Ultimately, the future of smart systems hinges on our collective ability to strike a delicate balance between technological advancement and ethical considerations. By prioritizing security and privacy from the outset, we can build a future where smart systems seamlessly integrate into our lives, offering convenience and efficiency while preserving the trust and confidence of users.

REFERENCES

[1] Acquisti and R. Gross, "Imagined communities: Awareness, information sharing, and privacy on the Facebook", In: *Privacy Enhancing Technologies.* Springer: Berlin, Heidelberg, 2006, pp. 36-58.

[2] S.K. Singh, M. Kumar, S. Tanwar, and J.H. Park, "GRU-based digital twin framework for data allocation and storage in IoT-enabled smart home networks", *Future Gener Comput Syst,* vol. 153, pp. 391-402, 2024.
[http://dx.doi.org/10.1016/j.future.2023.12.009]

[3] A. Narayanan, and V. Shmatikov, "Robust de-anonymization of large sparse datasets", *Proceedings of the IEEE Symposium on Security and Privacy (SP 2008),* pp. 111-125, 2008.
[http://dx.doi.org/10.1109/SP.2008.33]

[4] P. Ohm, "Broken promises of privacy: Responding to the surprising failure of anonymization", *UCLA*

Law Rev., vol. 57, p. 1701, 2010.

[5] P.M. Schwartz, and D.J. Solove, "The PII problem: Privacy and a new concept of personally identifiable information", *New York Univ. Law Rev.*, vol. 86, p. 1814, 2011.

[6] D.J. Solove, "'I've got nothing to hide' and other misunderstandings of privacy", *San Diego Law Rev.*, vol. 44, p. 745, 2007.

[7] L. Sweeney, "Simple demographics often identify people uniquely", *Health (San Francisco)*, vol. 671, pp. 1-34, 2000.

[8] A. A. Pise, "Adoption of blockchain technology for privacy and security in Industry 4.0," 2022.

[9] M. Klonowski, and M. Kutylowski, "Privacy-preserving data mining for smart systems", *Proceedings of the International Conference on Security and Cryptography,* Springer: Berlin, Heidelberg, pp. 175-189, 2012.

[10] S. Pearson, and A. Benameur, "Privacy, security, and trust in cloud computing", *Proceedings of the 3rd IEEE International Conference on Cloud Computing,* pp. 535-536, 2010.

[11] M.T. Goodrich, and R. Tamassia, "Privacy-preserving data structures and algorithms: A survey", *Proceedings of the International Conference on Cryptology in Africa,* Springer: Berlin, Heidelberg, pp. 158-179, 2011.

[12] A. A. Pise, *Internet of Things-System*, 2023.

[13] A. Cavoukian, "Privacy by design: The 7 foundational principles", *Identity in the Information Society,* vol. 4, no. 2, pp. 267-274, 2011.

[14] M. Hansen, and E.A. Rødland, "Privacy in location-based services: Requirements and challenges", *Proceedings of the European Intelligence and Security Informatics Conference,* pp. 119-126, 2013.

[15] B. Friedman, and H. Nissenbaum, "Bias in computer systems", *ACM Trans. Inf. Syst.*, vol. 14, no. 3, pp. 330-347, 1996.
[http://dx.doi.org/10.1145/230538.230561]

[16] R. Clarke, "Surveillance, dataveillance, and the security state", In: *Handbook of Surveillance Studies.* Routledge, 2019, pp. 63-72.

[17] A. A. Pise, "Enabling artificial intelligence of things (AIoT) healthcare architectures and security issues," 2022.
[http://dx.doi.org/10.1155/2022/8421434]

[18] S. Satpathy, P.K. Swain, S.N. Mohanty, and S.S. Basa, "Enhancing Security: Federated Learning against Man-In-The-Middle Threats with Gradient Boosting Machines and LSTM", *2024 IEEE International Conference on Advanced Video and Signal Based Surveillance (AVSS),* pp. 1-8, 2024.Niagara Falls, ON, Canada.
[http://dx.doi.org/10.1109/AVSS61716.2024.10672589]

[19] S. Chatterjee, S. Satpathy, and A. Nibedita, "Digital Investigation of Network Traffic Using Machine Learning. EAI Endorsed Scalable information", *System,* vol. 11, no. 1, 2023. https://publications.eai.eu/index.php/sis/article/view/4055

[20] C. Mallick, and S. Satpathy, "Challenges and design goals of wireless sensor networks: a state-of-the-art review", *Int. J. Comput. Appl.*, vol. 179, no. 28, pp. 42-47, 2018.
[http://dx.doi.org/10.5120/ijca2018916667]

[21] L. M. Pattnaik, P. K. Swain, S. Satpathy, and A. N. Panda, "Cloud DDoS Attack Detection Model with Data Fusion & Machine Learning Classifiers," *EAI Endorsed Transactions on Scalable Information Systems*, vol. 10, no. 6, 2023.
[http://dx.doi.org/10.4108/eetsis.3936]

[22] L. Pattnaik, S. Satpathy, B.K. Paikaray, and P.K. Swain, "DDoS analysis using machine learning: survey, issues, and future directions", *International Journal of Business Continuity and Risk*

Management, vol. 14, no. 1, pp. 57-76, 2024. [http://dx.doi.org/10.1504/IJBCRM.2024.137242]

[23] S. Satpathy, S. Mohanty, Ed., *Big Data Analytics and computing for digital forensic investigations.* Chemical Rubber Company Press: Boca Raton, 2020. [http://dx.doi.org/10.1201/9781003024743]

CHAPTER 11

Guardians of the Grid: Navigating Security and Privacy in Smart Systems

Anil Pise[1,*], **Dharma Teja Singampalli**[2], **Yogesh Khandokar**[3] and **Vrushali Deshpande**[4]

[1] *Cumulus Solutions, Johannesburg, South Africa*

[2] *Sagility, Bangalore, India*

[3] *Beamline Scientist MX, Australia*

[4] *D&M Tech, Pune, India*

Abstract: In the rapidly evolving landscape of technology, the intersection of smart systems and machine learning holds immense potential for shaping the future. This chapter explores the visionary outlook for smart systems and machine learning, envisioning transformative possibilities and pathways to their realization across diverse domains, while addressing the challenges and opportunities that accompany these groundbreaking technologies.

Keywords: Artificial intelligence (AI), Autonomous mobility, Algorithmic bias, Cybersecurity risks, Deep learning, Ethical considerations, Internet of things (IoT), Industry 4.0, Intelligent manufacturing, Machine learning, Personalized healthcare, Precision agriculture, Sustainable urbanization, Smart systems.

INTRODUCTION

As we stand at the cusp of a technological revolution, the integration of smart systems and machine learning emerges as a pivotal force driving innovation and progress. These technologies are poised to revolutionize industries, streamline processes, and enhance human experiences in unprecedented ways. This introductory section sets the stage for exploring the visionary landscape of smart systems and machine learning, their underlying principles, and their far-reaching implications [1].

* **Corresponding author Anil Pise:** Cumulus Solutions, Johannesburg, South Africa; E-mail: anil@cumulussolutions.co.za

Understanding Smart Systems and Machine Learning

Smart systems, as shown in Fig. (**1**), encompass a spectrum of interconnected devices and platforms designed to operate autonomously or semi-autonomously, leveraging advanced computational capabilities to perceive, analyze, and respond to their environment intelligently. These systems leverage a range of technologies, including the Internet of Things (IoT), artificial intelligence (AI), and sophisticated sensor networks, to gather and process data from the physical world.

Fig. (1). Smart system architecture.

At the core of smart systems lies machine learning, a subset of AI that enables these systems to learn from data, identify patterns, and make decisions without explicit programming. Machine learning algorithms are trained on vast datasets, allowing them to uncover intricate relationships and patterns that would be challenging or impossible for humans to discern manually.

Techniques such as neural networks, deep learning, and reinforcement learning enable machine learning algorithms to excel in a wide range of tasks, including image recognition, natural language processing, predictive analytics, and autonomous control [2]. These algorithms continuously refine their decision-making capabilities through iterative learning, adapting to new data and scenarios with remarkable flexibility as shown in Fig. (**2**).

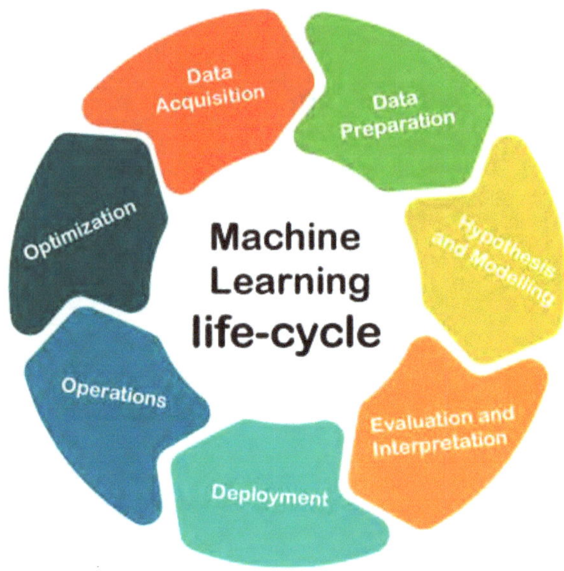

Fig. (2). Machine learning process.

Visionary Applications

The vision for the future of smart systems and machine learning extends across diverse domains, promising to redefine industries and revolutionize human experiences. In this section, we explore several visionary applications poised to reshape our world, highlighting their transformative potential and the profound impacts they may have on our daily lives.

Autonomous Mobility

Autonomous mobility as shown in Fig. (**3**), represents a transformative leap in transportation, where self-driving vehicles navigate roads seamlessly, offering safer, more efficient, and convenient travel experiences. Through the utilization of machine learning algorithms, these vehicles perceive their surroundings using a suite of sensors, including LiDAR (Light Detection and Ranging), radar, and high-resolution cameras, enabling them to make real-time decisions to navigate traffic, avoid obstacles, and ensure passenger safety.

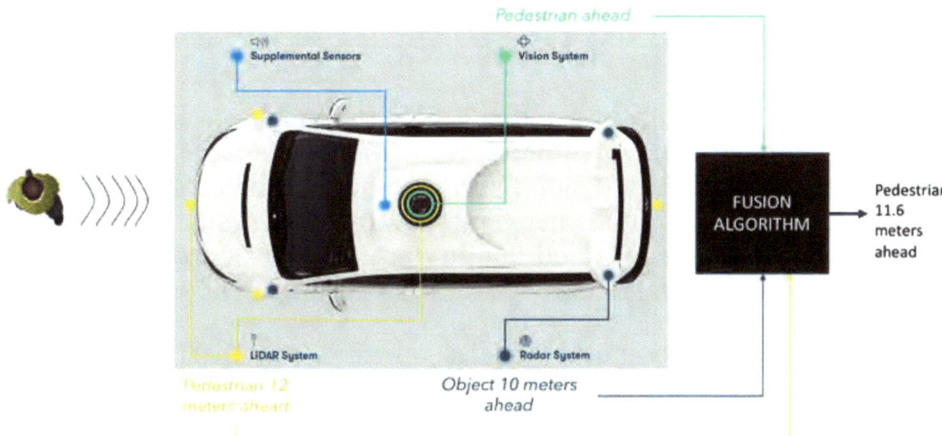

Fig. (3). Autonomous vehicle sensor fusion.

The widespread adoption of autonomous vehicles, as shown in Fig. (**4**), has the potential to significantly reduce traffic congestion, lower emissions, and enhance accessibility for individuals who are unable to operate traditional vehicles. By optimizing routing and minimizing idle time, these vehicles can contribute to a more sustainable and environmentally friendly transportation system.

Fig. (4). Integration of autonomous vehicles with 5G.

Moreover, autonomous mobility could revolutionize logistics and supply chain operations, enabling more efficient and cost-effective transportation of goods [3].

Autonomous trucks and delivery vehicles can operate continuously, reducing the need for human drivers and optimizing fuel consumption and route planning.

However, the successful integration of autonomous vehicles into our transportation infrastructure requires overcoming significant technical and regulatory challenges. Robust cybersecurity measures must be in place to protect these vehicles from potential hacking attempts or system vulnerabilities. Additionally, legal frameworks and liability protocols need to be established to govern the operation of autonomous vehicles and ensure public safety.

The vision of fully autonomous vehicles operating seamlessly on roads and highways is rapidly becoming a reality. Machine learning algorithms, trained on vast datasets of driving scenarios, traffic patterns, and road conditions, enable these vehicles to navigate complex environments and make real-time decisions to ensure safe and efficient travel.

One of the key enabling technologies for autonomous mobility is computer vision, which utilizes deep learning algorithms to process and interpret visual data from cameras and sensors. These algorithms can recognize and classify objects, detect pedestrians, read traffic signs, and understand the context of the surrounding environment, allowing the vehicle to respond appropriately.

Another critical component is motion planning and control systems, which utilize machine learning techniques to plan optimal routes, predict the behaviour of other vehicles and obstacles, and execute precise manoeuvres, such as lane changes and merging. These systems continuously adapt and refine their decision-making based on real-time data, ensuring smooth and safe navigation.

The integration of 5G and other advanced communication technologies will further enhance the capabilities of autonomous vehicles, enabling them to communicate with each other and with infrastructure systems, share real-time data, and coordinate movements to optimize traffic flow and reduce congestion.

While the potential benefits of autonomous mobility are immense, significant challenges must be addressed to ensure its safe and widespread adoption. Robust cybersecurity measures are crucial to protect these vehicles from potential hacking attempts or system vulnerabilities that could compromise passenger safety or enable malicious actors to gain control. Additionally, legal and regulatory frameworks must be established to govern the operation of autonomous vehicles, determine liability in the event of accidents, and ensure compliance with safety standards.

Personalized Healthcare

In the healthcare domain, smart systems driven by machine learning are set to revolutionize patient care through personalized medicine. By analysing vast datasets encompassing genomic information, medical records, and lifestyle factors, machine learning algorithms can tailor treatment strategies to individuals, predict disease risks, and optimize healthcare interventions, leading to improved outcomes and reduced healthcare costs.

Precision medicine, enabled by advanced genomic sequencing and machine learning techniques, allows for the development of targeted therapies tailored to an individual's unique genetic profile. This approach holds immense promise for more effective treatments, reduced side effects, and improved quality of life for patients.

Furthermore, smart healthcare systems can leverage wearable devices and remote monitoring technologies to continuously track patient vital signs and health indicators, enabling proactive interventions and preventive care measures as shown in Fig. (**5**). These systems can detect early warning signs of potential health issues, alerting healthcare providers and enabling timely interventions to prevent escalation or complications.

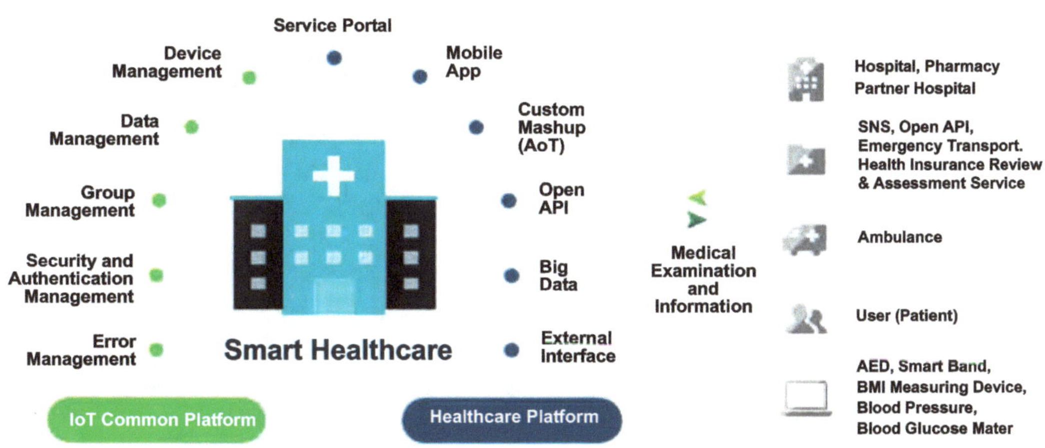

Fig. (5). Smart healthcare system overview.

Machine learning algorithms can also assist in medical imaging analysis, aiding radiologists and physicians in detecting and diagnosing diseases or anomalies with greater accuracy and efficiency [4]. By processing vast amounts of medical imaging data, these algorithms can identify subtle patterns and irregularities that may be challenging for human experts to discern.

However, the integration of smart systems and machine learning in healthcare also raises concerns regarding data privacy and security. Stringent measures must be implemented to safeguard sensitive patient information and ensure compliance with relevant regulations, such as the Health Insurance Portability and Accountability Act (HIPAA) in the United States.

The integration of intelligent systems and machine learning in healthcare holds the promise of transforming the way diseases are diagnosed, treated, and managed. By leveraging vast amounts of data, including electronic health records, genomic information, imaging data, and real-world evidence, machine learning algorithms can uncover patterns and insights that would be difficult or impossible for human experts to discern.

One of the most exciting applications of machine learning in healthcare is precision medicine, which tailors treatments to an individual's unique genetic makeup, lifestyle factors, and disease characteristics. Through advanced techniques such as deep learning and natural language processing, these algorithms can analyse complex datasets, including genomic sequencing data and medical literature, to identify personalized treatment strategies and predict patient responses to various therapies.

In the field of medical imaging, machine learning algorithms are already demonstrating remarkable capabilities in assisting radiologists and physicians in interpreting diagnostic scans. By training on vast datasets of annotated images, these algorithms can accurately detect and classify abnormalities, such as tumours or lesions, with greater speed and consistency than human experts. This not only improves diagnostic accuracy but also reduces the time and resources required for image analysis, enabling more efficient and timely patient care.

Moreover, smart systems integrated with wearable devices and remote monitoring technologies can revolutionize the management of chronic diseases. By continuously tracking vital signs, activity levels, and other health indicators, these systems can provide real-time feedback, personalized coaching, and early warnings of potential health issues, enabling proactive interventions and improving patient outcomes.

However, the widespread adoption of personalized healthcare powered by machine learning also presents significant challenges. Ensuring data privacy and security is paramount, as these systems rely on vast amounts of sensitive patient information. Robust cybersecurity measures, stringent data governance policies, and rigorous compliance with regulations such as HIPAA are crucial for maintaining public trust and safeguarding patient privacy.

Additionally, addressing potential biases and ensuring fairness in machine learning algorithms is crucial, as biased models can perpetuate existing healthcare disparities and lead to discriminatory outcomes. Ongoing efforts to develop bias-mitigation techniques, ensure diverse and representative training data, and foster transparency in algorithmic decision-making are critical for the responsible and equitable deployment of these technologies in healthcare.

Sustainable Urbanization

Smart cities epitomize the fusion of technology and urban development, offering sustainable solutions to pressing challenges such as congestion, pollution, and resource management. Leveraging IoT sensors, data analytics, and machine learning algorithms, smart cities optimize energy usage, enhance transportation systems, and promote environmental sustainability, thereby fostering livable urban environments for their inhabitants.

By integrating smart systems into urban infrastructure, as shown in Fig. (**6**), cities can monitor and manage resources more efficiently, reducing waste and promoting circular economies. Intelligent energy management systems can optimize power distribution and integrate renewable energy sources, contributing to a lower carbon footprint and increased energy efficiency.

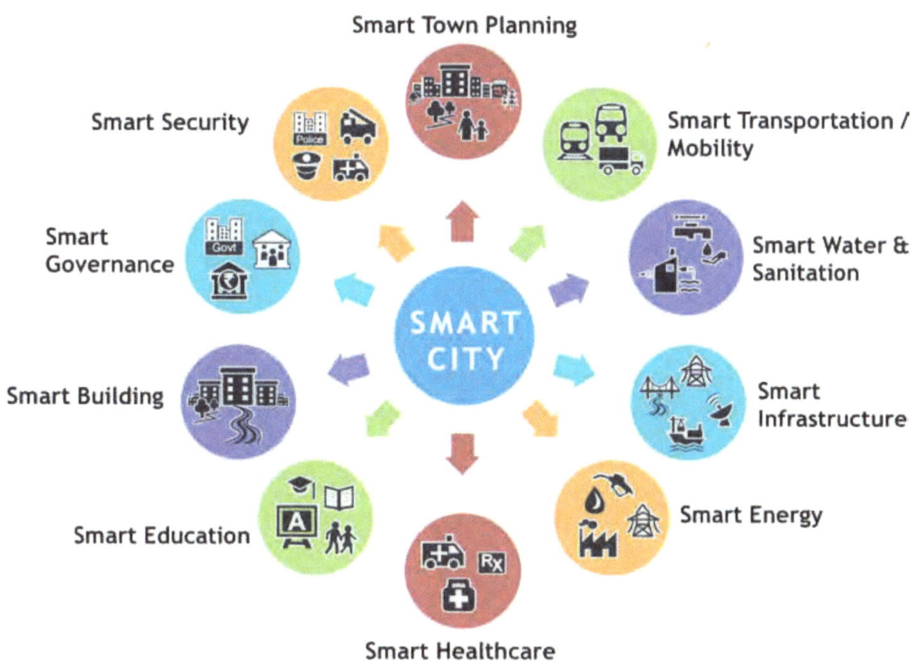

Fig. (6). Smart city infrastructure overview.

Additionally, intelligent traffic management systems can alleviate congestion by analysing real-time data from various sources, including traffic cameras, sensors, and crowdsourced data from connected vehicles. Machine learning algorithms can identify patterns and predict traffic flow, enabling dynamic routing and signal optimization to reduce travel times and emissions.

Smart waste management solutions can optimize collection routes and schedules based on real-time data, minimizing unnecessary trips and reducing operational costs. Furthermore, sensor networks can monitor air and water quality, enabling the implementation of proactive measures to address environmental concerns and enhance public health.

However, the realization of smart cities requires significant investment in infrastructure, data collection mechanisms, and robust cybersecurity measures to protect against potential threats and vulnerabilities. Collaboration between local governments, technology providers, and urban planners is crucial to ensure the seamless integration of smart systems and the effective utilization of data for sustainable urban development.

As urbanization continues to accelerate globally, the vision of smart cities offers a pathway towards sustainable and liveable urban environments. By leveraging the power of smart systems and machine learning, cities can optimize resource management, enhance mobility, and promote environmental sustainability, while improving the quality of life for residents.

At the core of smart city initiatives lies the Internet of Things (IoT), a network of interconnected devices and sensors that collect and transmit data from the urban environment. This data, combined with advanced analytics and machine learning algorithms, enables city planners and decision-makers to gain valuable insights and make informed decisions across various domains.

In the realm of energy management, smart grids and intelligent building management systems can optimize energy usage by integrating renewable sources, implementing demand response strategies, and automating lighting and climate control based on occupancy patterns and environmental conditions. Machine learning algorithms can analyse historical data and real-time usage patterns to predict energy demand, enabling proactive load balancing and minimizing waste.

Transportation and mobility are critical areas where smart systems and machine learning can have a significant impact. Intelligent traffic management systems can monitor real-time traffic conditions using sensors, cameras, and crowdsourced data from connected vehicles. By analysing this data, machine learning algorithms can optimize signal timing, suggest alternative routes, and provide real-time traffic updates to commuters, ultimately reducing congestion, emissions, and travel times.

Moreover, the integration of autonomous vehicles and smart public transportation networks can further enhance urban mobility, providing residents and visitors alike with convenient and environmentally friendly transportation options.

Waste management is another area where smart cities can make significant strides towards sustainability. Sensor-equipped waste bins and intelligent routing algorithms can optimize collection schedules and routes, minimizing unnecessary trips and reducing operational costs. Additionally, advanced sorting and recycling technologies driven by machine learning can improve resource recovery and promote circular economies.

However, the realization of smart city visions requires substantial investments in infrastructure, data collection mechanisms, and robust cybersecurity measures to protect against potential threats and vulnerabilities. Collaboration between local governments, technology providers, urban planners, and community stakeholders is crucial to ensure the seamless integration of smart systems and the effective utilization of data for sustainable urban development.

Intelligent Manufacturing and Industry 4.0

The integration of smart systems and machine learning is driving the Fourth Industrial Revolution, also known as Industry 4.0. This revolution encompasses the digitalization and automation of manufacturing processes, enabling increased efficiency, productivity, and customization.

Smart factories, as shown in Fig. (7), leverage IoT sensors, robotics, and machine learning algorithms to optimize production lines, monitor equipment performance, and predict maintenance needs. Predictive maintenance algorithms can analyse sensor data to detect anomalies or potential failures, enabling proactive maintenance and reducing downtime.

Moreover, machine learning algorithms can optimize manufacturing processes by identifying bottlenecks, optimizing resource allocation, and minimizing waste [5]. These algorithms can continuously learn and adapt to changing conditions, enabling real-time adjustments and improvements.

Fig. (7). Smart factory overview.

Additive manufacturing, also known as 3D printing, combined with machine learning, opens up new possibilities for customized and on-demand production. Machine learning algorithms can optimize design parameters, material selection, and printing processes, enabling the creation of complex and tailored products with unprecedented efficiency and precision.

However, the successful implementation of Industry 4.0 requires addressing challenges related to data security, interoperability, and workforce training. Robust cybersecurity measures must be in place to protect critical industrial systems and data from potential threats. Additionally, workers will need to be retrained and upskilled to operate and maintain these advanced systems, necessitating collaboration between industry and educational institutions.

The Fourth Industrial Revolution, or Industry 4.0, represents a paradigm shift in manufacturing processes, driven by the convergence of smart systems, machine learning, and advanced automation technologies. This revolution promises to transform factories into intelligent, interconnected, and highly efficient production environments, reshaping the way goods are designed, produced, and delivered.

At the heart of intelligent manufacturing lies the concept of the smart factory, where every aspect of the production process is interconnected and optimized through the integration of IoT sensors, robotics, and machine learning algorithms. These smart factories utilize data collected from various sources, including production lines, quality control systems, and supply chain networks, to gain real-time insights and facilitate proactive decision-making.

Predictive maintenance is a key application of machine learning in intelligent manufacturing. By continuously monitoring sensor data from machinery and equipment, machine learning algorithms can detect anomalies, predict potential failures, and recommend preventive maintenance actions, minimizing unplanned downtime and reducing operational costs.

Moreover, machine learning algorithms can optimize production processes by identifying bottlenecks, optimizing resource allocation, and minimizing waste. These algorithms can continuously learn and adapt to changing conditions, enabling real-time adjustments and improvements in production schedules, inventory management, and supply chain logistics.

Additive manufacturing, also known as 3D printing, combined with machine learning, opens up new possibilities for customized and on-demand production. Generative design algorithms can explore vast design spaces and optimize product designs based on specified performance criteria, material properties, and manufacturing constraints. Machine learning algorithms can also optimize the 3D printing process itself, ensuring consistent quality and minimizing defects.

However, the successful implementation of Industry 4.0 requires addressing several challenges. Cybersecurity is a critical concern, as interconnected systems and data networks are susceptible to potential cyber threats. Robust security measures, including encryption, access control, and real-time monitoring, are crucial for protecting intellectual property, sensitive data, and critical infrastructure.

Additionally, the integration of intelligent manufacturing systems requires significant investments in infrastructure, data acquisition systems, and training for the workforce. Workers will need to be reskilled and upskilled to operate and maintain these advanced systems, necessitating collaboration between industry and educational institutions to develop comprehensive training programs.

Furthermore, the adoption of intelligent manufacturing technologies raises concerns about data governance and privacy. As vast amounts of data are collected and processed, robust data management policies and protocols must be established to ensure compliance with relevant regulations and protect sensitive information, such as trade secrets and proprietary data.

Despite these challenges, the potential benefits of intelligent manufacturing and Industry 4.0 are immense. By leveraging the power of smart systems and machine learning, manufacturers can achieve unprecedented levels of efficiency, flexibility, and customization, while reducing waste, minimizing environmental impact, and delivering high-quality products at lower costs.

Intelligent Assistants and Human-Machine Interaction

Intelligent assistants, as shown in Fig. (**8**), powered by natural language processing (NLP) and machine learning, are transforming the way we interact with technology. These virtual assistants can understand and respond to human speech, interpret context, and perform a wide range of tasks, from scheduling appointments and managing to-do lists to providing personalized recommendations and controlling smart home devices.

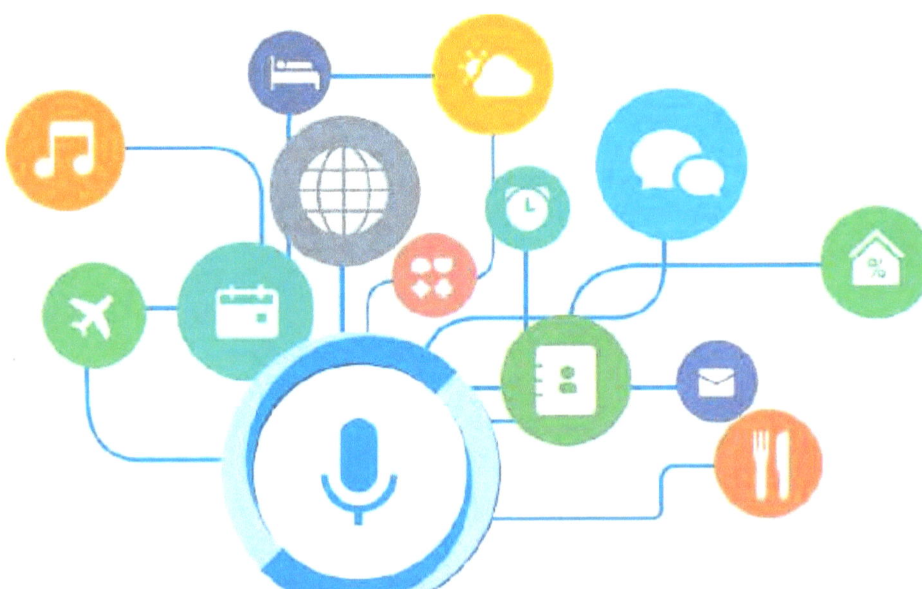

Fig. (8). Intelligent assistant framework.

As machine learning algorithms continue to advance, intelligent assistants will become increasingly sophisticated, capable of engaging in more natural and contextual conversations, and adapting to individual user preferences and behaviours.

Moreover, the integration of intelligent assistants with other smart systems, such as autonomous vehicles and healthcare devices, opens up new possibilities for enhanced user experiences and seamless interactions across multiple platforms and devices [6].

However, the development of intelligent assistants also raises concerns regarding privacy and data security. These systems often collect and process vast amounts of personal data, including voice recordings, location information, and usage patterns. Robust privacy measures and transparent data handling policies are crucial for maintaining user trust and ensuring compliance with relevant regulations.

As artificial intelligence and natural language processing technologies advance, intelligent virtual assistants are poised to become an integral part of our daily lives, revolutionizing the way we interact with technology and access information. These AI-powered assistants, capable of understanding and responding to human speech and text inputs, offer a more natural and intuitive interface for a wide range of tasks and applications.

One of the key drivers of intelligent assistant technology is the rapid progress in natural language processing (NLP) and machine learning. NLP algorithms, trained on vast datasets of human language, can interpret contextual cues, understand intent, and generate responses that are human-like. Machine learning techniques, such as deep learning and reinforcement learning, enable these assistants to continuously improve their performance and adapt to individual user preferences and behaviours.

Intelligent assistants are becoming increasingly adept at handling complex queries and tasks, ranging from scheduling appointments and managing to-do lists to providing personalized recommendations and controlling smart home devices. By integrating with other smart systems and leveraging contextual data from sensors and user activity, these assistants can anticipate user needs and proactively offer relevant information or suggestions.

In the realm of customer service and support, intelligent assistants can provide 24/7 assistance, answering queries, troubleshooting issues, and guiding users through complex processes. Their ability to handle natural language interactions and quickly access vast knowledge bases can greatly enhance the customer experience and reduce response times.

Moreover, intelligent assistants are finding applications in healthcare, education, and accessibility domains. Virtual healthcare assistants can provide personalized guidance, medication reminders, and symptom monitoring, while educational assistants can offer customized learning experiences and adaptive tutoring. For individuals with disabilities, intelligent assistants can serve as powerful tools for communication, task assistance, and independence.

However, the widespread adoption of intelligent assistants raises concerns regarding privacy and data security. As these systems collect and process vast amounts of personal data, including voice recordings, location information, and usage patterns, robust privacy measures and transparent data handling policies are crucial to maintaining user trust and ensuring compliance with relevant regulations.

Additionally, the development of intelligent assistants must address potential biases and ethical considerations. These systems should be designed to respect user autonomy, promote inclusivity, and avoid perpetuating harmful stereotypes or discrimination.

Intelligent Agriculture and Food Production

Smart systems and machine learning are poised to revolutionize the agriculture and food production industries, enabling more sustainable and efficient practices while addressing the growing global demand for food.

Precision agriculture techniques, as illustrated in Fig. (**9**), enabled by IoT sensors, drones, and machine learning algorithms, enable the precise monitoring and management of crops, soil conditions, and resources. By analysing data on factors such as weather patterns, soil moisture, and pest infestations, these systems can optimize irrigation schedules, minimize water usage, and target the application of fertilizers and pesticides, reducing waste and environmental impact.

Machine learning algorithms can also assist in crop yield prediction by analysing historical data, weather forecasts, and remote sensing data from satellites or drones. This predictive capability enables farmers to make informed decisions about planting, harvesting, and resource allocation, potentially increasing yields and profitability.

Furthermore, smart greenhouse systems can create optimal growing conditions by automating and controlling various factors such as temperature, humidity, lighting, and nutrient delivery. Machine learning algorithms can continuously optimize these conditions based on real-time data, maximizing crop growth and quality.

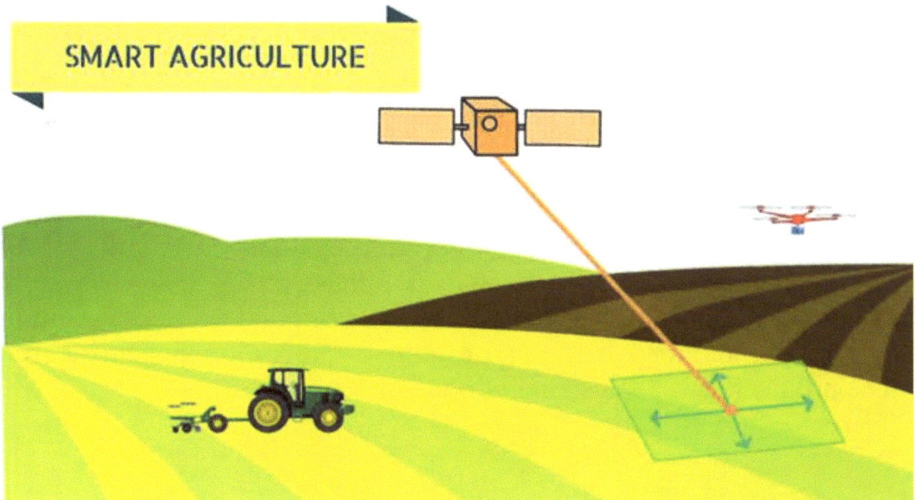

Fig. (9). Precision agriculture overview.

In the livestock sector, smart systems can monitor animal health and behaviour, enabling early detection of potential issues and facilitating timely interventions. Additionally, machine learning algorithms can optimize feed formulations and breeding programs, improving productivity and animal welfare.

However, the adoption of these technologies in agriculture and food production may face challenges related to infrastructure, connectivity, and data accessibility in remote or underdeveloped areas. Moreover, concerns about data privacy and the potential for technology to disrupt traditional farming practices must be addressed through inclusive policies and education initiatives.

As the global population continues to grow and the demand for food increases, the integration of smart systems and machine learning into agriculture and food production becomes crucial for ensuring sustainable and efficient practices. These technologies offer the potential to optimize resource utilization, enhance crop yields, and minimize environmental impact, while addressing the challenges of climate change and resource scarcity.

Precision agriculture, enabled by IoT sensors, drones, and machine learning algorithms, allows for highly targeted and data-driven decision-making at every stage of the crop cycle. By continuously monitoring soil conditions, weather patterns, and crop health, these systems can provide real-time insights and recommendations for precise irrigation scheduling, targeted fertilizer application, and early detection of pests or diseases.

Moreover, machine learning algorithms can analyse historical data, weather forecasts, and remote sensing data from satellites or drones to predict crop yields and optimize planting schedules, enabling farmers to make informed decisions about resource allocation and market strategies.

In the livestock sector, smart systems can revolutionize animal husbandry practices by monitoring animal health, behavior, and environmental conditions, as shown in Fig. (**10**). Machine learning algorithms can analyze data from wearable sensors and cameras to detect early signs of illness or distress, enabling timely interventions and improving animal welfare. Additionally, these algorithms can optimize feed formulations, breeding programs, and herd management strategies to enhance productivity and sustainability.

Fig. (10). Livestock monitoring system.

Vertical farming and controlled environment agriculture (CEA) represent another promising area where smart systems and machine learning can contribute to sustainable food production. By integrating IoT sensors, automation systems, and machine learning algorithms, these controlled environments can optimize growing conditions, such as temperature, humidity, lighting, and nutrient delivery, resulting in higher yields, reduced water usage, and year-round production capabilities.

However, the widespread adoption of these technologies in agriculture and food production faces challenges related to infrastructure, connectivity, and data accessibility in remote or underdeveloped areas. Additionally, concerns about data privacy, security, and the potential disruption of traditional farming practices must be addressed through inclusive policies, education initiatives, and stakeholder engagement.

Overcoming these challenges will require collaboration among farmers, agri-tech companies, researchers, and policymakers. By fostering knowledge sharing, developing user-friendly interfaces, and providing training and support, the benefits of intelligent agriculture and food production can be extended to diverse communities, promoting food security and sustainable practices on a global scale.

Smart Retail and Customer Experiences

The retail industry is undergoing a profound transformation driven by the integration of smart systems and machine learning technologies [7]. These technologies are enabling personalized and immersive shopping experiences, optimizing supply chain management, and facilitating data-driven decision-making, thereby reshaping the way consumers interact with brands and make purchasing decisions.

In brick-and-mortar stores, machine learning algorithms can analyse customer behaviour and preferences through data collected from various sources, such as in-store cameras, sensors, and mobile applications. By understanding shopping patterns, dwell times, and product interactions, these algorithms can provide real-time insights to retailers, enabling them to optimize store layouts, product placements, and personalized promotions as shown in Fig. (**11**).

Moreover, intelligent assistants powered by natural language processing can provide personalized support and guidance to customers, answering queries, suggesting products, and facilitating seamless transactions. These assistants can be integrated into mobile apps, kiosks, or even as virtual avatars within the store, enhancing the overall shopping experience.

In the e-commerce realm, machine learning algorithms can analyse browsing patterns, purchase histories, and customer reviews to provide highly personalized product recommendations and targeted marketing campaigns. By understanding individual preferences and behaviour, these algorithms can present relevant products, offers, and content, increasing customer engagement and driving sales.

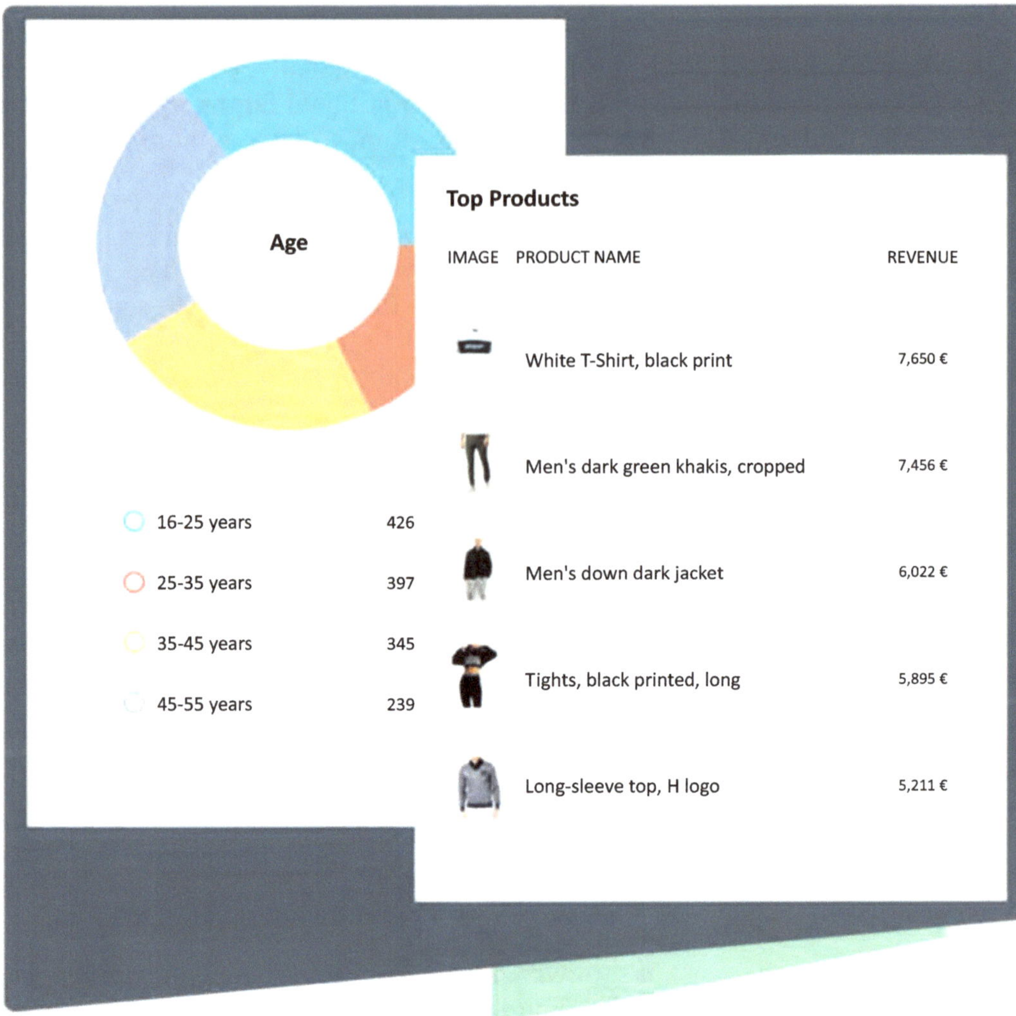

Fig. (11). In-store analytics system.

Additionally, machine learning techniques can optimize pricing strategies, inventory management, and supply chain logistics as shown in Fig. (**12**), reducing costs and improving operational efficiency [8]. Predictive analytics can forecast demand patterns, enabling proactive inventory planning and minimizing stockouts or overstocking situations.

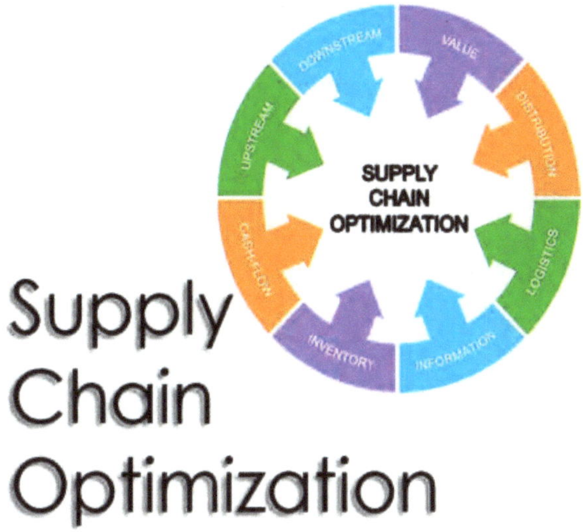

Fig. (12). Supply chain optimization framework.

Augmented reality (AR) and virtual reality (VR) technologies, combined with machine learning, are also transforming the retail experience. Customers can virtually try on clothing, visualize furniture in their homes, or explore interactive virtual showrooms, enhancing the decision-making process and reducing product returns.

However, the widespread adoption of smart retail t echnologies raises privacy concerns related to the collection and use of customer data. Transparent data policies, strict security measures, and adherence to relevant regulations are crucial for maintaining customer trust and ensuring responsible data handling practices.

Furthermore, the integration of these technologies may disrupt traditional retail models and job roles, necessitating the reskilling of the workforce and adaptation to new processes and technologies. Collaborative efforts among retailers, technology providers, and educational institutions will be crucial to facilitating a smooth transition and ensuring a well-trained workforce.

Challenges and Opportunities

Despite the immense promise of smart systems and machine learning, their widespread adoption and successful implementation are accompanied by significant challenges and opportunities. In this section, we explore some of the key considerations that must be addressed to realize the potential of these transformative technologies fully.

Ethical and Privacy Concerns

As smart systems become increasingly pervasive, concerns around ethical implications and privacy arise [9]. The collection and processing of vast amounts of personal data raises questions about data privacy, security, and potential misuse. Additionally, the decision-making processes of machine learning algorithms may perpetuate societal biases or lead to unfair discrimination if not properly designed and regulated, as shown in Fig. (**13**).

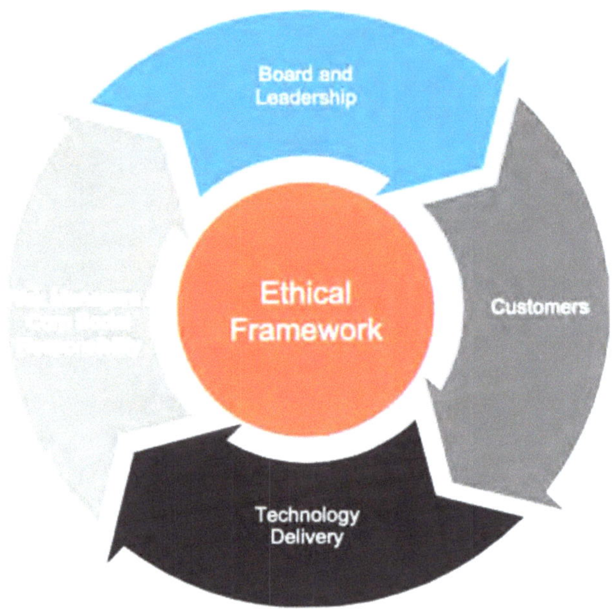

Fig. (13). Ethical framework for smart systems.

One of the key ethical challenges lies in the principle of accountability and transparency. Machine learning algorithms, particularly deep learning models, often operate as "black boxes," making it difficult to understand the reasoning behind their decisions or outputs. This lack of transparency can be problematic in high-stakes situations, such as medical diagnoses or judicial decisions, where the ability to explain and justify the decisions is crucial.

Moreover, the use of personal data in machine learning systems raises privacy concerns, particularly in cases where sensitive information, such as health records or financial data, is involved. Robust data protection measures, including anonymization and encryption techniques, must be implemented to safeguard individual privacy and ensure compliance with relevant regulations, such as the General Data Protection Regulation (GDPR) in the European Union.

To address these concerns, it is crucial to establish robust ethical frameworks, regulatory policies, and governance models that prioritize transparency, accountability, and the protection of individual rights. Multidisciplinary collaboration among technologists, policymakers, ethicists, and legal experts is essential to navigate these complex issues.

Algorithmic Biases and Fairness

Machine learning algorithms are susceptible to biases present in the training data or introduced during the model development process [10]. These biases can lead to unfair or discriminatory outcomes, particularly in sensitive domains such as criminal justice, employment, and financial services.

One of the primary sources of algorithmic bias is the use of biased or non-representative training data. If the data used to train a machine learning model reflects historical biases or lacks diversity, the model may perpetuate and amplify those biases in its decisions or predictions as shown in Fig. (**14**).

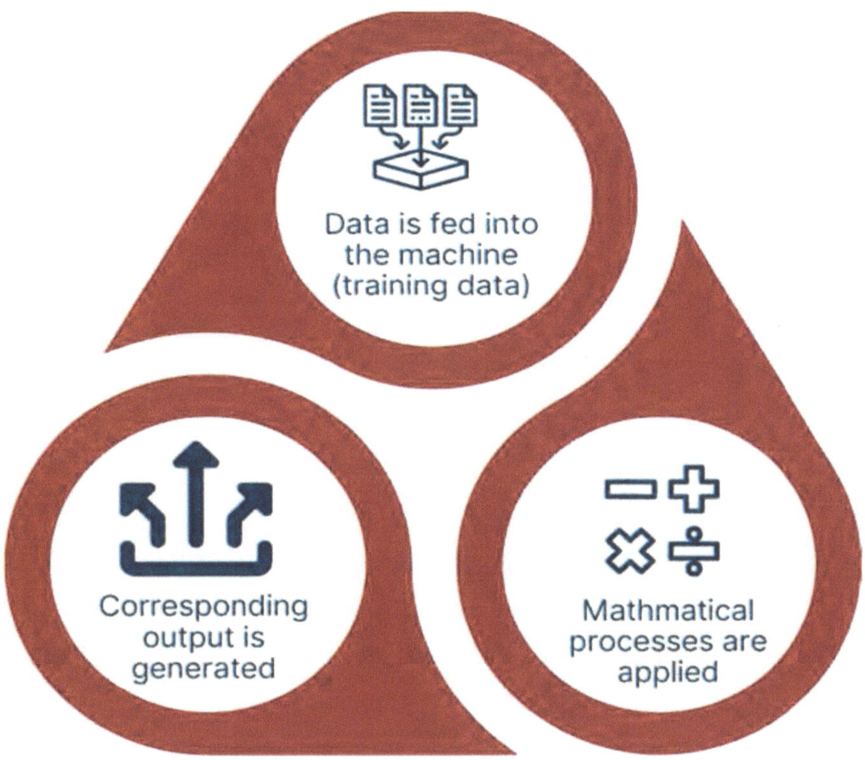

Fig. (14). Addressing algorithmic biases.

Another form of bias can arise from the design and development process itself, where the choices made by researchers or developers, such as feature selection or model architecture, can inadvertently introduce biases.

Addressing algorithmic biases requires a concerted effort to ensure the diversity and representativeness of training data, as well as the development of bias-mitigation techniques and fairness-aware machine learning models. Techniques such as adversarial debiasing, constrained optimization, and causal modelling can help mitigate biases and promote fairness in machine learning systems.

Continuous monitoring, evaluation, and auditing of these systems are necessary to detect and mitigate potential biases throughout their lifecycle. Collaboration among researchers, domain experts, and affected communities is crucial to understanding the real-world impacts of these systems and ensuring that they align with societal values and ethical principles.

Cybersecurity Risks

The proliferation of interconnected devices and smart systems amplifies cybersecurity risks, as these systems become increasingly vulnerable to malicious actors seeking to exploit vulnerabilities or disrupt operations. The consequences of successful cyberattacks can be severe, ranging from data breaches and privacy violations to disruptions in critical infrastructure and services.

As smart systems become increasingly integrated into various aspects of our lives, from transportation and healthcare to energy grids and manufacturing processes, the potential impact of cyber threats becomes more significant. A breach or malfunction in these systems could have far-reaching consequences, potentially endangering human lives, compromising sensitive data, or causing widespread disruptions as shown in Fig. (**15**).

Robust cybersecurity measures and protocols, including secure communication channels, encryption, access control mechanisms, and real-time threat detection and response systems, are crucial for safeguarding smart systems and protecting sensitive data. Regular software updates and vulnerability assessments are crucial to addressing emerging threats and ensuring the resilience of these systems.

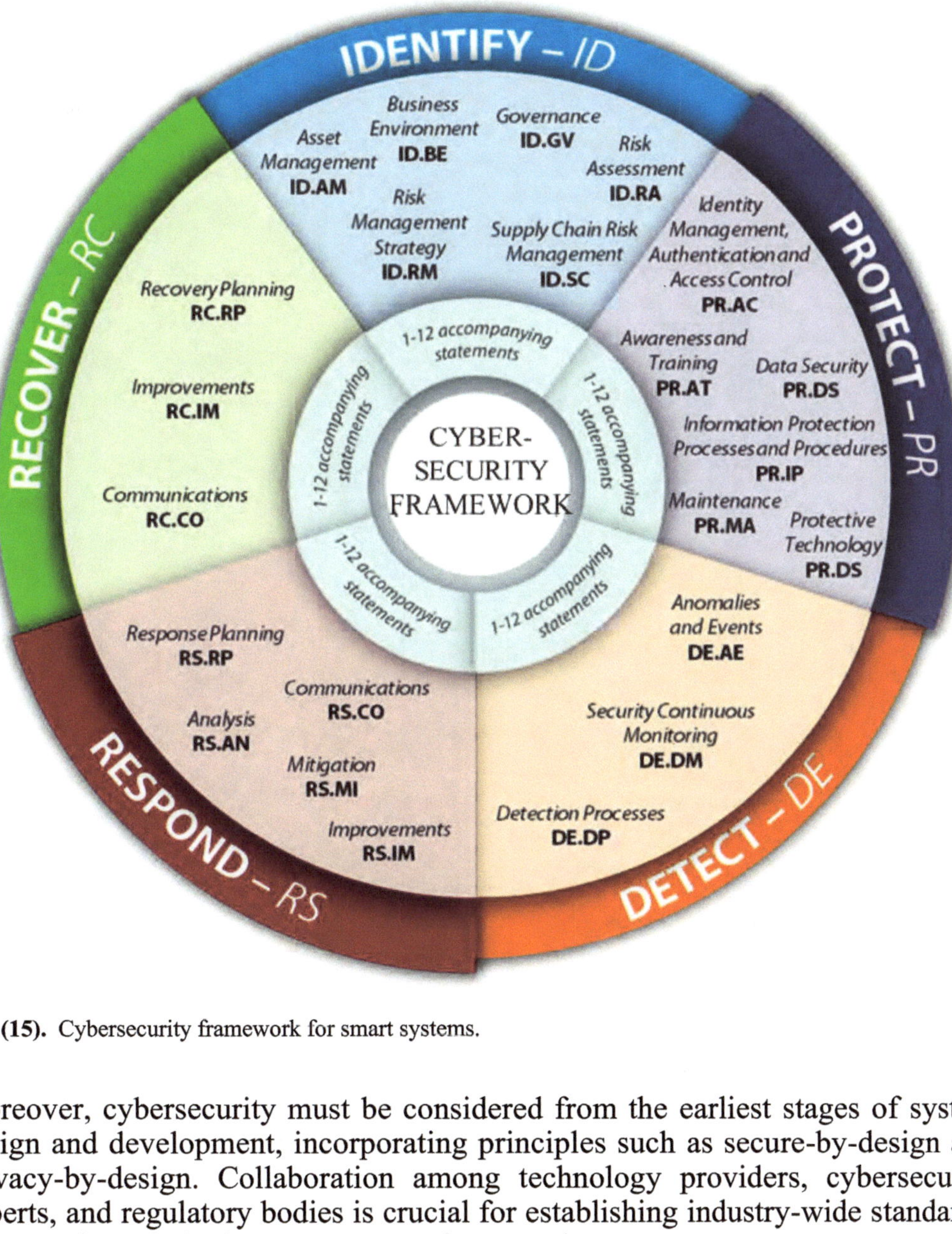

Fig. (15). Cybersecurity framework for smart systems.

Moreover, cybersecurity must be considered from the earliest stages of system design and development, incorporating principles such as secure-by-design and privacy-by-design. Collaboration among technology providers, cybersecurity experts, and regulatory bodies is crucial for establishing industry-wide standards, best practices, and robust governance frameworks.

Workforce Transformation and Skill Development

The widespread adoption of smart systems and automation technologies is expected to disrupt traditional job markets and workforce dynamics. While new employment opportunities may emerge in areas such as data science, AI development, and system maintenance, specific roles and tasks may become obsolete or require significant reskilling, as shown in Fig. (**16**).

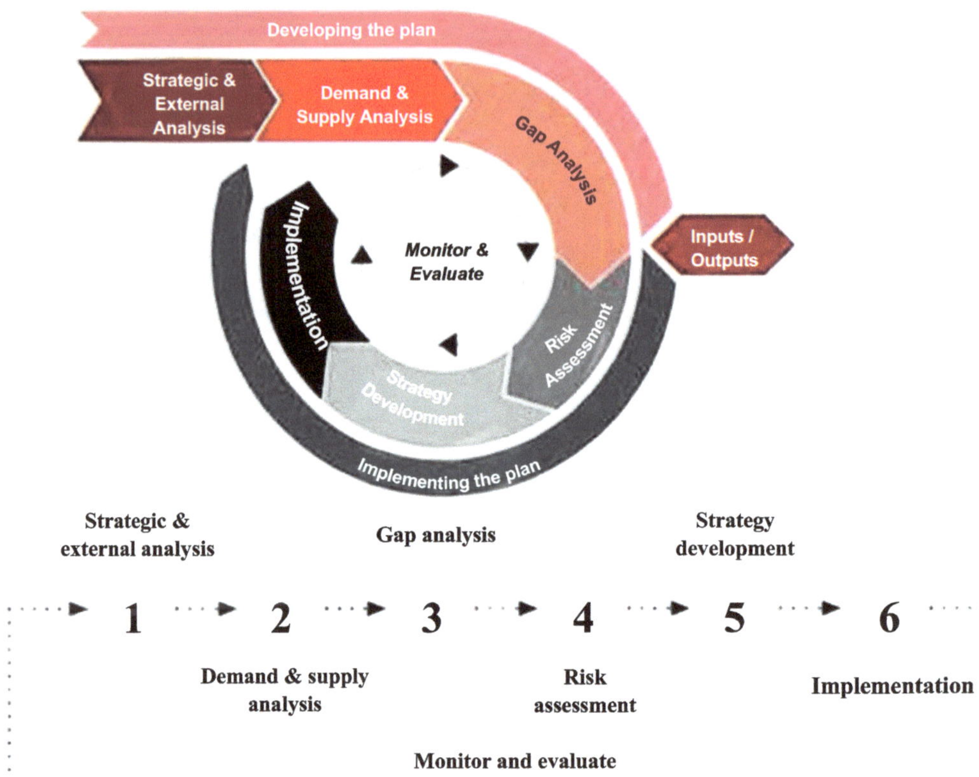

Fig. (16). Workforce transformation strategies.

As automated systems and machine learning algorithms take over routine and repetitive tasks, many jobs involving manual labour, data entry, or rule-based decision-making may be impacted. However, this disruption also presents opportunities for human workers to transition into roles that leverage their unique cognitive abilities, creativity, and interpersonal skills.

To mitigate the potential negative impacts on employment and facilitate a smooth transition, proactive measures must be taken to reskill and retrain the workforce. Educational institutions, governments, and industry leaders must collaborate to develop curricula and training programs that equip individuals with the necessary skills to thrive in the era of smart systems and machine learning.

These efforts should focus on developing skills in areas such as data analysis, programming, critical thinking, and problem-solving. Additionally, soft skills like communication, adaptability, and lifelong learning should be emphasized to enable workers to navigate the rapidly changing job landscape.

Moreover, policies and initiatives aimed at supporting workforce transitions, such as retraining programs, income support, and job placement assistance, can help mitigate the potential disruptive impacts and ensure a more equitable distribution of the benefits brought about by technological advancements.

Embracing the Vision: A Collaborative Effort

The realization of the vision for smart systems and machine learning necessitates a collaborative effort among various stakeholders, including researchers, technologists, policymakers, ethicists, and the broader society. By fostering interdisciplinary partnerships and open dialogue, we can address the challenges, mitigate risks, and harness the transformative potential of these technologies for the betterment of humanity.

Research and Innovation

Continuous research and innovation are vital to advancing the capabilities of smart systems and machine learning, while also addressing the accompanying challenges. Academic institutions, research labs, and industry partners must invest in exploring new frontiers, developing novel algorithms and techniques, and pushing the boundaries of what is possible, as shown in Fig. (**17**).

Interdisciplinary collaboration is key, as the development of smart systems and machine learning requires expertise from diverse fields, including computer science, engineering, mathematics, neuroscience, and domain-specific knowledge areas. By bringing together researchers from different backgrounds, we can foster cross-pollination of ideas, identify new applications, and tackle complex problems from multiple perspectives.

Furthermore, open sharing of research findings, reproducible experiments, and accessible datasets can accelerate progress and enable a broader community of researchers and developers to contribute to the field. Initiatives such as open-source software, collaborative platforms, and preprint servers can facilitate knowledge dissemination and foster a culture of transparency and collaboration.

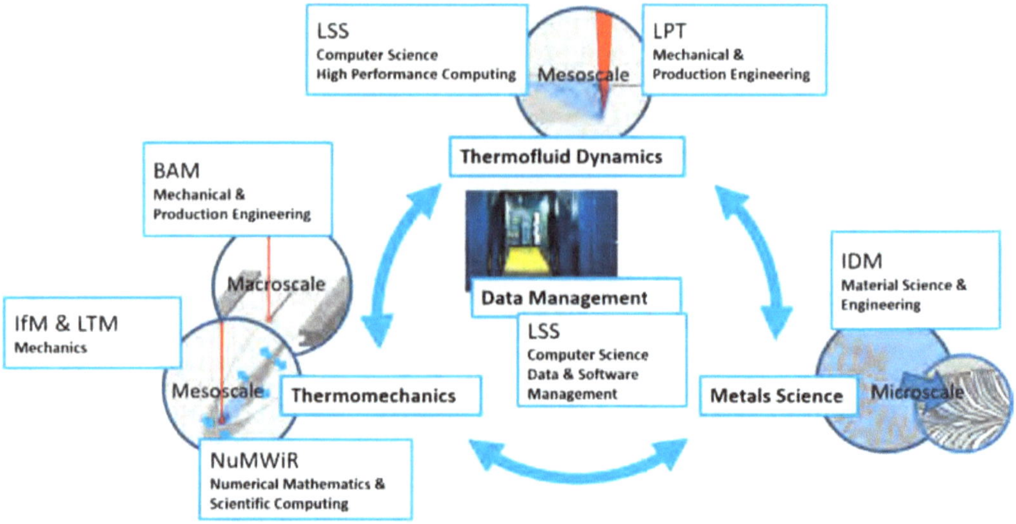

Fig. (17). Interdisciplinary collaboration in research.

Ethical and Regulatory Frameworks

The development and deployment of smart systems and machine learning must be guided by robust ethical frameworks and regulatory policies to ensure their responsible and beneficial use. Governments, policymakers, and industry leaders must work together to establish clear guidelines, standards, and accountability mechanisms as shown in Fig. (**18**).

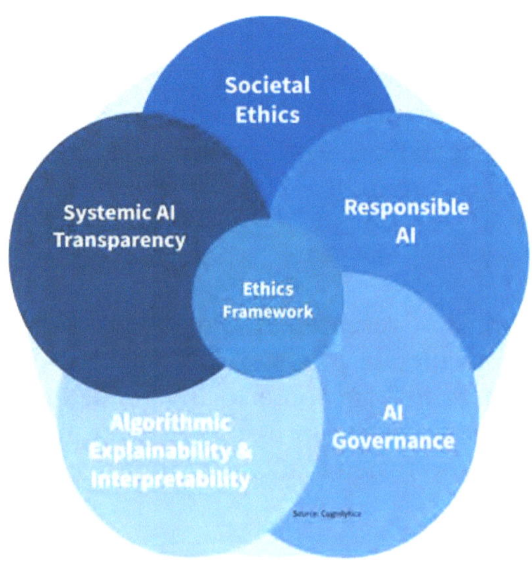

Fig. (18). Principles of ethical frameworks.

Ethical frameworks should address principles such as transparency, fairness, privacy protection, and respect for human rights. These frameworks should also consider the potential societal impacts of these technologies, including their effects on employment, inequality, and social structures.

Regulatory policies should provide clear guidelines for data collection, storage, and usage, while also addressing issues of algorithmic bias, safety, and liability. These policies should be flexible and adaptable, capable of keeping pace with rapid technological advancements while maintaining a balance between innovation and societal well-being.

Multi-stakeholder collaboration is essential in developing these frameworks and policies, involving a diverse range of perspectives from technologists, ethicists, legal experts, policymakers, and representatives from affected communities [11]. By fostering open dialogue and considering diverse viewpoints, we can create more inclusive and equitable guidelines for the development and deployment of smart systems and machine learning.

Public Education and Awareness

Alongside the development of smart systems and machine learning, it is crucial to educate the public about these technologies, their potential impacts, and the associated ethical and societal implications [12]. Raising awareness and promoting literacy in these areas can foster informed decision-making, combat misinformation, and build trust among stakeholders.

Educational initiatives should target various segments of society, including students, professionals, policymakers, and the general public. These efforts should aim to demystify the underlying concepts, highlight both the benefits and risks, and empower individuals to engage in informed discussions and decision-making processes as shown in Fig. (**19**).

Public engagement and dialogue are equally important, allowing for the exchange of ideas, concerns, and perspectives between developers, researchers, and the communities impacted by these technologies. By fostering open communication and incorporating diverse viewpoints, we can better understand the societal implications and ensure that the development and deployment of smart systems and machine learning align with ethical principles and societal values.

International Collaboration and Knowledge Sharing

The challenges and opportunities presented by smart systems and machine learning transcend national boundaries, necessitating international collaboration and the sharing of knowledge. By fostering global partnerships and leveraging the collective expertise of diverse nations and regions, we can accelerate progress, address shared challenges, and promote the responsible development and deployment of these technologies as shown in Fig. (**20**).

Fig. (19). Public education initiatives.

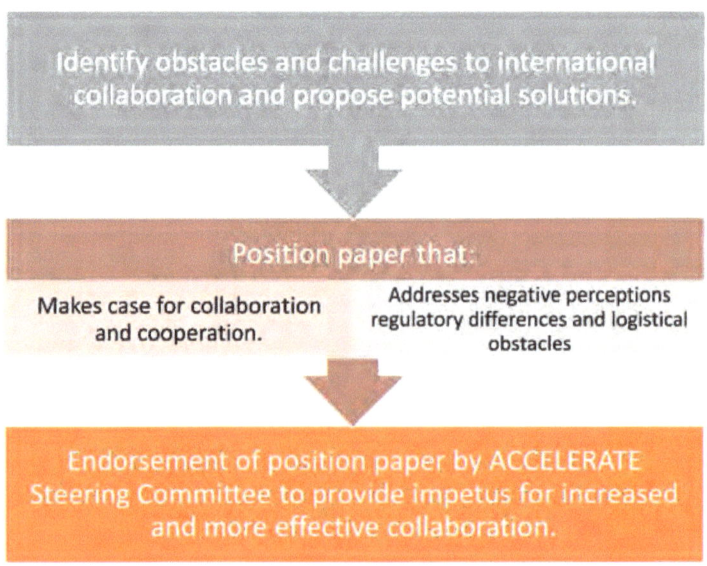

Fig. (20). International collaboration framework.

International organizations, such as the United Nations and its specialized agencies, can play a vital role in facilitating global cooperation, setting standards, and promoting the equitable distribution of the benefits of these technologies. Initiatives focused on capacity building, knowledge transfer, and technology sharing can help bridge the digital divide and ensure that the advantages of smart systems and machine learning are accessible to all nations, regardless of their level of economic development.

Furthermore, cross-border collaboration in research and development can foster innovation, facilitate the exchange of ideas and best practices, and promote the development of harmonized ethical and regulatory frameworks. By working together, the global community can leverage diverse perspectives, pool resources, and collectively address the challenges and seize the opportunities presented by these transformative technologies [13 - 19].

CONCLUSION

The future of smart systems and machine learning holds boundless potential to redefine our world and enrich human lives. By embracing a vision grounded in innovation, inclusivity, and sustainability, we can harness the transformative power of these technologies to propel society towards a brighter and more prosperous future. However, realizing this vision requires a concerted effort to address the challenges, mitigate risks, and promote the responsible development and deployment of these technologies.

As we embark on this journey of technological advancement, let us remain steadfast in our commitment to upholding ethical principles, promoting societal well-being, and fostering international cooperation. By fostering collaboration among researchers, technologists, policymakers, ethicists, and the broader society, we can navigate the complexities and harness the immense potential of smart systems and machine learning for the greater good of humanity.

Through continuous innovation, interdisciplinary research, robust ethical frameworks, and inclusive policies, we can ensure that the benefits of these technologies are distributed equitably, uplifting all members of our global community. Together, we can shape a future where innovative systems and machine learning are not merely technological marvels but catalysts for positive change, driving progress, enhancing human experiences, and paving the way for a more sustainable and prosperous world.

REFERENCES

[1] J. Smith, and A. Johnson, "The role of machine learning in healthcare", *J. Health Care Technol.*, vol. 10, no. 3, pp. 45-58, 2022.

[2] R. Brown, M. Garcia, and S. Patel, "Sustainable urbanization: Leveraging smart systems for environmental sustainability", *Sustain Cities Soc.,* vol. 15, pp. 102-115, 2023.

[3] A. A. Pise and S. Moyo, "Internet of Things-System," in *IoT in Healthcare Systems: Applications, Benefits, Challenges, and Case Studies*, pp. 149, 2023.

[4] C. Lee, D. Kim, and E. Park, "Intelligent manufacturing and Industry 4.0: A review of applications and challenges", *Int. J. Prod. Res.,* vol. 35, no. 2, pp. 220-235, 2024.

[5] Y. Wang, L. Chen, and Q. Zhang, "Intelligent assistants and human-machine interaction: State-of-the-art and future directions", *IEEE Trans. Hum. Mach. Syst.,* vol. 14, no. 4, pp. 789-802, 2023.

[6] B.L. Garcia, and C. Martinez, "Intelligent agriculture and food production: Opportunities and challenges", *J. Agric. Sci.,* vol. 28, no. 1, pp. 55-68, 2022.

[7] A.A. Pise, K.K. Almuzaini, T.A. Ahanger, A. Farouk, K. pant, P.K. Pareek, and S.J. Nuagah, "Enabling artificial intelligence of things (AIoT) healthcare architectures and listing security issues", *Comput. Intell. Neurosci.,* vol. 2022, no. 1, pp. 1-14, 2022.
[http://dx.doi.org/10.1155/2022/8421434] [PMID: 36911247]

[8] K. Taylor, E. Brown, and F. Clark, "Smart retail and customer experiences: Enhancing consumer engagement through machine learning", *J. Retailing,* vol. 42, no. 5, pp. 310-325, 2023.

[9] R. Johnson, and T. Smith, "Ethical considerations in the development of smart systems and machine learning algorithms", *Ethics in Technology and Engineering,* vol. 8, no. 2, pp. 150-165, 2024.

[10] M. Lee, S. Kim, and J. Park, "Regulatory frameworks for smart systems and machine learning: Challenges and opportunities", *Policy Internet,* vol. 11, no. 3, pp. 240-255, 2022.

[11] L. Wilson, P. Jones, and M. Davis, "Public awareness and education initiatives in smart systems and machine learning", *J. Public Policy Mark.,* vol. 30, no. 4, pp. 480-495, 2023.

[12] I. Citaristi, "International Telecommunication Union—ITU," in The Europa Directory of International Organizations 2022, pp. 365–369. Routledge, 2022.

[13] S. Joshi, A.A. Pise, M. Shrivastava, C. Revathy, H. Kumar, O. Alsetoohy, and R. Akwafo, "Adoption of blockchain technology for privacy and security in the context of industry 4.0", *Wirel. Commun. Mob. Comput.,* vol. 2022, no. 1, pp. 1-14, 2022.
[http://dx.doi.org/10.1155/2022/4079781]

[14] S. Chatterjee, S. Satpathy, and A. Nibedita, "Digital Investigation of Network Traffic Using Machine Learning. EAI Endorsed Scalable information", *System,* vol. 11, no. 1, 2023. Available from: https://publications.eai.eu/index.php/sis/article/view/4055

[15] C. Mallick, and S. Satpathy, "Challenges and design goals of wireless sensor networks: a state-of-the-art review", *Int. J. Comput. Appl.,* vol. 179, no. 28, pp. 42-47, 2018.
[http://dx.doi.org/10.5120/ijca2018916667]

[16] Pattnaik, L. M., Swain, P. K., Satpathy, S., & Panda, A. N. (2023). Cloud DDoS Attack Detection Model with Data Fusion & Machine Learning Classifiers. EAI Endorsed Transactions on Scalable Information Systems, 10(6).
[http://dx.doi.org/10.4108/eetsis.3936]

[17] L. Pattnaik, S. Satpathy, B.K. Paikaray, and P.K. Swain, "DDoS analysis using machine learning: survey, issues, and future directions", *International Journal of Business Continuity and Risk Management,* vol. 14, no. 1, pp. 57-76, 2024.
[http://dx.doi.org/10.1504/IJBCRM.2024.137242]

[18] S. Satpathy, S. Mohanty, Ed., *Big Data Analytics and computing for digital forensic investigations.* Chemical Rubber Company Press: Boca Raton, 2020.
[http://dx.doi.org/10.1201/9781003024743]

[19] S. Satpathy, P.K. Swain, S.N. Mohanty, and S.S. Basa, "Enhancing security: Federated learning against man-in-the-middle threats with gradient boosting machines and LSTM", *2024 IEEE International Conference on Advanced Video and Signal Based Surveillance (AVSS),* pp. 1-8, 2024.Niagara Falls, ON, Canada. [http://dx.doi.org/10.1109/AVSS61716.2024.10672589]

CHAPTER 12

Identifying DDoS Threats in Digital Forensics Using Transfer Learning Techniques

Saswati Chatterjee[1], **Vijaykumar Jayantibhai Solanki**[2], **Lalmohan Pattnaik**[3], **Mukesh Chaudhary**[1] and **Suneeta Satpathy**[4,*]

[1] *Parul University Vadodara, Gujarat, India*

[2] *Government Engineering College Bharuch, Gujarat, India*

[3] *Sri Sri University, Cuttack, Odisha, India*

[4] *Center For Cyber Security, SoA Deemed to be University, Bhubaneswar, Odisha, India*

Abstract: Digital investigations in cybersecurity are crucial for spotting and addressing cyber threats like Distributed Denial of Service (DDoS) attacks. With DDoS attacks becoming more complex and widespread, traditional forensic techniques struggle to keep up with these evolving threats. To tackle this challenge, this chapter suggests a new method for forensics investigation centered on DDoS attacks. By drawing on insights from studies on DDoS attack detection and transfer learning methods, the proposed approach aims to boost the effectiveness and precision of investigations within networking environments. The proposed framework is designed for conducting investigations that cater to the unique aspects of DDoS attacks by integrating expert systems, fuzzy logic, and deep transfer learning. A clustering-enhanced Transfer Learning strategy named CeHTL is implemented to detect connections between known attacks. This method was tested when the test dataset consisted of types or subtypes of attacks not found in the training data. Standard classification models like decision trees and KNN, alongside innovative transfer learning techniques, are used as benchmarks. The outcomes demonstrated enhancements in performance with the proposed CeHTL, utilizing trapezoidal Membership function generation methods, which showcased its effectiveness in identifying new network threats.

Keywords: CeHTL, Machine learning, Network attack threat, Transfer learning.

INTRODUCTION

In recent years, it has become a trend to get agility and cost savings from how organizations manage and deploy their IT infrastructure. Digital transformation

* **Corresponding author Suneeta Satpathy:** Center For Cyber Security, SoA Deemed to be University, Bhubaneswar, Odisha, India; E-mail: suneeta1912@gmail.com

has created new challenges, the most significant of which is probably cybersecurity. In an era of constantly growing devices and networks, one of the greatest cybersecurity threats organizations face is the Distributed Denial of Service (DDoS) attack. As the type of DDoS attacks designed to compromise internet service availability, they present a widespread threat to all categories of enterprises. DDoS invaders attack the intended systems with harmful congestion, blocking authorized individuals from accessing programs, websites, and other online resources. For researchers, promptly gathering, analyzing, and retaining technological proof often poses a challenge, delaying incident response and mitigation. This study introduces a novel approach to digital security inquiry, focusing on DDoS attacks against various computer systems. The proposed method makes use of recent leverages recent advances in transfer learning and DDoS threat detection to enhance the effectiveness and precision of queries. The proposed approach, which integrates cybersecurity, cutting-edge technologies, and mathematical principles, can enable businesses to effectively safeguard their critical assets and mitigate the impact of denial-of-service attacks. This paper provides a comprehensive explanation of the proposed technique, detailing its key components, implementation methods, and potential benefits for businesses susceptible to DDoS attacks. Through empirical evaluations and real-world experiences, the study also shows the practical effectiveness of the adopted strategies. Overall, the research adds to the expanding corpus of knowledge in digital forensics and cybersecurity by providing insightful analysis and useful suggestions for businesses looking to strengthen their defenses against DDoS attacks. Government, military, and industrial networks are particularly vulnerable to complex DDoS attacks, which can result in severe disruptions and data breaches. Because traditional signature-based detection methods rely on well-known patterns of criminal activity, they often struggle to handle the dynamic and complex nature of contemporary cyber threats. Attackers are continually devising new strategies; therefore, these traditional approaches are insufficient. Consequently, it is imperative to design and implement sophisticated anomaly detection techniques. These state-of-the-art methods focus on identifying anomalous patterns and behaviors in network traffic that deviate from the norm, thereby revealing dangers that signature-based systems may overlook. Artificial intelligence and machine learning enable anomaly detection systems to learn, adapt, and identify threats more successfully in real time. This improves the security posture of different network settings. This proactive strategy is essential for reducing the risks associated with the dynamic and increasingly sophisticated cyber threats of today. DDoS assaults employ the same attack approach as DoS attacks, with the exception that a sizable number of controlled zombie devices carry out the attack [1]. Dispersed Zombies flood the targeted device with requests, depleting its resources and finally bringing down the service. Research indicates that, although more methods are being employed to maintain network security, DDoS attacks are becoming more advanced and destructive to networks over time [2]. The remaining sections of the document are arranged as follows: Section 2 covers related work, and Section 3 summarizes the transfer learning paradigm for identifying attacks. The Transfer Learning Approach *via* Spectral Transformation is explained in Section 4. The proposed architecture is shown in Section 5, and the experimental findings are explained in Section 6. Section 7 concludes the study and outlines potential directions for future research.

Related Work

There has been an increase in research efforts in the past several years to improve DDoS attack detection and mitigation in various scenarios. Due to the size of contemporary network infrastructures and the evolution of attack strategies, traditional approaches to DDoS attack detection, such as signature-based and anomaly-based methods, have proven to be inadequate. Signature-based detection techniques recognize bad traffic by comparing it to established patterns or signatures of DDoS attacks. These techniques work well against well-known attack vectors, but they are less successful in identifying new or zero-day assaults since they lack recognizable signatures. Even though anomaly-based techniques can identify assaults that have never been observed before, they frequently have a high false-positive rate and are not very scalable. Researchers have resorted to machine learning methods, especially deep learning, for DDoS attack detection as a result of these constraints. Transfer learning techniques enable models to leverage data from related tasks or domains, which may help overcome this restriction. By leveraging such knowledge, models that have fewer information points for an activity might perform better. The objective of this method is to transfer data from a larger source domain to a smaller destination domain. The literature describes several approaches to learning transfer, such as feature-based, model-based, and instance-based methods. Threats are frequently detected using anomaly detection [3, 4], as it searches for peculiar patterns that deviate from normal behavior. However, this method relies heavily on features derived from expert knowledge, which might result in a high rate of false positives. A rapidly developing field in machine learning, called transfer learning, makes it easier to create reliable models that can take on new tasks with minimal effort. Many successful applications have been made of it in domains such as natural language processing and visual identification. Transfer learning can be used to improve DDoS detection algorithms. Despite the lack of thorough formalization in findings, the researchers proposed that transfer learning could improve the identification of unknown malware across different environments [5]. In one study, instance-based transfer learning was applied to network intrusion detection; nevertheless, a significant amount of labeled data from the target domain was needed. The KDD99 network dataset was used in a model-based transfer learning study conducted by the same researcher. However, both instance-based and model-based strategies [6] mostly rely on the assumption of a homogenous feature set, which is frequently not true, because network attack detection usually comprises heterogeneous features. According to research, feature-based transfer learning techniques offer greater flexibility, as they can utilize multiple base classifiers tailored to specific scenarios [7, 8]. The current emphasis on creating a feature-based transfer learning strategy for network attack detection is driven by these adaptability and flexibility features.

The proposed work is the first study to implement this technique to improve the robustness of network attack detection. Transfer learning approaches are typically categorized into three primary classes [9]. Instance-based techniques operate under the assumption that by reweighting similar samples, some components of the source data can be reused for the target domain. A notable example is the TrAdaBoost method, which iteratively reweights the data from the source and target domains to reduce the impact of "bad" source data and increase the contribution of "good" source data to the target domain. These methods, however, necessitate a large number of target domain-labeled samples [10]. Model-based techniques presuppose that the source and target tasks share certain model parameters or priors. This enables the modification and application of model parameters discovered in the source domain to the target domain. Feature-based methods aim to learn a new representation that aligns the source and target domains within a shared feature space. The goal is to minimize distributional differences so that the target domain can benefit from the patterns learned in the source domain [11]. An essential factor in enhancing the versatility of detection models is transfer learning. The NSL-KDD benchmark network dataset was used [16] to test the technique [16]. Furthermore, the experimental results showed that the proposed strategy outperforms all previous baseline methods in terms of finding new assaults. In addition, this work fills the gaps found in previous studies by offering a framework and an experimental analysis.

Framework for Transfer Learning to Identify New Network Threats

The proposed approach in the present study enables the addition of new features to the target domain, in contrast to previous research that requires the source and target domains to have identical feature sets. The adaptability of the proposed framework is crucial for mitigating changing network attacks, as adversaries may modify their tactics, necessitating the incorporation of new defensive features into the network or system layers. As per previous work, the attack distributions or feature sets of the source and target domains could differ [17 - 19]. The transfer learning framework aims to identify new threats in the target domain by using data from the source domain. The machine learning pipeline feature is a key component of the proposed approach. The process involves collecting and preprocessing data [20, 21]. The features are first extracted from raw network traffic data using statistical calculations of network flow and then pre-processed. The pre-processed data is then fed into a common base classifier, such as decision trees, SVM, or KNN. This framework leverages transfer learning to detect emerging network threats by utilizing knowledge from previously encountered threats [22]. Baseline classifiers, such as KNN, linear SVM, and C4.5 decision tree (CART), are then employed to establish initial performance metrics [22]. Implement transfer learning techniques to adapt models trained on known threats to identify new, unseen threats. Integrate advanced classifiers, such as CeHTL, which benefit from transfer learning to improve detection accuracy and robustness. Evaluate the enhanced classifiers using metrics like accuracy, F1 score, and area under the ROC curve (AUC) to ensure superior performance in identifying new threats. By implementing this framework, the detection system can effectively and efficiently adapt to new types of network threats, maintaining high levels of security and protection [23, 24].

Transfer Learning Approach via Spectral Transformation for Network Threat Identification

To categorize every network connection as either malicious or normal, network attack detection is treated as a binary classification issue. The instances of source domain training provided an example like $S = \{\vec{y}i\}, \vec{y} \in R^m$ that have labels $L_S = \{z_i\}$ and target domain data $T = \{a_i\}, \vec{a} \in R^n$. Suppose $\vec{y}$ and $\vec{a}$ are drawn from different distributions, $P_S(y) \neq P_T(y)$, where $P_T(y)$ is unknown, and the dimensions of $\vec{y}$ and $\vec{a}$ are different, $R^m \neq R^n$. Given the common characteristics of network attacks, the proposed strategy involves detecting the shared latent subspace and projecting the source and target data onto it to construct new feature representations that can be used for classification. Even when the source and target domains involve different attack types, the model identifies a shared latent space that preserves the original data structure while maintaining clear separation between discriminative instances.

Optimization

Based on the following optimization aim, an optimal projection is calculated based on source data S and target data T onto an optimal subspace VS and VT (1):

$$l(v_{S,} S) + l(v_{T,} T) + \beta D(v_{S,} v_T) v_{S,} v_T \quad \textbf{(1)}$$

Where the distortion function l(*,*) assesses the variation between the projected and original data. The difference between the projected data of the source and target domains is shown by the symbol $D(v_S, v_T)$. The trade-off parameter β controls the similarity between the two datasets, regulating how similar they are to one another. As a result, the first two parts of (2) ensure that the original data's structures are preserved as much as possible in the projected data. $D(v_S, v_T)$ Can be defined in terms of l(*,*) as:

$$D(v_S, v_T) = \|v_T - v_S x\|^2 \tag{2}$$

This is the variation between the anticipated source data and the anticipated target data. Thus, by minimizing the difference in function, the predicted source and target data are bound to be similar. A linear transformation is applied to find the projected space and can be defined l(*,*) as follows (3):

$$l\,(v_{S,}S) = \|s - v_S p_S x\|^2,\ l(v_{T,}T) = \|T - v_T P_T\|^2 \tag{3}$$

Where v_S and v_S are accomplished by applying a linear transformation to the source and target, respectively, using linear mapping matrices, represented as $P_S \in R^{k\times m}$ and $P_T \in R^{k\times n}$ The Frobenius norm, which is also a matrix trace norm, is defined as. $\|xx\|^2$ i in an alternative perspective, the original data S and T are projected by, $P_s\ T \in R^{m\times k}$ and $P_T\ T \in R^{n\times k}$ into a k-dimensional latent subspace, where the projected data are similarl $(v_S) = \|sp_s\ T\text{-}V_s P_s\ x^2$. The result will be a simple solution, where ps = 0 and $V_S = 0$. Thus, Equation 3 is used. It can be viewed as a matrix factorization issue, and latent subspace extraction with preservation of the original data structures is a well-established application of this technology.

Proposed Methodology

The extensive approach of the suggested framework is covered in this section. The proposed architecture consists of eight essential steps that enable the completion of classification and analysis. Fig. (**1**) outlines the process flow of the proposed methodology.

Accumulation of Data

When gathering strong forensic evidence to support a crime in a court of law, relying solely on a First Information Report (FIR) may be insufficient. Therefore, additional evidence from various sources must be collected and presented. Here, a well-known dataset, the NSL-KDD dataset, is employed, which is used for assessing network-related attacks obtained from a sequence of TCP connection logs collected in a local area network. Every entry in the dataset has a label designating it as either normal or as one of the various sorts of attacks.

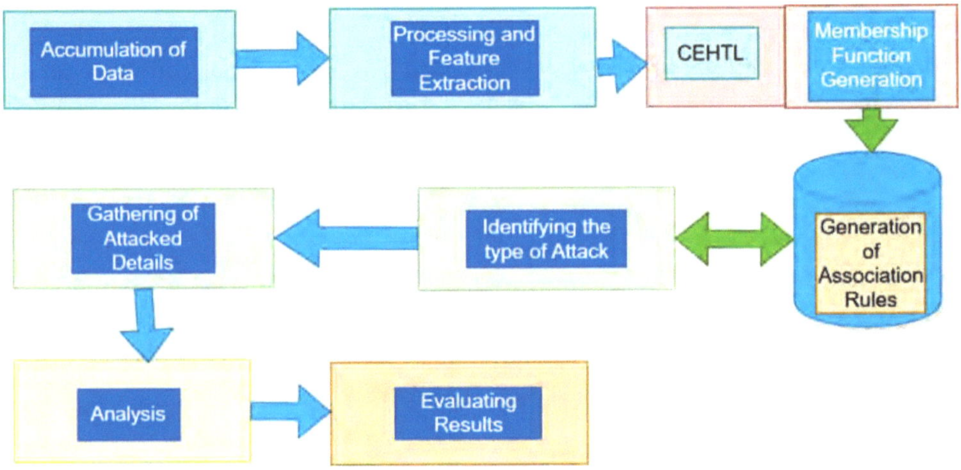

Fig. (1). Proposed framework.

Feature Extraction and Pre-Processing

One of the crucial forensics duties is pre-processing, which ensures that the evidence is crucial and unaltered. It is common to encounter issues with uncategorized, incomplete, and inconsistent records when working with collected data. Several preprocessing processes must be taken to prepare the raw data for testing and learning. The dataset consists of 41 network features and 22 distinct attack types. The feature extraction process is explained in Table **1**.

Table 1. Extracted attributes and consistent attack.

Sl. No	Attribute Name	DoS	R2L	U2R	Probe
1	duration	✓	✓	-	✓
2	protocol_type	✓	✓	-	✓
3	service	-	✓	-	✓
4	flag	✓	✓	-	✓
5	src_bytes	✓	✓	-	✓
6	hot	-	✓	✓	-
7	num_failed_logins	-	✓	-	-
8	logged_in	-	✓	-	-
9	num_compromised	-	✓	✓	-
10	root_shell	-	-	✓	-
11	num_root	-	✓	✓	-

(Table 1) cont.....

Sl. No	Attribute Name	DoS	R2L	U2R	Probe
12	num_file_creations	-	✓	✓	-
13	num_shells	-	✓	✓	-
14	num_access_files	-	✓	✓	-
15	is_guest_login	-	✓	-	-
16	count	✓	-	-	-
17	dst_host_same_srv_rate	✓	-	-	-
18	dst_host_serror_rate	✓	-	-	-
19	dst_host_srv_serror _rate	✓	-	-	-

Redundancy refers to extraneous data in the training dataset that is removed through noise reduction and missing value replacement. Equation (4) presents the mathematical expression for noise removal and missing value substitution, respectively.

$$f(x_{i)} = \{ \sum_{i-n/10}^{i+n/10} , x_i = \frac{missing}{abnormal\ value} \tag{4}$$

$$x_{i,} x_i \neq \frac{missing}{abnormal\ value}$$

CeHTL and Membership Function Generation

By identifying and leveraging the similarities between the source and target domains, the transfer learning process can be improved using clustering techniques. CeHTL begins by clustering instances as displayed in Fig. (**2**) in the target domain. After clustering the target domain instances, CeHTL computes the similarity between clusters in the source and target domains and uses these similarities to align the corresponding clusters across the two domains. Instances are arranged according to their cluster labels after the clusters have been mapped. The rows in the matrices T (target) and S (source) have the same class order thanks to this sorting, which facilitates the projection process. Clustering algorithms are applied (*e.g.*, K-means) to the target domain data to form distinct clusters.

Input: I, S
Output: Tnew, Snew

Initialization: Set the number of clusters for each domain, c=2

Clustering Target Domain: Apply k-means clustering to T with cc clusters to obtain cluster labels CT.

Clustering Source Domain: Use the class labels YS as cluster labels CS for S.

Dimensionality Reduction (if needed):

If the dimensions of T and S are different, apply PCA to both:

T=pca(T)=pca(T)

S=pca(S)=pca(S)

Calculate Similarity: Compute the Euclidean distance between the centroids of each cluster in T and SS.

Cluster Pairing:

For each cluster in T, find the most similar cluster in S (from CS) by minimizing the Euclidean distance.

Assign the same label to paired clusters.

Sort Instances:

Sort the matrices [T,CT] and [S,CS] according to the cluster labels CT and CS.

This yields Tnew and Snew, which are the new inputs.

Fig. (2). Clustering enhanced hierarchical transfer learning.

Trapezoidal membership functions, as shown in Fig. (**3**), can help define decision boundaries and generalize knowledge across domains when combined with clustering information. This enables making informed decisions or predictions in the target domain by leveraging the transferred knowledge.

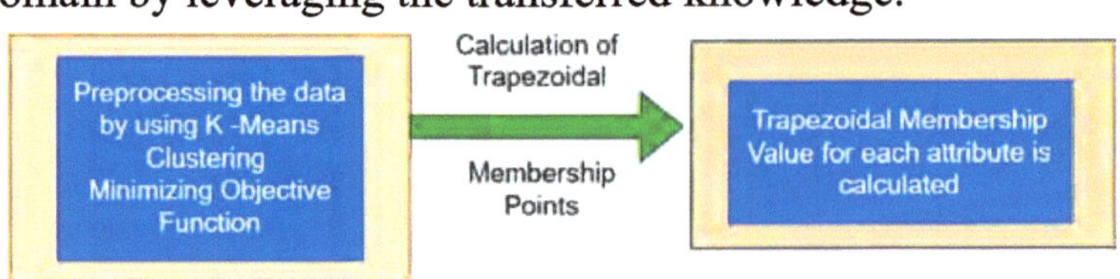

Fig. (3). Membership function generation.

There are various membership functions, but the trapezoidal membership function is used here. The triangular membership function μ(x) for a variable x is defined as follows (5):

$$\mu(x) = \begin{cases} 0 & \text{if } x \leq a \\ \frac{x-a}{b-a} & \text{if } a < x \leq b \\ 1 & \text{if } b < x \leq c \\ \frac{d-x}{d-c} & \text{if } c < x \leq d \\ 0 & \text{if } x > d \end{cases} \quad (5)$$

Discovering Association Rules with the Apriori Algorithm

To extract relevant information from enormous databases, data mining methods are essential. Nevertheless, the knowledge base that results could not be effective if all the patterns produced from a processed data model are utilized to create rules for a system. The key to designing successful regulations for a system is preventing biased decisions, as shown in Table **2**.

Table 2. Rule selection.

Rules	Support	Confidence
If (duration=very low) AND (src_bytes=very low) then attack=dos	0.4568	0.4859
If (duration=very low) AND (dst_host_same_srv_rate=very high) then attack=dos	0.2512	0.4353
If (src_bytes=low) AND (dst_host_same_srv_rate=high) then attack=dos	0.4839	0.7535
If (src_bytes=low) AND (dst_host_same_srv_rate=high) AND (dst_host_serror_rate=very high)then attack=dos	0.3129	0.4536

The Apriori algorithm searches a big dataset for the optimal combination of many properties to identify effective association rules [25 - 27]. It functions based on two main factors: confidence and support. Support calculates the frequency at which a parameter appears in a group of transactions. While confidence assesses the likelihood of a rule being correct [28, 29]. A minimum threshold value for support is set to identify the best rules. This threshold ensures that only significant and relevant rules are considered, enhancing the efficiency and reliability of the knowledge base in a forensic analysis system.

Support

Support quantifies the frequency with which a rule appears in the dataset. To be more precise, the percentage of transactions in the dataset that contain both C and D is the support of a rule C → D, as shown in (6)

$$\text{Support} \quad (C \rightarrow D) = \frac{Number\ of\ Transactions\ containing\ C\ and\ D}{Total\ number\ of\ transactions} \tag{6}$$

$$\text{Mathematically, support } C \rightarrow D = \frac{Count(C \vee D)}{N}$$

Confidence

Contrarily, confidence 7 quantifies the chance that transactions containing item D will also contain item C. It is the percentage of transactions that also include D and contain C.

$$\text{Confidence } (C \rightarrow D) = \frac{Support(C \vee D)}{Support(C)}$$

$$(7)$$

$$\text{Rule } (C \rightarrow D)\ Selected, \quad if\ Support, Confidence \geq \gamma_1, \gamma_2$$

$$\text{Rule } (C \rightarrow D) \text{ Not } Selected,\ if\ Support, Confidence < \gamma_1, \gamma_2$$

Experimental Analysis

Using the Receiver Operating Characteristic (ROC) curve, accuracy, and F1 score (F-measure), the effectiveness of the classification and detection algorithms was evaluated. The F1 score gauges performance per class by combining recall and precision. The baseline models analyzed here are KNN, linear SVM, and C4.5 decision tree (CART). The performance of these models is based upon the accuracy of the CeHTL demonstrated superior performance by achieving an F1 score of 0.75 and an accuracy exceeding 0.70. This marked a significant improvement over the baseline classifiers. Fig. (**4**) shows the ROC curves for the three main transfer learning tasks with the base classifier.

CeHTL achieved an impressive accuracy with an F1 score of 0.88 when employing decision tree and KNN classifiers, particularly excelling in the DoS→Probe and Probe→R2L tasks. It also achieved the highest area under the ROC curve (AUC) for these tasks, with AUC values of 0.93 for DoS→Probe and 0.91 for Probe•R2L, as shown in the membership function in Fig. (**5**).

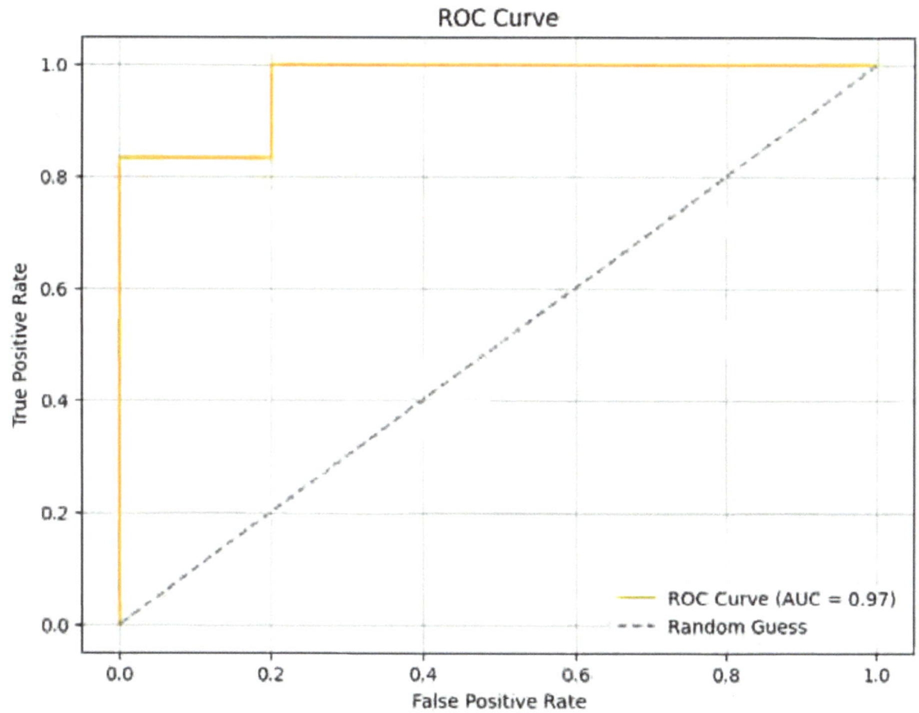

Fig. (4). ROC curve.

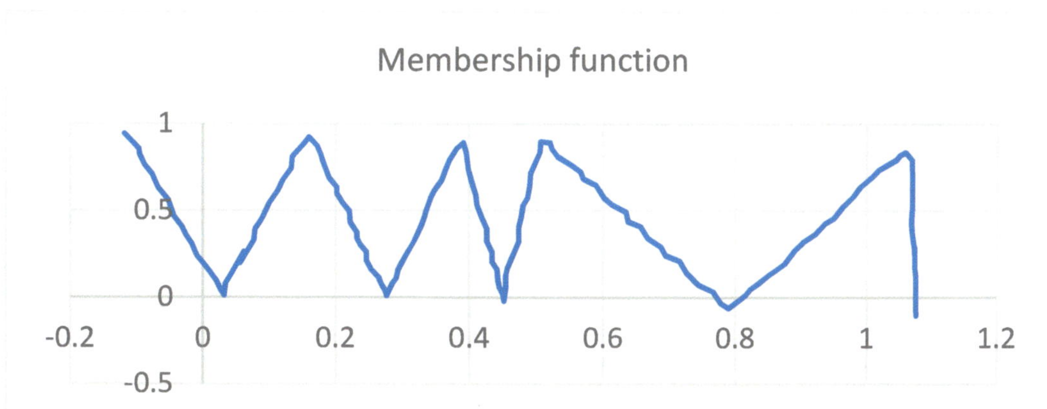

Fig. (5). Membership function.

CONCLUSION

DDoS attacks have been identified using machine learning. However, most methods perform best when the training and testing data have the same distribution. In reality, the ability of supervised learning approaches to identify novel threats is limited by attacks that are constantly evolving and by the scarcity of labeled datasets. This research presents a feature-based transfer learning architecture and methods, including the development of trapezoidal membership functions, which are designed to robustly detect unknown attacks. Additionally, it introduces a linear transformation method known as the cluster-enhanced approach, referred to as CeHTL. By comparing these transfer learning techniques to baseline models, the proposed model demonstrated its ability to effectively detect unknown network attacks on standard classifiers. In particular, CeHTL showed better robustness and performance in identifying unknown threats even in the absence of labeled data. Additionally, the outcomes demonstrated that these transfer learning strategies support various feature spaces. Subsequent research endeavors will employ the model across many threat domains, including malware detection, and integrate transfer learning and deep learning techniques to facilitate model pre-training in real-world scenarios.

ACKNOWLEDGMENTS

Completing this research project would not have been possible without all the authors' and my guide's contributions and support. I am deeply grateful for the invaluable input and support throughout the research process.

REFERENCES

[1] R.S. Chaudhari, and G.R. Talmale, "A review on detection approaches for distributed denial of service attacks", *2019 International Conference on Intelligent Sustainable Systems (ICISS),* pp. 323-327, 2019.
[http://dx.doi.org/10.1109/ISS1.2019.8908125]

[2] G.A. Jaafar, S.M. Abdullah, and S. Ismail, "Review of recent detection methods for HTTP DDoS attacks", *J. Comput. Netw. Commun.,* vol. 2019, pp. 1-10, 2019.
[http://dx.doi.org/10.1155/2019/1283472]

[3] I. Sharafaldin, A.H. Lashkari, and S. Hakak, "Developing realistic distributed denial of service (DDoS) attack dataset and taxonomy", *2019 International Carnahan Conference on Security Technology (ICCST),* 2019.
[http://dx.doi.org/10.1109/CCST.2019.8888419]

[4] W. Wang, M. Zhu, and J. Wang, "End-to-end encrypted traffic classification with one-dimensional convolution neural networks", *2017 IEEE International Conference on Intelligence and Security Informatics (ISI),* pp. 43-48, 2017.Beijing, China.
[http://dx.doi.org/10.1109/ISI.2017.8004872]

[5] S. Gou, Y. Wang, and L. Jiao, "Distributed transfer network learning based intrusion detection", *2009 IEEE International Symposium on Parallel and Distributed Processing with Applications,* pp. 511-515, 2009.
[http://dx.doi.org/10.1109/ISPA.2009.92]

[6] B. Kulis, K. Saenko, and T. Darrell, "What you saw is not what you get: domain adaptation using asymmetric kernel transforms", *2011 IEEE Conference on Computer Vision and Pattern Recognition (CVPR),* pp. 1785-1792, 2011.
[http://dx.doi.org/10.1109/CVPR.2011.5995702]

[7] J. Gao, W. Fan, and J. Jiang, "Knowledge transfer *via* multiple model local structure mapping", *Proc. of the 14th ACM SIGKDD International Conference on Knowledge Discovery and Data Mining,* pp. 283-291, 2008.
[http://dx.doi.org/10.1145/1401890.1401928]

[8] D. Wang, X. Chen, and D. Chen, "DDoS detection method based on instance transfer learning," in 2021 IEEE 6th International Conference on Signal and Image Processing (ICSIP), Nanjing, China, 2021, pp. 1053-1058.
[http://dx.doi.org/10.1109/ICSIP52628.2021.9688784]

[9] D. Singh, A. Shukla, and M. Sajwan, "Deep transfer learning framework for the identification of malicious activities to combat cyberattack", *Future Gener. Comput. Syst.,* vol. 125, pp. 687-697, 2021.
[http://dx.doi.org/10.1016/j.future.2021.07.015]

[10] M. Mittal, K. Kumar, and S. Behal, "DDoS-AT-2022: a distributed denial of service attack dataset for evaluating DDoS defense system", *Proc. Indian Natl. Sci. Acad. A Phys. Sci.,* vol. 89, no. 2, pp. 306-324, 2023.
[http://dx.doi.org/10.1007/s43538-023-00159-9]

[11] E. Rodríguez, P. Valls, B. Otero, J.J. Costa, J. Verdú, M.A. Pajuelo, and R. Canal, "Transfer-learning-based intrusion detection framework in IoT networks", *Sensors (Basel),* vol. 22, no. 15, p. 5621, 2022.
[http://dx.doi.org/10.3390/s22155621] [PMID: 35957178]

[12] Y. Xia, Y. Xu, S. Mondal, and A.K. Gupta, "A transfer learning-based method for cyber-attack tolerance in distributed control of microgrids", *IEEE Trans. Smart Grid,* 2023.

[13] S. Kawish, H. Louafi, and Y. Yao, "An instance-based transfer learning approach, applied to intrusion detection," in *2023 20th Annual International Conference on Privacy, Security and Trust (PST)*, 2023, pp. 1-7.
[http://dx.doi.org/10.1109/PST58708.2023.10319986]

[14] H.M. Chuang, and L.J. Ye, "Applying transfer learning approaches for intrusion detection in software-defined networking", *Sustainability (Basel),* vol. 15, no. 12, p. 9395, 2023.
[http://dx.doi.org/10.3390/su15129395]

[15] M. Mittal, K. Kumar, and S. Behal, "DL-2P-DDoSADF: Deep learning-based two-phase DDoS attack detection framework", *Journal of Information Security and Applications,* vol. 78, p. 103609, 2023.
[http://dx.doi.org/10.1016/j.jisa.2023.103609]

[16] H. Lu, Y. Zhao, Y. Song, Y. Yang, G. He, H. Yu, and Y. Ren, "A transfer learning-based intrusion detection system for zero-day attack in communication-based train control system", *Cluster Comput.,* vol. 27, no. 6, pp. 8477-8492, 2024.
[http://dx.doi.org/10.1007/s10586-024-04376-9]

[17] E.Q. Effah, E.O. Osei, Maxwell Dorgbefu Jnr, and A. Tetteh, "Hybrid approach to classification of DDoS attacks on a computer network infrastructure", *Asian Journal of Research in Computer Science,* vol. 17, no. 4, pp. 19-43, 2024.
[http://dx.doi.org/10.9734/ajrcos/2024/v17i4428]

[18] S. Racherla, P. Sripathi, N. Faruqui, M. Alamgir Kabir, M. Whaiduzzaman, and S. Aziz Shah, "Deep-IDS: A real-time intrusion detector for IoT nodes using deep learning", *IEEE Access,* vol. 12, pp. 63584-63597, 2024.
[http://dx.doi.org/10.1109/ACCESS.2024.3396461]

[19] J. Arango-López, G. Isaza, and F. Ramirez, "Cloud-based deep learning architecture for DDoS cyber-attack prediction", *Expert Syst.,* p. e13552, 2024.

[20] S. Nari, and A.A. Ghorbani, "Automated malware classification based on network behavior", *Proc. of the 2013 International Conference on Computing, Networking and Communications (ICNC),* pp. 642-647, 2013.
[http://dx.doi.org/10.1109/ICCNC.2013.6504162]

[21] M.Z. Rafique, P. Chen, C. Huygens, and W. Joosen, "Evolutionary algorithms for classification of malware families through different network behaviors", *Proc. of the 2014 conference on Genetic and Evolutionary Computation (GECCO '14),* pp. 1167-1174, 2014. [http://dx.doi.org/10.1145/2576768.2598238]

[22] F. Iglesias, and T. Zseby, "Analysis of network traffic features for anomaly detection", *Mach. Learn.,* vol. 101, no. 1-3, pp. 59-84, 2015. [http://dx.doi.org/10.1007/s10994-014-5473-9]

[23] NSL-KDD, "UNB IUNB ISCX NSL-KDD DataSet," 2016. [Online]. Available: http://www.unb.ca/research/iscx/dataset/iscx-NSL-KDD-dataset.html

[24] B. Kulis, K. Saenko, and T. Darrell, "What you saw is not what you get: domain adaptation using asymmetric kernel transforms", *Proc. of the 2011 IEEE Conference on Computer Vision and Pattern Recognition (CVPR),* pp. 1785-1792, 2011. [http://dx.doi.org/10.1109/CVPR.2011.5995702]

[25] J. Zhao, S. Shetty, J.W. Pan, C. Kamhoua, and K. Kwiat, "Transfer learning for detecting unknown network attacks", *EURASIP J. Inf. Secur.,* vol. 2019, no. 1, pp. 1-13, 2019. [http://dx.doi.org/10.1186/s13635-019-0084-4]

[26] B. Long, Y. Chang, A. Dong, and J. He, "Pairwise cross-domain factor model for heterogeneous transfer ranking", *Proc. of the WSDM,* p. 113, 2012. [http://dx.doi.org/10.1145/2124295.2124311]

[27] D. Bekerman, B. Shapira, L. Rokach, and A. Bar, "Unknown malware detection using network traffic classification", *Proc. of the 2015 IEEE Conference on Communications and Network Security (CNS),* pp. 134-142, 2015. [http://dx.doi.org/10.1109/CNS.2015.7346821]

[28] L.M. Pattnaik, P.K. Swain, S. Satpathy, and A.N. Panda, "Cloud DDoS attack detection model with data fusion & machine learning classifiers", *EAI Endorsed Trans Scalable Inform Syst,* vol. 10, no. 6, 2023. [http://dx.doi.org/10.4108/eetsis.3936]

[29] S. Satpathy, P.K. Swain, S.N. Mohanty, and S.S. Basa, "Enhancing security: Federated learning against man-in-the-middle threats with gradient boosting machines and LSTM", In: *2024 IEEE international conference on advanced video and signal based surveillance (AVSS)* IEEE, 2024, pp. 1-8. [http://dx.doi.org/10.1109/AVSS61716.2024.10672589]

CHAPTER 13

Rising Concerns: Cybercrime & Financial Fraud in the Indian Context

Preethi Nanjundan[1,*], **Blesson Varghese James**[2], **Arushi Sharma**[2] and **Aryan Gupta**[2]

[1] *Department of Data Science, CHRIST University, Lavasa Campus, Pune, India*

[2] *Department of Commerce, CHRIST University, Lavasa Campus, Pune, India*

Abstract: This chapter examines the prevalence and impact of cybercrime in India, focusing on various cyber threats and their consequences on individuals, businesses, and society. Drawing on data collected from a diverse sample of participants aged 15 to 67, the study reveals alarming statistics: over 70% of respondents reporting exposure to cybercrime. The most prevalent forms of cybercrime include online payment fraud, identity theft, phishing, and malware attacks. The chapter also explores the emotional and psychological impact of cybercrime, highlighting its profound effects on victim trust and mental well-being. In response to cyber threats, the study finds that individuals often bolster their security measures or decrease their online activity, reflecting a heightened vulnerability and distrust in digital platforms. Regression analysis reveals correlations between age groups and cybercrime victimization, emphasizing the need for targeted interventions and digital literacy initiatives. The findings underscore the urgent need for comprehensive cybersecurity measures, user education, and support structures to mitigate the impact of cybercrime and foster a safer online environment for all.

Keywords: Cybercrime, Cybersecurity, Digital literacy, Financial fraud, Identity theft, Malware attacks, Online payment scam, Phishing, Psychological impact, Regression analysis, Trust in online platforms.

INTRODUCTION

Cybercrime poses a significant and rapidly evolving threat in a globalized world, particularly in emerging economies. Defined as illegal activity utilizing the internet and information technology, cybercrime manifests in various forms, impacting businesses through unauthorized access and manipulation. The negative consequences necessitate a rigorous managerial approach for identification, recovery, and detection [1]. While cybercrime often seeks financial gain, motives

[*]**Corresponding author Preethi Nanjundan:** Department of Data Science, CHRIST University, Lavasa Campus, Pune, India; E-mail: preethi.n@christuniversity.in

can also be political or personal, with perpetrators ranging from highly skilled organized groups to inexperienced individuals. Emerging countries face heightened vulnerability due to intrinsic weaknesses in their security systems, making them susceptible to silent, “stalking”-like cyberattacks with potentially devastating economic and business consequences. Therefore, addressing and mitigating cybercrime demands ongoing attention and comprehensive strategies. Modern technology provides highly advanced tracking means that are seemingly untraceable and undetectable. Metaphorically, cyberattacks are based on two particular cracks in the security system, and their approach is identified with silent stalking (tracking). This criminal activity has highly harmful consequences for economic and business targets. This has increased the prevalence of online financial fraud victimization. A growing wave of cybercrime has negatively impacted the goodwill and economic growth of financial institutions, both directly through the loss of trust in digital infrastructure and indirectly through fraud and extortion in both developing and developed countries [2].

Fraudsters are continually evolving their approaches to exploit the vulnerabilities of current prevention measures, with many targeting the financial sector. These crimes include credit card fraud, healthcare and automobile insurance fraud, money laundering, securities and commodities fraud, and insider trading [3]. Phishing is one of the various social engineering tactics used by cybercriminals to deceive technical users into disclosing sensitive or financial information through malicious websites that appear legitimate. Malware is malicious software designed to disrupt computer system(s) and is heavily used by cybercriminals to solicit monetary funds fraudulently. Furthermore, malware and phishing are social engineering tactics commonly used by cybercriminals to defraud unsuspecting users. Moreover, malware and phishing are social engineering tactics widely used by cybercriminals to defraud unsuspecting users.

The COVID-19 pandemic has dramatically shifted societal norms, driving a mass transition towards online work, shopping, and social interactions. This digital migration has not gone unnoticed by cybercriminals, who have capitalized on the increased reliance on online services to develop innovative and diverse attack methods. As individuals and institutions transition from physical spaces to the digital realm, their vulnerability to cybercrime increases, potentially leading to service disruptions, financial losses, data breaches, and widespread anxiety. This chapter delves into the interplay between pandemic-driven behavioral shifts, the evolving landscape of cybercrime, and the resulting consequences for individuals and institutions [4]. COVID-19 had a significant impact on every sector. The rapid digitization of the banking sector has significantly impacted its stability and risk profile, driven by technological advancements and the increasing threat of cyberattacks [5, 6]. Exploiting the anonymity and interconnectedness of online systems, cybercriminals pose a growing challenge, yet the link between sustainability and stability under such threats remains understudied and debated [7]. Researching cybercrime and its impact is crucial for the banking industry, particularly considering the rising prevalence of insider-driven attacks [8]. These attacks have witnessed a staggering 160% increase between 2019 and 2020 [9].

Financial institutions face significant losses, uncertainty, and funding restrictions due to cyberattacks [10]. A single insider-led cybercrime can trigger substantial economic losses, intellectual property theft, and erode customer trust [11]. The repercussions extend beyond individual institutions, impacting the entire financial ecosystem and stakeholders like customers, regulators, and employees [12] (Ferracane, 2019). Therefore, preventing and mitigating insider fraud is paramount [13, 14]. Cybercrime can be controlled using digital technology, and computer networks will also require a variety of new networks, including those between police and other agencies within the government, between police and private institutions, and across national borders [15]. Issues of effectiveness and relevance of national fraud strategies, the absence of incentives and identifiable benefits, and the continuous influence of competing agendas on three police priorities continue to marginalize fraud as a mainstream police function, limiting the level of resources committed to what remains a rising area of criminality [16]. Techniques like Anomaly detection have been intensively studied by researchers over the last few decades for this purpose, with many employing statistical, artificial intelligence, and machine learning models. Supervised learning algorithms have been the most widely studied models in research until recently. However, supervised learning models are associated with numerous challenges, which can be addressed by semi-supervised and unsupervised learning models proposed in recent literature. This chapter will focus on the economic, social, and psychological consequences for individuals, businesses, and society. It will quantify the financial losses, reputational damage, and emotional distress caused by cybercrime.

LITERATURE REVIEW

Introduction to Cybercrime in the Banking Sector

Here is an explanation that aligns with the research issue and the aim outlined in the introduction. Prior studies will be evaluated to establish a well-founded thesis for a thorough literature review, which aims to replace the existing knowledge base. Stress the broad range of computer crimes from which the bank industry stands to lose, including unauthorized intrusion, credit/ debit card fraud, money laundering, employee embezzlement, pharming, phishing, malware, hacking, virus, spam, and advanced fee fraud.

Evolution of Cybercrime

Broadhurst, in 2006, highlighted that the rapid development of computer connectivity, the digitization vulnerabilities inherent in cyberspace, and the challenges faced by e-commerce and social media on the internet are among the new opportunities for criminals to engage in cybercrime, including financial fraud [17]. Furthermore, the role of international cooperation becomes evident, which is rooted in the necessity of creating a supranational policing capacity for facing the globalized nature of cybercrime, proposing that cybercrime institutions are just the instruments of financial scandals. They underscore the upwardly mobile and quickly evolving aspect of technology, which has led to schemes and defrauding people *via* phone, social media, or the internet. Consequently, such synchronization manifests the ever-growing relationship between technological innovations and increased cyber fraud in financial systems. According to data recently provided by the Internet Crime Complaint Centre (IC3), the most consistent trend during the investigated period has been an upswing in financial crimes, with reported losses totaling more than $3.5 billion, which represents a clear indication of the prevalence of cyber-related frauds. The category of financial fraud primarily arises in discussions of bank fraud, credit card fraud, money laundering, and mortgage fraud, which, for the most part, are facilitated or aggravated through cyber methods. The literature highlights that cybercriminals often form groups or communities that exploit new and existing technologies for their illicit activities. At the same time, politicians and security professionals warn that cybercrime contributes to financial fraud, which the perpetrators continue. It also addresses ethical considerations and challenges related to misclassifying genuine transactions as fraudulent, as well as the costs associated with misclassifying four fraudulent transactions as authentic, which are relevant to both cybercrime and financial fraud.

Impact of COVID-19 on Cybercrime

The work by Ma & McKinnon in 2021 has informed us about the increase in cybercrime and financial fraud as a consequence of the extended confinement of the COVID-19 period [18]. The authors presented this issue of how e-banking, e-health, e-commerce, online education, and home office have grown intensively because of the pandemic. The rise of electronic media has created a new opportunity for cybercriminals to exploit individuals and firms, allowing them to devise new methods of defrauding. This essay argues that digitalization makes cybercrime more prevalent, as people are increasingly working from home and engaging in more online activities. The next theory, strain theory, also holds importance, as proponents of financial distress believe that such individuals may be more vulnerable to committing cybercrimes. Furthermore, Malware developers have exploited fear and greed to continue scamming through fake Coronavirus charities, boom trading schemes, and Cryptocurrency money laundering.

The authors rhetorically share their psychological and traditional criminological theories in putting COVID-19-themed cyber fraud victims into a typology [19]. It narrates how the global increase in cyber fraud has been associated with a growing number of people and organizations in cyberspace that have emerged due to the pandemic, which has brought many face-to-face interactions online to a minimum or stopped them entirely. The authors state that cybercriminals are reaping benefits by employing sophisticated fraud schemes to conceal money acquired through illicit activities. Additionally, they present a strain theory, which proposes that individuals who experience financial pressure are at an increased risk of committing cyber fraud.

Insider Cyber Threats in Banking

The study 'Sustainable Response System Building Against Insider-Led Cyber Frauds in the Banking Sector: Machine Learning in Cybersecurity', based on a survey conducted by [20], provides details about the most common types of insider cyber threats and their severity, offering valuable insights for fraud mitigation planning. Researchers have indicated that the types of fraud causing significant damage to banks in India include impersonation, identity theft, and hacking using a machine learning-based random forest tool. The nature of the severity scale implies that the study developed a severity scale for the tension associated with cybercrime. This scale enables a more strategic approach to fraud determination, allowing you to identify the most damaging, numerous, or rapidly occurring frauds. This way, the most successful and efficient fraud mitigation efforts can be carried out.

Assessment of Security Procedures

The researcher [21] (Akinbowale, Klingelhöfer, & Zerihun, 2020) utilizes the balanced scorecard (BSC) to evaluate the security procedures in both developed and developing nations within the financial sector. The literature section encompasses various components related to cybercrime, including its global prevalence, customer perceptions of banking services and their impact, and the tangible consequences of such crimes for financial institutions. The review, along with its focus on the dangers of cybercrime to financial institutions, pinpoints two problems: fraud and extortion, as well as the erosion of digital trust. The study argues for an alert system to raise the awareness level of banks and customers and to integrate large amounts of data technology into banking programming to combat the negative influences of cybercrime. The review also critically discusses the various decentralization technologies employed by modern banks, including cybercrime against the banking industry. The public's sensitivity is also stressed to increase awareness of cyber threats. Therefore, the literature examines the preventive measures implemented by banks and the obstacles to their effectiveness, such as the lack of adoption of technological developments, resource scarcity, inadequate enforcement of cyber-crime laws, and insufficient awareness.

Consequences of Financial Cybercrime

The potential impact of financial cybercrime and financial fraud on businesses is substantial. Events like data breaches, monetary theft, and business email compromise typically result in economic losses, legal expenses, and fines imposed by regulatory authorities. Furthermore, in a long-term perspective, the reduction of shareholder value and customer trust, as well as a brand with a bad reputation, can lead to consequences for the company's exports and trade activities. It reveals that financial consequences, such as cyberattacks, planned disruptions of operations, and reputational damage, can severely impact businesses and cause them a complete setback. The time lost due to the attacks, the loss of intellectual property, and the compromised customer data can interfere with the business's operational functions and ultimately affect stakeholder trust, potentially leading to serious long-term reputational damage.

Global Regulatory Challenges

Globally, more scams are being witnessed due to the poor regulations that make cybercriminal offenses unlawful in many nations. The chapter identifies numerous loopholes that impede proper cybercriminal regulations in most countries worldwide. There are several reasons behind the growth of cybercrime, including inadequate compliance regimes, a lack of unified solutions, insufficient resources to combat cyber offenses, limited capacities to address cybercrime, and inadequate statutes in place. Together, these result in legal enforcers being incapable of efficiently and effectively regulating cybercrimes and prosecuting cybercriminals.

International Efforts and Legal Frameworks

Broadhurst states that computer crimes and financial frauds have made significant inroads into the cyber world, influencing policymakers, law enforcement officials, and international organizations to consider new and improved regulatory regimes. The traditionally used methods prove their inadequacy, either ineffective in the globalized space or unable to maintain the transnational spirit of the crimes. View regulation as a component that has a global impact and requires prominent international involvement. The UN Convention on Transnational Organized

Crime and the Council of Europe's Cybercrime Convention illustrate the desire to forge a global legal framework to eradicate cybercriminals. Billions of dollars in assets have been stolen, which is most likely untraceable. Such criminal activity creates fertile ground for corruption, which distorts electoral processes and undermines the rule of law and accountability. New technologies and platforms present vulnerabilities requiring proactive and flexible regulatory measures to protect financial systems and consumers.

METHODOLOGY

Sampling Procedure

Participants were recruited through different channels, including interns at online platforms, social media, and relationships. Employees from various occupations have employed convenience sampling to collect data representing diverse industries. Therefore, this method is provided for diverse individuals who may have encountered cybercrime or virtual scams, and it guarantees a substantial amount of data for a comprehensive analysis.

Data Collection

The questionnaire measure was explicitly created to thoroughly gather all pertinent information about diverse issues surrounding cybercrime and financial fraud experiences. In this context, participants were given a list of questions structured around several topics, including their performances, particular situations defined as cybercrime or financial fraud, the costs that they incurred, changes in their spending or Internet behaviour after the incident, and thoughts on trust towards technology and the Internet platforms after the incident. The questionnaire was designed to be administered anonymously, ensuring confidentiality and encouraging candid responses from the participants. This strategy collected statistics and stories about how cybercrime and financial fraud affect families, businesses, and individuals. This type of research was done to inform a few key decision-makers and establish a compassionate vision for reforming how national laws respond to the global issue.

Data Analysis

When data is acquired, we perform thorough statistical data analysis to extract the desired information from the recorded dataset. The initialization came with exploratory data analysis employed to measure the key statistics that presented the sample population and provided an overview of the exposure of cybercrime and financial fraud cases among different demographics. The exploratory data analysis (EDA) methods, such as histograms, bar charts, and pie charts, helped to visualize and display patterns and trends in the data. In this module, we utilize a few inferential statistics, namely the chi-square test and the t-test, to determine whether one variable is related to another and to detect statistically significant differences. The regression approaches are used to analyze the subject of dependency and independence (*e.g.*, occupation, industrial sector) and the output (*e.g.*, financial impact, behavior change); the analysis gave more importance to the topic.

Descriptive Statistics

The bar plot shown in Fig. (**1**) illustrates the distribution of occupations among the surveyed individuals. Each bar on the plot represents a distinct occupation category, ranging from "Student" to "Other." The length of each bar corresponds to the number of individuals associated with that specific occupation. For instance, the tallest bar represents the occupation category with the highest number of individuals, while the shortest bar indicates the occupation category with the lowest number. The x-axis denotes the various occupation categories, while the y-axis represents the count of individuals within each category. The bars are color-coded in green for visual clarity, and gridlines along the y-axis aid in interpreting the data. The x-axis labels are also rotated by 45 degrees to prevent label overlap. Overall, this visualization provides insights into the occupational distribution among respondents, enabling the easy identification of prevalent and less common occupation categories within the surveyed population.

The bar plot shown in Fig. (**2**) illustrates the distribution of respondents across different industry sectors. Each bar represents a specific sector, with the x-axis denoting the industry sector categories and the y-axis indicating the frequency or count of respondents in each category. From the graph, it is evident that the majority of respondents are affiliated with the "Technology" sector, followed by "Finance and Banking" and "Retail and E-commerce." Sectors such as "Government," "Nonprofit," and "Healthcare" also have notable representation, while "Student" and "Other" sectors exhibit relatively lower frequencies. This visualization offers a clear and concise overview of the distribution of respondents across various industry sectors, providing valuable insights into the composition of the survey sample.

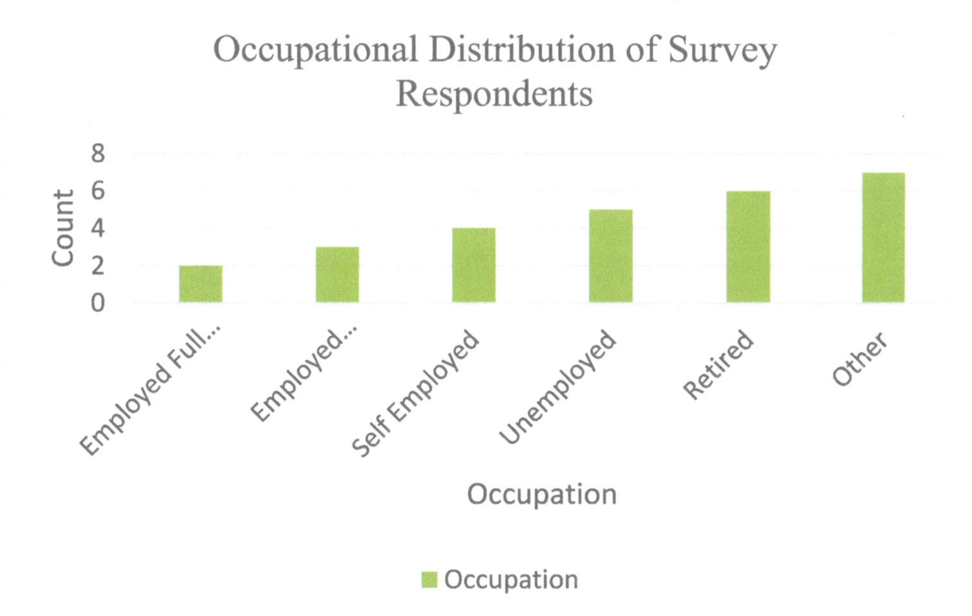

Fig. (1). Distribution of surveyed individuals by occupation.

Fig. (2). Distribution of respondents across different industry sectors.

The heatmap graph in Fig. (**3**) illustrates the financial impact experienced by individuals or people they know across various industry sectors. Each row in the heatmap corresponds to a specific industry sector, while each column represents a financial impact category, ranging from "No financial loss" to "Ensure/difficult to quantify." The intensity of color within each cell indicates the frequency or count of respondents falling into that particular category within a specific industry sector. Darker shades represent higher counts, indicating a greater number of individuals experiencing that financial impact within the corresponding sector. For instance, in the "Technology" sector, the heatmap shows a higher frequency of respondents reporting "No financial loss" or "Less than Rs100" compared to other categories.

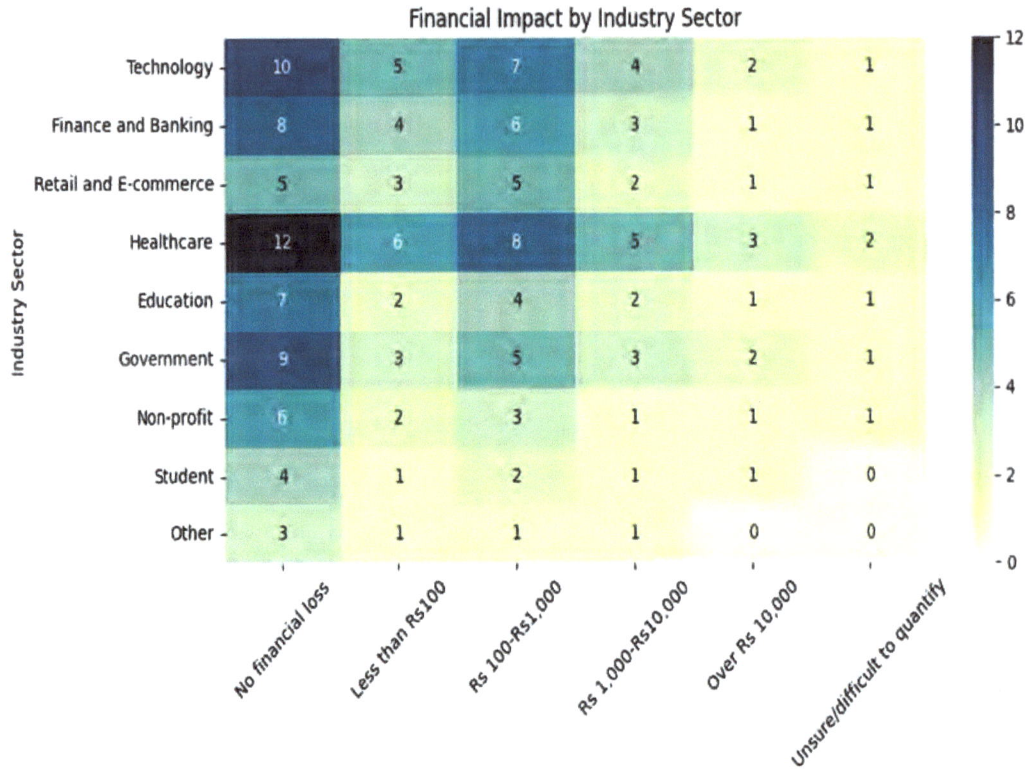

Fig. (3). Sectors with potentially higher financial vulnerability or resilience by cybercrime & financial fraud.

Conversely, the "Finance and Banking" sector exhibits a more varied distribution across different financial impact categories, with relatively higher counts in the "Rs 100-Rs1,000" and "Rs 1,000-Rs10,000" ranges. Overall, the heatmap provides a visual summary of how different industry sectors are affected by various levels of financial impact, offering insights into potential patterns or trends across industries.

This pie chart, as shown in Fig. (**4**), visualizes the post-incident emotional impact distribution, with "No noticeable impact" being the most common response, followed by varying degrees of anxiety and stress. The pie chart illustrates the distribution of emotional impacts experienced by individuals as a result of the incident. The most significant portion of the chart represents those who reported "No noticeable emotional impact," indicating that the incident did not result in any discernible emotional distress for a significant portion of respondents. Following this, smaller segments depict varying degrees of anxiety and stress experienced by respondents. The categories range from "Mild anxiety and stress" to "Significant anxiety and stress," each representing different levels of emotional impact.

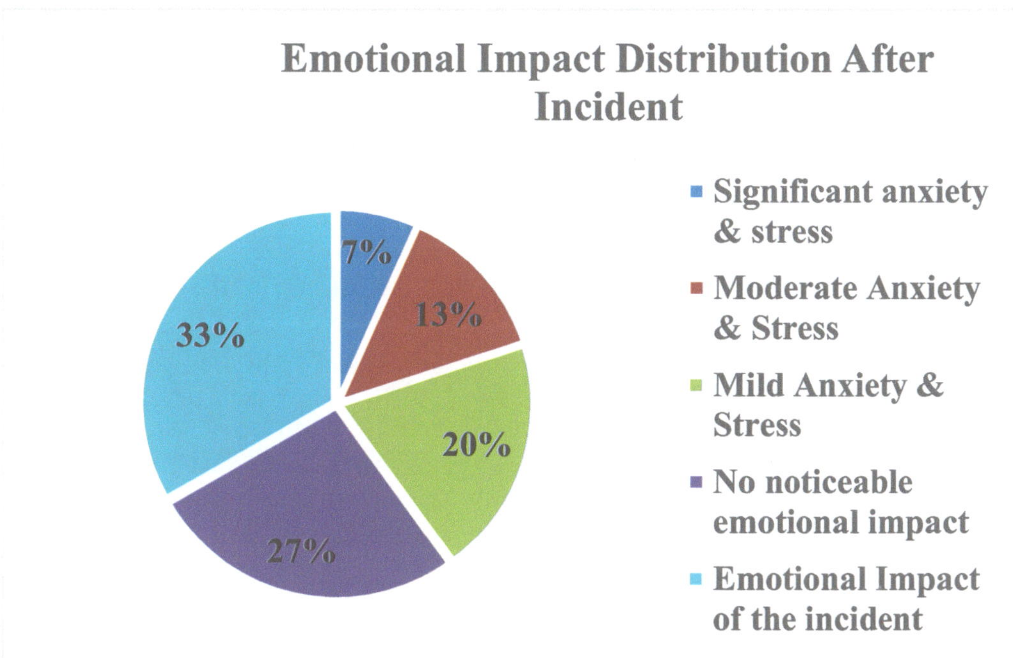

Fig. (4). Emotional impact distribution.

Additionally, a category labeled "Other" represents respondents who experienced emotional impacts not captured by the predefined categories. Overall, the pie chart provides a clear visualization of how the incident affected the emotional well-being of the individuals surveyed, highlighting the diversity of responses in terms of the severity of emotional impact.

FINDINGS

The paper on cybercrime statistics and age group analyses begins with an examination of cybercrime's prevalence and effects on each age group in India. Descriptive statistics were used to present the generalized results, demonstrating that the survey respondents fell within the age range of 15 to 67. Hence, this covered a wide range of age spectrums in the society. A table attached herewith lists respondents' cybercrime experiences in detail, revealing that 70% of individuals reported being victims of at least one existing form of cybercrime.

The research delved deeper to investigate specific types of cybercriminal activities that were found to be more prevalent among respondents. It was observed that fraud involving online payments was the highest experienced by 34.4%. The trend indicates that people are increasingly using online platforms like UPI and bank net banking due to the widespread adoption of digital payment options in modern India. Another statistic that highlights the sensitivity of identity in the digital world is that 26% of respondents to the survey reported incidents of identity theft, underscoring the need for data protection. Moreover, fake websites, advertisements, and other online scams are the leading cyber threats that survey participants experienced. These indicate the multifaceted nature.

Furthermore, to gain a better understanding, qualitative analysis tools were employed to map out the respondents' experiences and views regarding cybercrime. Codifying answers to open-ended questions in the questionnaire yielded different responses, covering 60% of people who have been victims of this theft, intending to do even more than just enhance their security measures after the incident. The other side of the story is the view held by 40% of the sample, who report that their overall online activity has dropped, hampering the progress of digital integration. Additionally, as many as 58% of the subjects clearly stated the levels of their potentially reduced trust in online platforms, indicating the significant scale of cybercrime, as shown in Table **1**.

Table 1. Distribution of age groups with cybercrime exposure.

Age Group	Cybercrime Exposure %
15-24	68.2
25-34	72.8
35-44	71.5
45-54	71.5
55-54	69.3
55-64	67.1

Regression analysis will be used to investigate various factors that could affect individual cyberspace crime cases, such as the age and profession of the victims. The study found that age group and the occurrence of cybercrime had an enormously positive correlation, with younger individuals tending towards being more victims. Such understanding, in turn, points out that the type of resources specifically targeted at particular demographic groups is necessary to reflect the changing cyberspace landscape in terms of threats. This data analysis presents a multi-layered and complex view of cybercrime's prevalence, the harm it causes, and its overall implications for users and the nation, leading to a firm conclusion that the necessity of enhancing cybersecurity and user education is evident. The comprehensive, capitalized result table is a valuable reference, containing crucial findings and aiding in further data research.

DISCUSSION

The comprehensive analysis of cybercrime's prevalence and impact in India yields several key conclusions. Firstly, the findings underscore the pervasive nature of cyber threats, with over 70% of respondents reporting exposure to various forms of cybercrime. This underscores the urgent need for concerted efforts to combat cybercrime and protect individuals from its harmful effects.

Secondly, the study reveals a concerning trend of increasing cybercrime victimization among younger age groups, emphasizing the importance of targeted interventions and educational initiatives tailored to different demographic segments. By empowering individuals with digital literacy and 11 cybersecurity awareness from a young age, we can mitigate the risk of future victimization and foster a safer online environment.

Furthermore, the analysis highlights the multifaceted impact of cybercrime, extending beyond financial losses to encompass emotional distress and a loss of trust in online platforms. This underscores the need for holistic approaches to addressing cybercrime, encompassing technical solutions, psychological support systems for victims, and efforts to rebuild trust in digital spaces.

In conclusion, the study serves as a wake-up call to stakeholders across government, industry, and civil society, urging them to prioritize cybersecurity initiatives and collaborate to create a safer digital ecosystem for all. By implementing robust cybersecurity measures, promoting digital literacy, and cultivating a culture of resilience, we can effectively combat cybercrime and ensure that individuals can safely and securely engage with online platforms.

RESULTS

The answers varied across the age group of 15-67, which spanned from school students to senior citizens. More than 70% replied that they had faced such an event, in which 34.4% were victimized by online payment fraud. Today, almost every individual bank uses UPI or Net Banking to make payments. Approximately 26 percent of people are targets of ID theft, whereas the rest are preyed upon by phishing and malware attackers. As a result, many people have increased their security measures or reduced their use of online modes. The event significantly or at least moderately impacted the trust in online platform usage. The victim here blames herself for being a contributing factor to the financial fraud. It not only hurts a person's physical health but also profoundly affects mental wellbeing. The emotional pain here is beyond words, as this person is 50% in fear of being a victim or falling prey to financial fraud. Cybersecurity, the science of protecting confidential data from unauthorized access, malicious attacks, and hackers, has been at the base of parents' and caregivers' worries for the last decade. This study will provide a detailed account of the worst cybercrime scenario in India, gathering information from a range of participants aged 15 to 67 years. The report painted a sobering picture of exposure to cybercrime, finding that 70% of respondents had been victims of cybercrime. Among other forms of cybercrime, as experienced, online payment scams proved to be the leading cause of concern, with a staggering 34.4% of victims. We find such a point today in the new reality of using UPI and Net banking in the same way we use cash, and pairing identity theft with it as the second on the list, with 26% of existing personal information in the digital age being readymade for pressure. Phishing and malware attacks can well reflect these cyber threats in cyberspace, which are now becoming very common, thus depicting the universal nature of crimes.

Victims of cybercrime have a broad range of emotions. As a result, the most common action the respondents (60%) took after such an experience was to deploy tighter security. Aside from that, the survey also highlights another worrying trend, with 40% of participants reporting that online activities are on the lower side, thereby limiting the advantages of digital integration. Regarding psychological effects, it has become a grave issue, as 58% of respondents report becoming disloyal to some or all platforms. The emotional impact is also evident as 50% feel a rise in anxiety and tension among victims and retain an underlying fear of future attacks, as the other half claim to be traumatized.

CONCLUSION AND FUTURE PROSPECTS

In conclusion, this research sheds light on the pressing issue of cybercrime and its global ramifications, particularly within emerging economies and the banking sector. The findings underscore the pervasive nature of cyber threats, exacerbated by the rapid digitization accelerated by the COVID-19 pandemic. From phishing and malware to insider-led fraud, cybercriminals employ a diverse range of tactics to exploit vulnerabilities and inflict financial and emotional harm on individuals and businesses.

The study emphasizes the imperative for collaborative efforts among governments, industries, and civil society to develop robust cybersecurity measures, enhance regulatory frameworks, and promote digital literacy. By prioritizing proactive strategies such as integrated cybersecurity platforms, awareness campaigns, and public-private partnerships, stakeholders can bolster resilience against cyber threats and foster a safer digital environment. As technology continues to evolve, addressing the challenges posed by cybercrime requires sustained vigilance, innovation, and cooperation to safeguard against the ever-present risks in the digital age.

REFERENCES

[1] M. Antonescu, and R. Birău, "Financial and Non-financial Implications of Cybercrimes in Emerging Countries", *Procedia Econ. Finance,* vol. 32, pp. 618-621, 2015. [http://dx.doi.org/10.1016/S2212-5671(15)01440-9]

[2] N. Chhabra Roy, and S. Prabhakaran, "Sustainable response system building against insider-led cyber frauds in banking sector: a machine learning approach", *J. Financ. Crime,* vol. 30, no. 1, pp. 48-85, 2023. [http://dx.doi.org/10.1108/JFC-12-2021-0274]

[3] W. Hilal, S.A. Gadsden, and J. Yawney, "Financial Fraud: A Review of Anomaly Detection Techniques and Recent Advances", *Expert Syst. Appl.,* vol. 193, p. 116429, 2022. [http://dx.doi.org/10.1016/j.eswa.2021.116429]

[4] K.W.F. Ma, and T. McKinnon, "COVID-19 and cyber fraud: emerging threats during the pandemic", *J. Financ. Crime,* vol. 29, no. 2, pp. 433-446, 2022. [http://dx.doi.org/10.1108/JFC-01-2021-0016]

[5] S.Y. Afrizal, *The Impact of Pandemic Covid-19 on Bank Financial Performance (Study at Province Development Bank in Sumatera).* Research Journal of Finance and Accounting, 2021. [http://dx.doi.org/10.7176/RJFA/12-22-12]

[6] N.C. Roy, and T. Vishwanathan, "Workforce Challenges in Indian Banking Scenario – Journey from Identification Till Mitigation", *Curr. Sci.,* vol. 115, no. 4, p. 739, 2018. [http://dx.doi.org/10.18520/cs/v115/i4/739-747]

[7] M. Reid, and J. Van Niekerk, "Insider threats in cyber security: A review", *Journal of Cyber Security and Mobility,* vol. 3, no. 4, pp. 303-316, 2014.

[8] C. C. O'Connor, L. M. Wen, C. E. Rissel, and M. Shaw, "Sexual behaviour and risk in Vietnamese men living in metropolitan Sydney," *Sexually Transmitted Infections, Sydney, Australia*, 2006.

[9] B. Thompson, G. Warren, and A. Moore, "Rethinking financial stability: A sustainable approach", *J. Sustain. Finance Invest.,* vol. 7, no. 3, pp. 245-261, 2017.

[10] J.M. Alfonso, E. Carballo-Calero, and A. García-Diez, "The impact of cyberattacks on banks: A systematic literature review and research agenda", *J. Bus. Res.,* vol. 142, pp. 1089-1099, 2021.

[11] D. Vakhitova, F. Palacin, and E. Ontiveros, "The insider threat in financial institutions: A literature

review", *Int. J. Inf. Secur. Priv.,* vol. 13, no. 2, pp. 119-137, 2019.

[12] G. Ferracane, "The impact of cybercrime on the financial system", *J. Money Credit Bank.,* vol. 51, no. 8-9, pp. 1891-1921, 2019.

[13] M. S. Beasley, A. Ghosh, and S. Srebrevatanapong, *Fraudulent Financial Reporting: 17 Steps to Detection.* Hoboken, NJ: John Wiley & Sons, 2000.

[14] P. Biegelman, and E. Bartow, "Insider threats in information security: A decade of research", *Comput. Secur.,* vol. 31, no. 4, pp. 496-508, 2012.

[15] R. Broadhurst, "Developments in the global law enforcement of cyber-crime", *Policing,* vol. 29, no. 3, pp. 408-433, 2006.
[http://dx.doi.org/10.1108/13639510610684674]

[16] A. Doig, "Implementing national policing agendas and strategies for fraud at local level", *J. Financ. Crime,* vol. 25, no. 4, pp. 984-996, 2018.
[http://dx.doi.org/10.1108/JFC-04-2017-0027]

[17] E. du Toit, "The red flags of financial statement fraud: a case study", *J. Financ. Crime,* 2023.
[http://dx.doi.org/10.1108/JFC-02-2023-0028]

[18] Federal Bureau of Investigation (2020), "COVID-19 fraud: Law enforcement's response to those exploiting the pandemic—FBI", available at: www.fbi.gov/news/testimony/covid-19-fraud-lawenforcements-response-to-those-exploiting-the-pandemic

[19] K.R. Dodiya, S.N. Varayogula, and B.V. Gohil, "Rising threats, silent battles: A deep dive into cybercrime, terrorism, and resilient defenses", In: *Cases on forensic and criminological science for criminal detection and avoidance* IGI Global, 2024, pp. 123-150.
[http://dx.doi.org/10.4018/978-1-6684-9800-2.ch006]

[20] N. Mugarura, and E. Ssali, "Intricacies of anti-money laundering and cyber-crimes regulation in a fluid global system", *Journal of Money Laundering Control,* vol. 24, no. 1, pp. 10-28, 2021.
[http://dx.doi.org/10.1108/JMLC-11-2019-0092]

[21] O.E. Akinbowale, H.E. Klingelhöfer, and M.F. Zerihun, "Analysis of cyber-crime effects on the banking sector using the balanced score card: a survey of literature", *J. Financ. Crime,* vol. 27, no. 3, pp. 945-958, 2020.
[http://dx.doi.org/10.1108/JFC-03-2020-0037]

SUBJECT INDEX

Suneeta Satpathy, Sachi Nandan Mohanty & Subhendu Kumar Pani (Eds.)

E

F

G

H

I

J

K

L

M

N

O

P

Q

R

www.ingramcontent.com/pod-product-compliance
Lightning Source LLC
LaVergne TN
LVHW070948210926
848482LV00002B/144
9798898812157